A Street
in a Town
Remembered

A Street in a Town Remembered

Carole Shelby Carnes

NAUTILUS PUBLISHING

For information contact Nautilus Publishing, 426 South Lamar Blvd., Suite 16, Oxford, MS 38655.

In some cases, names of individuals have been changed in the interest of privacy.

ISBN: 978-1-936946-34-1 (hardcover)
978-1-936946-35-8 (paperback)

The Nautilus Publishing Company
426 South Lamar Blvd., Suite 16
Oxford, Mississippi 38655
Tel: 662-513-0159
www.nautiluspublishing.com
www.AStreetInATown.com

First Edition

Front cover design by Le'Herman Payton.

Library of Congress Cataloging-in-Publication Data has been applied for. Printed in the United States of America.

10   9   8   7   6   5   4   3   2   1

For

Virginia Landis Bass
First to read this book and encourage me

and

Frederick Fauntleroy Preaus
my most southern friend
(1937-2006)

and

Fergus, Rowdy, and Nipper
who sat beneath my computer

Shelby and Poitevent families who came to live in Shelby, Mississippi

Shelby

Moses Darwin Shelby m. Mary Jane Irwin
b.1815   d. 1871   b.1819   d.1880

Issue:

1. Evan b. 1839 d. 1864 (medical student killed in civil war)

2. Isaac   m. (1866)   Ellen August Poitevent
    b. 1840 d.1883   b.1846 d.1884

Issue:

a. Darwin Poitevent Shelby   m.(1899) Anna Liner
   b. 1867 d. 1922   b.1879 d.1958
   Issue:
   i. Sarah Frances Shelby
      b.1900 d.1903
          ii.   Zula Shelby m. Thomas Brown
                 b.1903 d.1965 b.1903 d.1952
             issue: Shelby Thomas Brown b. 1943
          iii.   May Shelby   m. 1932   Ernest Hayes Carnes
                 b.1905 d.1969   b.1895 d.1963
             issue: Carole Shelby Carnes (Tucker)
                     b. 1940
          iv.   Eleanor Shelby m. Ray Booth
                 b.1907 d.1976   b.1910 d. 1983

 b. Mary Jean (called Madia) m. 1895 Dr. James Murnan
   b.1868 d.1938   b. in Ireland 1860s d.1920s
 c. Ellen Walton Shelby m. 1888 John McEwen
   b.1870 d.1926
   issue: Norman McEwen, Kennedy Shelby McEwen, Donald
McEwen (lived elsewhere but spent considerable time on the street)

Issue of Norman and his wife Dorothy:
Ellen Shelby McEwen (Taylor) b.1920 d. 1980

3. Minnie Shelby m. Fred Nelson
  b. 1850 d.1931 (lived in Memphis)

4. Mary Louise
  b. 1851 d. 1931

5. David
  died as a child 1864

Dr. Thomas Neil Shelby Jr. m. Isabella Elizabeth Gibbs
(both died about 1863 from Malaria), no children, moved to Bolivar County
with his brother Moses Dawin Shelby, the town of Shelby was built on his
plantation.

Jacob Poitevent   m. Mary Jane Gause
    b.1818 d.1878   b.1823 d. 1878

Issue: 9 children

1.   Marguerite Anne "Maggie"
        b.1843 d.1892 (teacher) spinster

2. Ellen Augusta Poitevent m. 1866 Isaac Shelby
        b.1846 d.1884   b.1840 d.1883

3. Jane Eliza Poitevent   m. George Barnes Shelby
        b.1848 d.1938   b.1844 d.1909
Issue:
a. Janora Shelby
    b.1879 d.1885
b. Thomas Fletcher Shelby
    b.1874 d.1875
c. Frederick Poitevent Shelby   m. 1938 Ruth Benoit Edwards
        b.1979 d.1957   b.1880s d.1956
d. George Barnes Shelby m. Willie Joe Gwin
        b.1886 d.1959   b.1888 d.1960
    Issue:
    i. George Shelby (died about 1911) a child
    ii. Edgar Gwin Shelby m. 1944 Nan Wilkinson Brettell
        b.1910 d.1985   b.1915 d.2007
    Issue:
    Bobbie Lou Brettell Shelby (Green)
    b.1938
    Becky Brettell Shelby (Smith)

b. 1941

Jo Gwin Shelby (Mayhew)

b.1945 d.2011

iii. Frederick Poitevent Shelby

b.1912 d.1944

iv. Jane Shelby

died at about 79, brain damaged from birth

4. Lula Fletcher Poitevent m. William Cornell

b.1860 d.1936   b.1851 d.1930

Issue:

a. Marguerite

b.1892 d.1897

b. Thomas Jacob

b.1899 d.1901

5. Thomas Jacob Poitevent. m. 1898 Mary Ellen Maddox

b.1862 d.1915   b.1877 d.1959

Issue:

a. Isabel   m (early 1920s)   William Barksdale

b.1900 d.1981   b.1896 d.1977

Issue (neither lived in Shelby):

Mary Jane Barksdale (Milligan) b.1924 d.2009

Thomas Isabelle Barksdale (Maynard) b.1931

b. Mary   m. late 1920s   John Redwine

b.1902 d.1994   d. late 1930s

Issue: Mary Elizabeth Redwine (Soper) b. 1936 d. 1989

c. Janula   m. (late 1930s)   Charles Davis

b.1907 d.1987   b.1905 d.1952

Issue:

Janula (Jan) Poitevent Davis (Clark) b. 1942

As the year reached 2000 I telephoned Annie Anderson in Shelby, Mississippi, and spoke to a young lady with a middle-American accent.

"Miss Annie is out. She's at church."

Her accent continued to perplex me for it was not from the Deep South.

"Who is this?" I asked.

"Kimberly."

"Oh, Madie's daughter."

"How did you know?"

"I know a lot about you. I have heard for years that you are very smart. What are you doing these days?"

"Now that I have finished high school, I'm thinking of going to law school and I plan to study pre-law at Baylor University."

"Not a bad idea. I'm a lawyer. It's as stimulating a way to make a living as any."

"Who are you?" she asked.'

"Don't you know who I am? Your family and my family have lived together for five generations in the Mississippi Delta."

"That is interesting. I don't know anything about that. I would like to know."

My thoughts went back to a street in a town...

 Introduction

I have always had difficulty with directions apart from up and down. Right, left, north, south, and east were matters that have made me pause for reflection. But the West was always clear. It remains a vision of the afternoon sun behind the Mississippi River and Holmes Lake, light penetrating through the cold stark winter afternoons, seeping into our living room, focusing on particles of dust over the coffee table while my mother poured coffee, passed a plate of fudge, peanut butter, or caramel candy, and told stories. When she grew bored with stories we played with the Ouija board, which sometimes did flips in the air, cursed, read the thoughts of guests, and occasionally made some accurate predictions into the future. As an only child I heard so many stories that the dead were to me as alive as the living. The further she went into the past, the more my mother romanticized, reflecting the past with a sepia *Gone with the Wind* tint. I have reconstructed the earliest days of my story from books, documents, letters, photographs, many of which I found in an old leather trunk; after that I rely on my mother's stories dictated in 1969, and my own indelible recollections of her stories. [Ouija has been omitted from this tale, which is solely limited to the past.] Although I saw this world through the eyes of my relations and close friends, I believe that they represent a kaleidoscope of a part of America. I knew that beginning and I watched it pass away.

I was born on the 29th of September 1940, and lived in a small town called Shelby in the Mississippi Delta. My mother's family had settled this area in 1852, when my great-great-grandfather, Moses Darwin Shelby, emigrated with his wife, Mary Jane Irwin, his younger brother, Dr. Thomas Neil Shelby, and his wife, Elizabeth Gibbs, called Bella. They came from their considerably more civilized plantations near Port Gibson, Mississippi (Claiborne County) to travel a hundred and sixty miles north to this yet uncultivated land in Bolivar County, covered with such a dense growth that the slaves had to cut a passage from the Mississippi River with cane knives and axes. Of course, there were no roads. The few settlements near our plantation were on the Mississippi River, notably Carsons Landing, Concordia, Gunnison, and Prentiss, the county seat, (long since under water), and replaced by Rosedale, where the first courthouse was built in 1836. At Concordia and Gunnison were two other planter families who came to live on our street, the Blanchards and the Wilsons. A gravestone in the old Concordia cemetery, now covered in weeds and bramble, marks Robert M. Wilson's demise. He returned to the area to help his friends in the 1879 epidemic of yellow fever, to which he succumbed. His relations claimed that he was a descendant of one James Wilson, a Scot, who signed the Declaration of Independence. It was a tough environment into which some of the early settlers of the United States had penetrated.

Three other families who did not remain in the area accompanied the Shelby families. They cultivated the completely flat land, well watered by the alluvial silt that flowed from the Mississippi River. Deer, panthers, wolves, and bear roamed; rattlesnakes and water moccasins crawled. The paths in the woods were known only to the vanished Native Americans and the forest animals. Slaves had to throw up levees in low places, maintained at the planters' expense.[1] The General Levee Board was not established until 1858.[2]

---

1 Sillers, Florence Warfield ed. and Members of Mississippi Delta Chapter of Daughters of the American Revolution and the County History Committee, History of Bolivar County Mississippi, the RePrint Company, Spartanburg, South Carolina, 1976 "Shelby" by Lucy S. Weissenger, part of the early history taken from an article by Mrs. Janie P Shelby, 370-71

2 Cobb, James C, The Most Southern Place on Earth, The Mississippi Delta and the Roots of Regional Identity by Oxford University Press, 1992,

Moses Darwin Shelby was thirty-seven when he moved to the Delta. He and his wife reached reasonable ages before retiring to Memphis, Tennessee. The graves of his brother, Thomas and his wife, Bella, believed to have been victims of malaria, rest on a mound surrounding a cistern on their plantation, which was to become the site of the town of Shelby.[3]

My great grandparents met a similar fate in their late thirties and early forties. They were captives of the land, ideal for planting cotton, but not for civilization. Despite these odds Mississippi became the largest cotton-producing area in the States by 1880. A major portion of this crop came from the alluvial Delta.[4]

Moses Darwin Shelby had bought thousands of acres from the government and the largest site was his plantation named "Monochonut", so named by the Native Americans, for the water lily that grew in profusion in low places. Mr. Humes' plantation, Wildwood, joined Moses. Next was the plantation of Dr. Thomas Shelby (now the town of Shelby) and north of that was land belonging to Mrs. Clementine Evans, a widow, called "Lucknow." I have no idea why this farm in the Mississippi Delta was named for the cantonment in Utter Pradesh, India, the site of the Siege of Lucknow. This land was later bought by my grandfather, Darwin Poitevent Shelby, in about 1890. I still own part of that land.

The railway between Vicksburg and Memphis was first completed in 1884, and a branch went through my grandfather's land in 1892. The town changed its name from Shelby, because another town in Mississippi was called Shelby, to Bellevue (reputed to have been named for the unfortunate Bella). It later resumed the name of Shelby.[5]

New York, 29

3 Shelby, Cass Knight, The Paternal Ancestry of May (Shelby) Carnes, Hollidaysburg, Pennsylvania, July, 1954, 22

4 Encyclopedia Britannica, 9th ed. Edinburgh: Adam and Charles Black, 1878, 523

5 Sillers 370-371

Darwin Shelby and gin hands standing and sitting on bales of cotton, his house in the background, not a tree or a house in sight, 1890s.

During the years between the original settlement and the formation of a town, a third generation was born into this wilderness. They were the patriarchs of my childhood.

The farmhouse in which I lived was built on my grandfather's plantation, and the space in front of this house became a street. As in so many small towns, the street told its story. There was no plan; a shanty town faced a tree-lined street of pleasant houses built of cypress, followed by two blocks of stores, the City Hall and the Methodist Church, the latter built on a lot donated by a generous Jewish settler, Mr. Godfrey Frank.[6] After the church was another tree-lined street of pleasant houses. The borders were marked by two American icons, the Gulf station and the Texaco station. Except for those icons it was not unlike a town in Africa.

When the town was incorporated in 1903 with a population of 520, there were no streetlights and livestock roamed at large. In 1904 my great uncle, Dr. J. R. Murnan, was elected mayor and artesian water and a sewage system were installed. Later came a walk of wooden planks and a stock law. By 1920 the population had grown from 520 to 1,300, with churches, a school, business houses, and a center for ginning cotton.[7]

Our house was meant to have been a bachelor's accommodation. My grandfather lived there with Dr. James Murnan, who was to marry my great aunt. The house of no particular style, except early farm, was built of cypress. Surrounded by porches, it resembled a steamboat. There was a service yard on the back acre with a dove house, a cook's house, an outside toilet for servants, a "windmill", and space for a few horses. There were no trees. The house faced our cotton gin and behind the gin were the commissary and a row of tenant houses belonging to our plantation.

The street in front of our house eventually became U. S. Highway 61, after my grandfather died. He declared that he had no idea such a town would grow around him or else he would have settled in Hushpuckana, a

6 Sillers 372

7 Sillers 372

settlement four miles north of Shelby, and never larger than three or four houses.

As the service yards gradually disappeared, this area became a smart residential neighborhood in the 1950s. The letter H with the cross bar extended would appropriately describe the plan of the town. The cross bar was the main street with two traffic lights. At Christmas these signals were supplemented with strings of colored lights, quite bewilderingly to the unsuspecting traveler along a US Highway for many blinked out during the season, leaving the remaining lights to compete with the traffic lights. Holmes Lake, where the native monochonut flower once bloomed, was scarcely more than a large ditch that crossed the town and ran behind our tenant houses. Mixed wild flowers grew along the railway bank in the spring, and the lake was lined with cypress trees that rooted in the water. We faced an oil mill, a compress for bales of cotton, a cotton gin, and a water tower. Small pockets of residential houses formed within the perimeters of the H. The town never exceeded 2500 people. There were two schools (we called one a white school and the other colored), and four churches: Methodist, Baptist, Presbyterian, and Catholic (before the Baptist split and became First and Second Baptist Churches). It seemed significant in its time, and yet Shelby, Mississippi, was one of those many places throughout America that did not appear on many maps and never would.

In reflection, this was as cosmopolitan as Bleaker Street in New York City. There were members of the early colonial families: the Henrys, descendants of Patrick Henry; Mrs. Thomas, a close cousin of Jefferson Davis; the Poitevents, Huguenots who had arrived in Charleston in 1685 to escape persecution; the Shelbys, and my cousin Joe Gwin Shelby, a lateral descendent of Cardinal Hughes, who founded St. Patrick's Cathedral in New York. Later came the Wilsons, descendants of a signature of the Declaration of Independence. On the other side of the street were Jews from Poland who first lived in the back of their store. The majority of the people who lived across the street were dark: Africans, people intermarried with Africans and the Native Americans, Chinese (who often had children who were part African American as well), and people from the Middle East whom we called Assyrians. Italians from Sicily dotted the edges of the street.

Living in this limited space gave one a lasting sense of separateness. The all-embracing factor was the weather. Clouds formed and we prayed for them to give rain or withhold it. Crickets screamed louder and louder during a drought. The earth cracked. Blooms on the cotton would drop into the cracks or squares would not fill out. In the autumn, called "fall" in the South, there was the reassuring chug of the cotton gin, the smells of cottonseed oil and fire. This season marked the end of our year.

Part One

Peering into the Trunk

(1852-1903)

The Settlers

The Shelby families in America are all related for they descend from one Evan Shelby, born in Wales in 1693, and his wife Catherine. Records indicate that they were part of the rural peasantry who had come from York and intermarried with the Welsh. They liked to imagine that they were descendants of Vikings as Shelby was not a Welsh name, but a genealogist who spent twenty years on the subject was only able to find the name of one Shelby on a parish roll in Treason, Cardiganshire, where he was given a coat, and no connection to the more illustrious Selbys of York, except that they were members of the Church of England.

Evan and Catherine Shelby and about five children came to Pennsylvania when they were in their early forties, in about 1735. Another child was born in the new world. There is no known last name for Catherine. Several ladies in that family at that time appear to have lost their last names. Subsequent biographers and history seem to agree that they were brave and photographs of the later generations show straight noses, wide set gray eyes, sandy hair, broad Welsh foreheads, and perfect teeth.

When my first Shelby ancestors (about six greats), Evan and Catherine, settled in the province of Pennsylvania, the state had a polyglot population of English, Welsh, Scots, northern Irish, Germans, Swiss and some Frenchmen, all attracted by the low priced lands and the tolerant government of William Penn, who had been given the land by a Royal Charter. That same year Evan obtained a license for three hundred acres in the Cumberland Valley and quickly acquired more land until his property crossed what was later called the Mason-Dixon Line into Maryland. He bought a plantation of two thousand five hundred acres, known as Maiden's Choice, encompassing four square miles. There he built a stone house and owned a mountain comprising 200 acres, named "the Mountain of Wales" and soon acquired about four thousand acres in the vicinity of his home. He lived for another twelve years until 1751, leaving five sons and three daughters. What must Catherine have thought of this quick rise in her family's fortune, as one son became a general and other children married into the Polks and Alexanders, major colonial families in Maryland and Virginia?[8] Despite the laws of primogeniture that passed Maiden's Choice to his son Evan Jr., Evan was still able to give each of the four younger sons several hundred acres, a start in life. The new world had fulfilled every promise for the likes of Evan and Catherine in just sixteen years.

Their oldest and most distinguished child, Evan Jr., became a Captain in the French and Indian War, where he was reputed to have killed a Native American chief with his bare hands. He later reached the rank of General in the American Revolution. This was the stock from which these soldiers of that war would come. General Evan Shelby's son, General Isaac Shelby, distinguished himself in the Battle of Kings Mountain during the American Revolution when he and John Sevier with other volunteers defeated the British and Loyalist forces. Isaac went on to become the first governor of Kentucky. Numerous places throughout the States have been named for him and other members of the family. In 1818, his last years, General Isaac was commissioned by the United States Government with General Andrew Jackson to procure the treaty with the Chickasaw Indians for the purchase of land west of the Tennessee River.

I descend from a younger son of Evan and Catherine, Moses Shelby, who also served in the American Revolution, and his son Moses Jr. This branch moved to North Carolina before the American Revolution (the Carolinas were at that time one state). After two generations in North Carolina and a brief time in Georgia, Moses Jr. and his younger brother William,

---

8 Galloway, Howard S., Shelby Family, printed by author, Mobile, Alabama, Gill Printing Co. 2-8

How Shelby County Got Its Name

MEET GEN. ISAAC SHELBY—Probably this is the first time you have ever seen the picture of the man for whom Shelby County is named. His picture is very rare. This is the centerpiece of the 35-foot long photo-montage mural over the bar in Hotel Claridge's new Shelby Room, lounge and grill, which opened last night.

Al Patterson, assistant hotel manager and record keeper, spent 10 days in Cossitt Library and the Goodwyn Institute looking thru 75 books of the history of Shelby County, Tennessee, and Kentucky to find that picture.

"Any real credit for finding Gen. Shelby's picture goes to the ladies of the Goodwyn Institute," said Mr. Patterson. "They had to go thru every book on Tennessee they had before they found it."

The picture finally turned up in a history of the United States printed by the Southern Historical Publication Society.

Gen. Shelby, Mr. Patterson discovered, was a Kentucky governor and treaty commissioner, born 1750 and died 1826. He was brought up a frontiersman, worked on his father's plantation. He was a lieutenant in his father's Finecastle Company, and history is full of accounts of his skill and gallantry in battle, leading his men against savage Indians.

His most outstanding military feat was in the battle of King's Mountain in 1780, when he and John Sevier, with volunteers they had organized, defeated overwhelmingly British and Loyalist forces.

In 1818 he was commissioned by the U. S. Government with Gen. Andrew Jackson to hold a treaty with the Chickasaw Indians for the purchase of land west of the Tennessee River. Eight counties in the United States are named after him. A brief history of Shelby County appears on the back of the Shelby Room menu.

The mural about Gen. Shelby's picture contains 16 pictures of what Lawrence H. Levy, hotel manager, considered Shelby County's most important scenes.

Clipping from the Memphis Commercial Appeal (1950s) depicting General Isaac Shelby who, along with Andrew Jackson, negotiated the treaty with the Chickasaw Indians and for whom Shelby County is named.

who was married, moved to Kentucky. William died there in 1817. In 1811 Moses Jr. decided to move to New Orleans (still in Spanish hands). The family embarked on flat boats with their furniture and slaves to follow a steamboat down the Ohio and Mississippi rivers. Their boats were wrecked by the effect of the Great New Madrid Earthquakes of 1811-1812. All of the passengers survived and came ashore near Memphis, rather scantily clad. Moses Jr. and his family then continued to the Natchez (Mississippi) Territory, where they settled in Claiborne County. He acquired land near Port Gibson four years before Mississippi was admitted to the Union. The Choctaw and Creek nations were still troublesome, and stockades had to be built on their plantation to protect them from an attack. Even the wives were armed with rifles. Over 160 years later I married a descendant of Moses Shelby.

The lives of these ancestors followed a similar pattern of acquiring large tracts of land, dying in middle age and leaving behind four or five children. They were a nomadic lot, taking their young children with them in search of ever more promising new territory. Some children lived, many perished. Apart from a few doctors and quite a few soldiers (Generals Evan [the French & Indian War] and Isaac [the American Revolution] and Generals Joe and John [the Civil War]), they all appeared to have been planters. The last outpost of my mother's branch of this family was the street in this town called Shelby, Mississippi.[9]

*

The writer David Cohn described the Mississippi Delta as "a strange and detached fragment thrown off by the whirling comet that is America." His other famous quotation was that "the Mississippi Delta begins in the lobby of the Peabody Hotel in Memphis [Tennessee] and ends on Catfish Row in Vicksburg [Mississippi]." Although it would one day come to symbolize the Old South, only 10 percent of Delta land was cleared by 1860, making it scarcely more than a sparsely inhabited plantation frontier as the

9 Shelby 1-23

antebellum area drew to a close.[10]

About fifteen thousand years ago, during the final cycle of worldwide melting glaciers, the Mississippi River and its tributaries cut deep valleys into the Lower Gulf coastal plane, causing the level of the sea around the mouth of the Mississippi to rise. Sediment-laden streams backed up, flooding the Mississippi valley. One of the many basins marking the irregular surfaces of this alluvial bed is the Yazoo-Mississippi Delta. The area is located several hundred miles north of the mouth of the Mississippi River. It is approximately 200 miles long and 70 miles at its widest point.[11]

Long before the landmarks of the Peabody Hotel and Catfish Row existed, an early population, The Mounds People inhabited the area from A.D. 1000 to 1450. In these times, prehistoric in Mississippi, the population belonged to what anthropologists call the "Mississippian Culture." Little is known of their way of life except from the early explorers and a few archeologists. These Native Americans were semi-domesticated and largely dependent on horticulture. Their major settlements had political and religious centers and a yearly resident population. They were situated on abandoned channels or oxbow lakes in the river tributary areas, near good sandy loam land. They appeared advanced in technology with carvings in stone, using marine shell and fresh-water pearls in decoration and some stone tools. The ceramics were better than any produced in later periods and were often highly decorated with carefully molded effigies of animals and humans. In the place called Mounds (Winterville), near Greenville, the people lived away from the mounds, and only a few of the highest ranking tribal officials lived on the mounds, of which there were twenty-three, including the largest fifty-five foot high Temple Mound. A great fire, the cause a mystery, during the late 1300s consumed the original building on the Temple Mound at Winterville. By A. D. 1450 the Winterville mound site appears to have been completely abandoned. These tribes probably had a civilization

10 Cobb preface vi

11 Cobb 1

similar to that of the Natchez nation, the Mississippi tribe documented by French explorers and settlers in the early 1700s. The Natchez society was divided into upper and lower ranks, with a person's social rank determined by heredity through the female line.[12]

By the time the Europeans arrived in 1540, what had been a highly civilized portion of North America was occupied by small autonomous tribes with little knowledge at best of the greatness of their past. But there had been at least three examples of this Mississippian culture in the Delta. One was at Buford, a site near Sumner (40 miles west of Shelby), another approximately forty miles south of Shelby, in Winterville. The Buford settlement did not fare well, but there was a third, somewhat later, settlement in Hushpuckena (four miles north of the Street).[13]

This rich Delta jungle seems to have been slumbering when Hernando de Soto began an excursion from Florida to Mississippi in 1539. He claimed the Yazoo Delta for Spain, but made no attempt to establish settlements in that part of Mississippi. Then France claimed the Illinois area of the Mississippi Valley in 1671. Subsequent missions by Jolliet, Marquette, LaSalle, and Tonti planted French settlements along the Mississippi River in the late seventeenth century as bases for their lucrative fur trade. After the French and Indian War the Delta fell into British hands as a result of the 1763 Treaty of Paris. The area passed to the United States at the end of the Revolutionary War. Only a handful of whites visited the place at this point, which was called the Mississippi Territory, and according to Cobb, a scholar described the Delta as "a seething lush hell." Even after Mississippi gained

---

12   Anon, Winterville Mounds (Pamphlet), undated, Jeffery P. Brain, Winterville: Late Prehistoric Culture Contact in the Lower Mississippi Valley, 1989, Mississippi Department of Archives and History, Greenville, Mississippi.

13   McLemore, Richard Aubrey ed. (1973) A History of Mississippi (2 Vols) University & College Press of Mississippi, Jackson, (Vol. I) 61-4.

statehood in 1817, the Delta continued to lie fallow.[14]

Very few people who live in the Mississippi Delta today have much knowledge or interest in the vanquished Native Americans who lived there at that time. We have to think twice about whether Choctaw or Chickasaw inhabited our area. Many plantations boast a mound and, if plowed, pottery will appear, alternating between rude gray with cross marks to bits of carefully crafted and painted pieces, as well as a plentiful supply of glass beads, no doubt left by the traders. The Chickasaw tribes were in the north, around Walls, Mississippi, near Memphis and east. The Choctaw populated our part of the Delta and the interior regions. Only small isolated groups (notably the Natchez) seemed to have retained any degree of social and political control once held by their ancestors.[15]

Theses tribes shared a similar culture. The Choctaw, numbering about 20,000, and the Chickasaw and Natchez, each about 4,500, spoke a common tongue, Muskhogean, reputed to have been a courteous, gentle, musical language, resembling singing birds. No tribe had a written language, but each had a rich folklore, transmitted orally by their elders. Tales included a creation epic, an account of their migration from the "setting sun" to the "land of the great river," and of a flood from which people and wild creatures were saved from rising waters by rafts. The sun was the most important deity, but there were also lesser spirits—evil ones. The tribes followed a common law system, with ownership of common land vested in each tribe. Principal crimes were homicide, blasphemy, theft, and adultery. Relatives of the victim were expected to seek out and kill the perpetrator of the crime. If he could not be found, his brother could substitute. Lesser crimes were punished by public whipping. They practiced both monogamy and polygamy. Often a man wed a woman and her sisters, so that he need maintain only one household. They were hunters and gatherers and plunders of conquered enemies.

14 Cobb 5-6

15 McLemore Vol. I 63

The first slave owners on the continent were the Native Americans who captured others in inter-tribal wars. Women especially esteemed acquiring slaves, for this privilege changed their status from drudge to overseer. In order to prevent escape, Native American slaveholders mutilated their slaves' feet by cutting nerves or sinews just above the instep. They could labor but could not flee.[16]

After the long struggle of French-inspired wars climaxing in the Seven Year's War, with the Peace of Paris in January 1, 1763 and the British takeover, the Native American tribes in Mississippi were drastically reduced, as these wars involved heavy casualties from the tribes. Exposure to European disease also sapped the population. The Chickasaw had preyed on other Mississippi tribes, and they continued to capture slaves for the British to be sold to the Carolinas and the West Indies. The French Wars destroyed the Natchez nation in 1731, but survivors had settled among the Chickasaw and Cherokee. The remnant Yazoo tribes became for generations the source of slaves for Chickasaw raiders. Thus, by 1763 there were essentially two tribes remaining in the Mississippi Delta: the Chickasaw and the Choctaw.[17]

Apparent among these Mississippi tribes by 1763 was the rapid growth of mixed-blood families (mixed with French and English traders who had lived among the tribes for several generations). More assertive than their full-blood counterparts, they came to comprise a sort of aristocracy in the tribes. The descendants of Greenwood Leflore of the Choctaw tribe in Greenwood, fifty miles east of Shelby, were an example. Greenwood Leflore was the son of a Canadian trader and explorer, Louis LeFleur, and a Choctaw woman, the niece of the chief. Greenwood was elected chief of the tribe in 1830 and educated in Nashville, Tennessee. He became the first Principal Chief of the Choctaw Nation, previously governed by regional chiefs. He signed the Treaty of Dancing Rabbit Creek, ceding tribal lands

16 For more detailed discussion about the Indians of the Mississippi Delta, McLemore Vol I 61-65, 84

17 McLamore 65-75

in Mississippi to the United States and moving the Choctaws west to Indian Territory, now Oklahoma. He was condemned as a traitor by his tribe but among white men his prestige grew with his wealth. By the 1840's he was a Mississippi politician, a fixture of Mississippi high society, and a personal friend of Jefferson Davis. He represented his country in the House of Representatives and the Senate for one term and once addressed them in Choctaw in reply to another senator's speech in Latin. He never joined the Confederacy and relied upon the U.S. government to protect his interest, but they could not fulfill their part of the contract during the Civil War, when he lost his 15,000 (appx) acres and died in his mansion, Malmaison, with its imported French antiques. His fortune and life ended less then four months after Appomattox. I believe that his family stayed in Mississippi for a long time and became well off once more. Malmaison was burned down in 1942.[18]

The intermarried people also had the effect of destroying the clan associations based on wisdom and bravery. Mixed-blood parentage was based on accommodation to the emerging new order. The full-blooded Native Americans increasingly withdrew or transported themselves out of their confusion with rum and brandy supplied by the traders. The takeover of management of tribal affairs led to an abandonment of ancient self-sufficiency and Native Americans turned more to agriculture.

When Mississippi became a state, the questions of jurisdiction, taxation, and land titles made it impossible for the Choctaw and Chickasaw nations to exist within a federal jurisdiction. Missionaries of all denominations came to Mississippi between 1799 and 1827, preaching temperance and attempting to provide succor for the tribes when they were pressured to sign removal treaties that forced them to abandon their ancient homeland and migrate west over the Trail of Tears to a new home in the Indian Territory (Oklahoma). By the treaty of Dancing Rabbit Creek in 1830 (Leflore), the Federal government agreed to pay removal expenses, provided emigrants

18 Workman 134

with blankets, powder, shot, and enough money and goods to subsidize them in the West for one year until they could raise a crop. Those Choctaw who chose to remain in Mississippi each received 640 acres of land; each child over ten years of age, 320 acres; and each child under ten, 160 acres. Approximately 5,000 Choctaw remained in Mississippi and received allotments and came to be called Mississippi Choctaw, to distinguish them from the others. By 1818 the Chickasaw had by a series of treaties been stripped of all eastern land in Mississippi except territory in northeast Mississippi. Intense pressure by the settlers and state and federal officials finally led the Chickasaw chiefs to sign a total cession treaty with the United States in 1832, which committed the Chickasaw nation to evacuate its eastern homeland upon the founding of a western estate. Finally in 1837 they signed the Treaty of Doaksville with the Choctaw nation, by which terms they were to join the Choctaw and colonize the western portion of the Choctaw nation in Indian Territory. The Choctaw removal was nearly completed by 1840, but scattered Chickasaw families were still moving to Indian Territory as late as 1850. Throughout the nineteenth century Native American families from allotted Mississippi Choctaw communities migrated to Indian Territory until 1900, when the Choctaw community in Mississippi numbered less than 2,000.[19] I never saw a Native American until I was fifteen and passed through the northeastern part of the state where two were standing by the side of the road.

Mississippi became the nation's twentieth state in 1814, when the Delta was still in the hands of the Choctaw. After these major treaties between 1820 and 1832, Bolivar, Coahoma and Tunica Counties were formed in 1836. White settlers and their African American[20] slaves began to trickle

19 McLemore 86-89

20   Colored/African American: The description of people who were brought from the African continent has had so many terms of usage in the last fifty years, that I have used the words that were polite at the time when most of the events in this book took place, that was "colored" and "white".

into the river towns in the area. The terrain was not suitable for many settlers without slaves. Bolivar County's white population increased from 395 in 1850 to 1,193 in 1860 and the slave population increased from 2,180 in 1850 to 9,078 in 1860. Planters came from areas suffering from soil depletion. Despite rumors of the Delta being unhealthy, with its jungle-like vegetation and unpredictable climate, the move to this area offered the settlers the only hope of maintaining their accustomed standard of living. It was also an exciting adventure. The average value of a farm in Tunica, Coahoma, Bolivar, Washington and Issaquena Counties was in excess of $30,000 by 1860 and those whose total individual wealth exceeded one hundred thousand dollars rose from fourteen to eighty families during this period when the value of land tripled.[21] I suspect that my ancestors were among that small percentage, but I have no proof.

**

Moses Darwin Shelby, the grandson of Moses Jr. who capsized in the Mississippi River, was my great-great-grandfather. He had begun buying land when he came of age. The records show that he owned more than six thousand acres in Claiborne County, Mississippi, together with a thousand

---

I appreciate that the word "colored" became pejorative in the 1960's because of the "colored" and "white" drinking fountains and restrooms. The 'coloreds' then became 'Blacks', but many were not even dark brown. A large portion of the people whom I knew best were mixed with what was called 'Negro blood', Native American, white, and sometimes Chinese. I have occasionally used the word Negro, usually if it refers to a statute or to describe a person who has a portion of African American ancestry and referred to at the time of usage or in a quotation. I have used the words African American or black when speaking myself, but in dialogue before and until late 1960s I have used the word 'colored' which was polite at the times that the events took place. I certainly hope that no one will be offended.

21 Cobb 7-9 and 30

slaves.[22] One can surmise that adventure and the challenge of developing richer land led Moses and his brother Dr. Thomas Neil Shelby to come to the Mississippi Delta in 1852. He and his wife, Mary Jane (nee Irwin), already had five children when they arrived in the Delta.

Land, labor, medicine, and some means of education were all that the settlers needed. The death of Thomas Neil Shelby left them without a doctor. But Mary Jane and Moses must have been made of sturdy stock for four of their five children reached adulthood.

The few roads or tracks were almost impassable during the winter months when the deep fertile soil became a gummy mass. The only means of transportation was by horseback or wagon to which six mules were usually attached. Despite these primitive conditions the early settlers made every effort to maintain some social life and to meet for worship. A minister would come and hold services in different houses several times a year. In 1856 Moses Darwin Shelby had his slaves build a log house on the east end of Monochonut to be used as a church for the planter's families and their slaves and as a school for the white children. It was called Holmes Lake Methodist Church, South. (The Shelby family was Methodist-Episcopalian). Services were held for the white people in the morning and for the slaves in the afternoon. In 1868 this church was given to the black people and became St. Peter's Methodist Church, a landmark in the area for a long time.

Mrs. Jennie Elder Brander, the first teacher in this part of Bolivar County, taught the children of five families in a small house in the yard of Monochonut plantation until the church was built. She was replaced by Mr. Will Payne, a family friend from Grenada, Mississippi.[23]

The four children of Moses and Mary Jane who survived into adulthood were Isaac, Evan, Minnie and Mary (David died as a child during the Civil War). I have pictures of their two sons, Evan and Isaac. Isaac, my

22 Shelby 22
23 Sillers, ed, 371

great-grandfather, shared with his brother sandy hair, high foreheads, gray eyes, roman noses, full lips, and robust complexions.

The University of Mississippi, chartered in 1844, had its first session in 1848 with 80 students in the liberal arts. According to the *Historical Catalogue of the University of Mississippi (1849-1909)*, the student body in antebellum days was entirely different from that of later years. They claimed that the per capita distribution of wealth in Mississippi was larger in the years before the Civil War than in any other state. (This no doubt referred to white people only.) Not surprisingly the student body was composed of the sons of wealthy parents, many of who did not realize the importance of work or study. Their strengths lay in other directions. Isaac had graduated from the university with honor in 1860 and stayed on to study law. Evan left medical school to become a captain in the Confederate Army. His degree with honor was bestowed upon him in 1862, while he was serving in the Confederacy as a medical officer.

At the close of the spring session in 1861, there was some expectation that classes might resume in the fall. Four students appeared for matriculation. Realizing that the war would continue indefinitely, the faculty resigned and the doors of the institution were closed. In the spring of 1861, many students withdrew before the end of the session in order to enlist in the Confederate army. A company of students that became legendary was organized on the campus under the title "University Greys." The number on the roll of this company was 135. Losses from all causes numbered 111. Probably four-fifths of all the young men whose names appeared on the rolls as students of the University from its organization up to the beginning of the Civil War enlisted in the Confederate service.[24]

Moses Darwin Shelby formed his own company, The Bolivar Greys, of which he was the captain and his son Isaac a sergeant.[25] As the war ended

24 Anon, Historical Catalogue University of Mississippi, 1849-1909, pp. 133,139, 392-93, 9-11

25 Sillers, ed, 142

he was Colonel Shelby and his sons were captains.

When the clouds of war were gathering in the spring of 1860, Isaac Shelby acquired a friendship album in which his friends and fraternity brothers in Delta Kappa Epsilon wrote. Their style was fluid and eloquent, fashionable at that time. Only one was frivolous. They were a paradigm of the aspirations of that society with themes of friendship, adversity, Isaac's manly qualities, his good nature and big heart, exhortations to "noble thoughts and deeds", referring to things temporal and alluding to impending death.

One friend wrote, "You have told me Ike that you have no ambition other than to be a good citizen. You shall get none the less honor if you set well your part in this respect than he who aspires to be the child of power and the well paid grandee of fame."

Another referred to him as an Adventurous Knight, Swift Footed Knight, Gallant Knight, and signed the letter "Faithful Knight."

A friend from Port Gibson, Mississippi (Claiborne County) wrote, "Well I do remember the first day I saw you at the old country schoolhouse, and how my heart was drawn to you at the first sight of your good-natured countenance, ever since than I have known you as one of my best friends."

I take the liberty of reproducing two letters.

To My Old Friend Ike.

After nearly four years connection as friends and classmates, you have requested me to write a few lines in your album, as a token of eternal friendship. Ike, had I the eloquence of a Dem------ (unclear) or the inspired pen of Lah--- (unclear), then might I attempt to express the feelings of one who has ever from our first acquaintance as insignificant freshmen fully appreciated your talented and generous soul. And I shall ever be proud to hail you as a friend; for I believe you possess all the qualities, which constitute a <u>true man</u>. When in after years your manly brow shall be furrowed, your robust form bent, and your head whitened by the frost of many winters then you may think that the many hours that we have spent together talking over the scenes of the past and also of the ones we love, might have been employed better. So they might, but Ike they will ever be the sweet sessions (unclear) of my college days, and I hope the time will never come when they will be considered otherwise by me, and be assured if you have gained nothing else, by our association as friends, you gained the friendship, and that I will be your friend as long as life last. Ike I hope the one you profess to love will prove worthy of so virtuous (unclear) a knight and that you may live in peace and happiness, and when your race is run, may you enter the abode of the _good_."

J. W. Buchman
Buena Vista, Miss.

Written in pencil in a neat and precise hand beneath this letter are the words "severely wounded at the battle of Jonesboro, Georgia." The same pencil has recounted the fate of all but a few of these young men. "Died from disease contracted in the army." "Killed in the battle of ----- Maryland." "Wounded in the battle of Shiloh." "Died April 1962 at the Smithfield House, Chattanooga, Tennessee from disease." "Killed accidentally at Manassas, July 22nd 1861." "Killed at Gettysburg, Virginia." "Killed at Battle of Manassas, July 2nd 1861." "Killed in battle." "Killed in the seven days fight around Richmond."

The second letter tells a different tale. It is from Isaac's mother and was written while he was in a Northern prison of war camp.

My dear son,
Among the many names recorded in your Album, I know that the name of your Mother will have a welcomed place. ---- (unclear)

in all your lists of friends, you well know that your Mother is near-
est and truest, and her loves unchangeable. While life lasts, it nour-
ished and tended your helpless infancy and in the promises of your
youth and manhood it found its highest blessing and reward. When
my sons went out to battle for our sunny South my heart went with
you in prayer and faith and my loving care which your Mother can
most deeply feel and experience. Your noble brother has passed
away my son. He died as a brave, true Southman should, and many
hearts join in our mourning and desolation. He is gone. Close fol-
lowing after our angel David, to join our angel lad who waits for
us in heaven, and now you are our one, only son, doubly dear for
the trials and dangers you have passed, as well as for those gifts of
mind and heart that lead us to picture for you a bright and honored
life. And though you are absent and afraid in an enemy's land, your
Mother my dear boy is praying and hoping for you, praying that
in all your ways you will remember the God who blesses you with
friends, even in prison, and hoping she will soon look upon your
young bright face and listen to the joyous accents of your voice.
And she fervently prays that the God who has preserved your life
through four years of war and bloodshed will guard and spare you
through this fearful struggle of our country and enable you to fill
out a long term of life, distinguished as a true honorable man and
a humble God-loving Christian.

This is the prayer of your loving Mother,
Mary Jane Irwin Shelby
Monochonut, March 9th 1865

Months before the war ended, Isaac's brother Evan, a medical officer, was guarding the Mississippi River at a camp near Concordia. After the capture of Memphis, gunboats came down the River and it was necessary to patrol the river. Evan heard a noise of someone leaving the camp. He commanded the man to halt, but the insider, a deserter, shot and killed him. At this time Evan was engaged to marry Ellen Augusta Poitevent who lived in Grenada, Mississippi.

The letter continues:

> P. S.
>
> *My dear precious son, Just ten years today since this was written. Many afflictions have we passed through and we will have many more before another ten years passes. If we are faithful, we shall all form one unbroken family around our father's throne, no more to part, it is the prayer of your Mother, that you and your dear family, may live as long and be as happy as we have all been together. Be faithful my only dear boy and look to God for all things, is the prayer of,*
>
> *your loving Mother.*
>
> *Monochonut, March 19, 1875*
>
> *Ten more years from today where will we be?*

Someone wrote in pencil, "November 1885, Ah, where?

During the War, Stark's cavalry regiment was stationed in Bolivar County and selected the great bend of the river – now Lake Beulah – north of Prentiss and south of Beulah, as their place of action. The town of Prentiss, now Rosedale (the County seat, 20 miles from Shelby), was taken by Federal troops, who freed all of the criminals in the jail and burned the town.[26]

Federal troops came through Monochonut and burned the cotton that had been stored in anticipation of the end of the war, but they did a strange thing: they supplied the family with a trunk full of receipts on behalf of the Federal Government for property that they had destroyed. These documents remained in the same trunk in our storage room for years in the vain

---

26 Sillers, ed. 149-50

hope that the receipts might be honored.

There is another document found in the trunk: a ledger. It had later become a children's scrapbook containing cuttings from various newspapers. The book reveals a curious fact: following the Emancipation Proclamation in 1863, the slaves acquired last names and were charged for their supplies, yet they continued to work at Monochonut. Very few Confederates paid any attention to the decree for which Abraham Lincoln was most famous, as the two parts of the States were separate nations and at war. After the fall of Vicksburg in 1863, many people in Mississippi favored ending the war.

Nevertheless, General Charles Clark was elected governor as an anti-peace candidate and despite the sentiment there was only token opposition in the election. During his administration the Federal Army occupied the state capital, forcing him to move the capital to Macon and then to Columbus and back to Macon. Confederate troops from Alabama and Mississippi surrendered on May 6, 1865. The governor was arrested upon returning to Jackson to a hastily convened special session of the legislature. He was placed in prison at Fort Pulaski.[27] I don't know if any of my ancestors opposed Governor Clark, but I note that Colonel Moses Shelby's own grandfather, Moses Jr., had become impressed by religion shortly after his marriage and freed his slaves.[28] One can only surmise that the freeing of slaves may have been the reason for the Federal troops giving my great-great-grandfather receipts for the cotton they had burned. He could also have foreseen that the South would lose the war and freed his slaves in an effort to retain their support, as the loss of labor was the ever-abiding fear of the Delta.

27 On Line Publications of the Mississippi Historical Society, Charles Clark Twenty-Fourth Governor of Mississippi: 1863-1865, 2000-2004

28 Letter from Gov. Isaac Shelby to John Crittenden his aide-de-camp on the Upper Canada campaign in the war of 1812, documentation supplied in a letter from genealogist Cass K. Shelby to May Shelby Carnes Shelby, Dec. 15, 1953.

Isaac Shelby and his wife Ellen August Poitevent, great grandparents of the author, who died young after the Civil War, leaving five children.

Immediately after the Civil War the halls of the University of Mississippi were filled again, but with a class of students never seen before in any American college. They were the sons of parents who had been wealthy, but whose wealth had been swept away by the war. Perhaps half of these young men had served in the Confederate Army. With such preparation for college as the circumstances suggest they came with possibly as little scholastic attainments as those students who entered in 1848; but they came with a determination born of necessity. In later years the University achieved a much higher standard in scholarship.[29]

***

A dedicated lady came into our family when Isaac married Ellen Augusta Poitevent, called Ella, his brother's fiancée, on May 30th, 1866. She descended from Huguenots who came from the Orleanais and Maine provinces of France in 1685 to Orange Quarter, South Carolina, bringing a family group that numbered ten. The elder Poitevent (the name was originally Portevin) who came to the United States was named Antoine. The refugees were accompanied to South Carolina by a minister, Laurent Philippe Trouillard, the first pastor of the little colony of Orange Quarter. This colony intermarried with the other settlers in Orange Quarter. The land grants that they received were comparatively small (200 and 150 acres), but their assets were increased by intermarriage with a family named Bordeaux who had more land. The area in which they settled was a peninsula formed by the Cooper and Wando Rivers and was probably settled by these families before Old Charleston was removed to Oyster Point. They cultivated the vine, olive, and mulberry, and engaged in the manufacture of wine, oil and silk. A small church was erected and regularly attended by Huguenot families. They arrived briefly before Louis XIV revoked the Edict of Nantes on October 21st, 1685.[30]

29 Historical Catalogue of the University of Mississippi, 10-11

30 Maynard, Isabel Thomas Poitevent Barksdale, Poitevent Genealogy,

The Poitevents moved to North Carolina in 1836, and later three branches of this family traveled from Brunswick County, North Carolina to Mississippi. This was a trek lasting forty-seven days and covering over 900 miles before most members joined other relations in Hancock County, Mississippi. The journey was recorded in detail by a young lady, Miss Amelia P. Russ, a member of the group, who appears to have later married a Poitevent. They marched or rode on horses and lived off the land, buying essential supplies. Two branches of the family settled in the region of Hancock County on the Gulf of Mexico.[31] Ellen's branch descended from one John Poitevent, who settled in Grenada, Mississippi, a hill town located on the edge of the Mississippi, Delta, where he was buried in 1853.[32] They carried with them a belief that all superior culture came from France and they appeared to have for the most part intermarried with other Huguenot families in the States for the first two hundred years of their settlement in the country.

What caused Isaac to marry his brother's bereaved fiancée? Was she the loved one referred to by his friend six years earlier? That is doubtful. Their whole world had been turned upside down and the South was facing twelve gruesome years of Reconstruction.

I found a clipping from a newspaper, the name of which has disappeared, describing the pair on their wedding trip.

In the summer of 1866 the writer met an old friend and comrade, Captain Isaac Shelby with his young and blooming bride. The luxurious season, the happiness of themselves and those who attended them on this blissful tour, harmonized gloriously with the grand emotions of these two young hearts newly frightened with

---

Birmingham, Ala. 1967, 3-8

31 A Journal of Our Travels of Miss Amelia P. Russ, Hancock County, Mississippi, Feb 18 – April 14,, 1836

32 Maynard 28

the delightful burden of marriage. The manly port and character of the bridegroom, the grace and beauty of his dark eyed bride, challenged the admiration of all in that pleasant resort of refined people. In my whole memory I cannot recall a more propitious union.

Isaac was twenty-six, Ellen was twenty.

In 1866 Moses sold to Isaac his farming equipment, animals, and presumably land for the sum of $15,000. The deed which I found describes seventeen mules, three horses, five yoke of oxen, fifty head of cattle, thirty-nine head of sheep, fifty hogs, two wagons and harnesses, and all ploughs, hoes, and axes. The estate was considerably less than the one that he left in Claiborne County for this Delta adventure. It is difficult for me to comment on the price, for many people were leaving the Mississippi Delta at that time and most people would have divested themselves of United States currency for worthless Confederate dollars. The deed does not state the number of acres and there was no description of the land. I don't know where the money came from (probably the cotton crops). It appears not to have been a straw man conveyance because a promissory note indicates that Isaac met his obligation by paying his father $5,000 in 1865 and $10,000 the following year when the assignment was made.

Mary Jane had had her fill of the Delta. In 1867 she bought a house sitting on twenty-two acres lying two and one half miles east of Memphis, Tennessee and moved there with Moses and her two daughters, Mary and Minnie. Records indicate that this was partly paid by Mary Jane and no doubt the rest by her husband, who in the same year bought a lot in Elmwood Cemetery in Memphis for $340 and paid a man $60 to plant a hedge and trees on the lot. This bill contrasts sharply with a medical bill for $37, representing four visits and six prescriptions. These figures further contrast with an agreement with a company known as Lott, Butcher & Co., date

1867, to deliver to Isaac Shelby nine hands to work on his plantation for a year for the sum of $180, or twenty dollars a head, none of which would probably have been seen by the men who would work in order to eat. The slaves were free, but many years were to pass before free men were worth more than oxen and gravesites.

Monochonut was sold in 1871 for $400 taxes, owed to the Mississippi Levee Commissioners, and redeemed in the same year by Moses Shelby. After Mary Jane, Moses and their two daughters moved to Memphis in 1866, their daughter Minnie made her debut and married a Mr. Fred Nelson, who became a much beloved and wealthy relation for whom several people of our family were named. Moses and Mary Jane would certainly appear to have retained some money, but by the times of their deaths, there is no evidence of a considerable inheritance. I do not know what happened to the other daughter, Mary Louise. It is possible that she was not normal, because nothing in family records ever said anything about her and she lived into her eighties with the family of her sister Minnie. Moses died in 1871, the year that he redeemed Monochonut for taxes. He was sixty-two.[33]

Ellen, Isaac's wife, was reputed to have been a beauty. She had curly dark hair, large eyes, small lips and sloping shoulders. She was said to have gone about the plantation with a Bible in one hand and a medicine spoon in another administering to the former slaves. There was a white family who lived within riding distance. The young mother had a baby who failed to thrive. Ellen rode to her house and offered the help of a black woman on her plantation, who had enough milk for two babies. The young mother was suspicious and retorted that no "Negro" woman was going to nurse her baby. In an embryonic version of Ward of Court Proceedings, Ellen collected the infant, tied it to her back, rode away, and returned the healthy baby nine months later.

Isaac and Ellen's children were born in close succession. My grandfather Darwin Poitevent Shelby was born in March 1867, his sister Mary Jean

---

33 Shelby 23

(called Madia) the following year, and Ellen Walton in 1870. Two years later Isaac, Jr. was born, followed by Evan in 1874 and Fitzgerald in 1877, six children in ten years. Evan lived to be only three.[34]

In 1878 Ellen's sixteen-year-old brother, Thomas, traveled alone by horse from Grenada to Monochonut, through about sixty miles of cane, forest and mud to bring them news of Ellen's family.

At past five o'clock in the evening of August 11th 1878, Jacob Poitevent wrote to his wife's half brother Judge William Henry Fitzgerald, who lived in Friars Point, Mississippi:

> *Dear William,*
>
> *I suggest you have herd of our safe arrival at home from that delightful Sea Coast. I am still improving – but am sorry to say that we jumped out of the frying pan into the fire. We have the genuine Yellow Fever in our Town – it has been confined to three blocks commencing at Misters Old Stand on Main Street to Stevenson Carriage Factory running to the Depot. Had two deaths day before yesterday and 4 up to 4 o'clock today making 6 deaths from it. There are about 50 now sick – in these Blocks – of about 1 – sick in all in the Town – but don't suppose half is Yellow fever (deaths today are ....) about five more not expected to live (.......). I am well and all the family except Ora. She had a fever but clear of it today. Your sister went out to Dr. Fs this morning – looking for her back tonight – Dr. R. wants us to go out to his house. I am willing for family to go but your Sister wants me and all to ...will determine tomorrow. Maggie Coffman is very ill not expected to live (with Yellow Fever). Dr. H. is nearly worn out – the Odd Fellow has dispatched for nurses. Many leaving town frightened nearly to death but my people appear to take it calmly. Dr. Fitz has had the fever – in New York. I have been with it so we are not easily frightened.*

---

34 Shelby 23-24

*This Sunday evening the Town nearly looks desolate. Had a good
rain this evening and in hopes health will improve. Love to all.*
    Yours truly and in heart,

    J. Poitevent

Sixteen days later his wife, Mary Jane, was dead of the fever and he
died the following day. His nurse, thinking that he might recover, did not
tell him of his wife's death. Their two daughters Mary Gause and Ora also
died in the epidemic, ages twenty-seven and twenty-one. (Ora lingered in a
bad state for two years.)[35] The letters indicate that half the children went to
the country when Ora and Mary became ill and the parents could not leave.
The servants abandoned the house; Jacob Poitevent did the cooking, and
his wife the nursing. This is incorporated into another letter to his brother-
in-law asking for coffee. No one entered the death house for months.[36]
Their children Janie, Lula, and Thomas, and grand children, Darwin Poitevent Shelby, Madia Shelby Murnan and Gerald (Fitzgerald) Shelby, George
and Fred Shelby, Isabel, Mary and Janula Poitevent, came to live in Shelby
on our street.

Mary Jane Irwin Shelby died in 1880. Her son Isaac died of malaria
on October 14th, 1883. Ellen, too, is reported to have also died of malaria
three months later in 1884, but her cause of death is not certain for she
had been ill several months before her husband was stricken. She was not
yet thirty-eight, leaving five children between the ages of six and sixteen.

The writer who had met the couple as newlyweds continued with the
obituary.

    *In November of last year the brave and affectionate
    father was stricken down and the loving and tender moth-*

---

35 Maynard 47
36 Maynard 48-52

er, then lying ill followed him on January 7th 1884. Among her last words were those that came like a whispering of the death notes of the old mothers of Israel: 'God's will be done through all, I yield: I am glad to yield. I shall soon drink of the waters that flow at the Savior's feet.' She had not only faith, but the delight in Christ that follows faith, and though she grieved to part from her little ones, yet she was happy in the thought and fixed hope of soon meeting her loved ones before God's throne. Her consciousness and perception continued to the last, and joy, rather than fear, ruled at the parting hour.

Ellen's sister Janie Poitevent married George Barnes Shelby, Isaac's second cousin. They took over the management of Monochonut and the care of the extended family of children. Child mortality was expected. Two years later Isaac Jr. died at the age of fourteen. Janie and George added their own children, Fred and George and a daughter Janora, who died aged four in 1885 and there had also been a son, Thomas, who had died at age one in the preceding year. In 1886 Uncle George bought the remaining equity in Monochonut from the children of Isaac and Ellen. I am not certain why so little equity remained in the property, but it must be remembered that reconstruction lasted for twelve years following the war and there was also bad health. Mississippi was only re-admitted to the union in 1869. Ellen's older sister Margaret and youngest sister Lula Poitevent moved to the Delta. Lula married a gentle, elegant businessman, William Connell. Maggie (Margaret) died young, a teacher and a spinster. These people formed the nucleus of my relations who came to live on this street.

The Third Generation
(1880s and 1890s)

A third generation gradually moved into the small settlement, located a mile and a half east of Monochonut Plantation, which had been built on the land of Dr. Thomas Shelby and his wife Bella. The Delta began to thrive. The population continued to number nine or ten African American people for every white. A small melting pot soon developed as immigrants arrived. Some were carpetbaggers, others peddlers. "Every American community has its leaven of Jews. Ours arrived shortly after the Civil War with packs on their backs, peddlers from Russia, Poland, and Germany. They sold trinkets to the Negroes and saved. Today they are plantation-owners, bankers, lawyers, doctors, merchants; their children attend the great universities, win prizes, become connoisseurs in the arts and radicals in politics."[37]

There had been Jewish people in the river settlements since earliest times, notably Mr. Godfrey Frank and even a Rothschild.[38] The story of the Jews in the Mississippi Delta is enough material for a book. Their status in the society was equal to their education and contributions. There were no Jewish ghettos in the Mississippi Delta. William Alexander Percy wrote, "Jews too much like natives even to be overly prosperous."[39] Later there was an influx of families from south Mississippi who came from Wilkinson and Amite Counties to live in Shelby. They were the Tolars, the Wilkinsons, the Smiths, the Dentons, the Doolittles, the Roberts, and the McLeans

---

37 Percy, William Alexander, Lanterns on the Levee, Recollections of a Planter's Son , with introduction by Walker Percy, Louisiana State Press, Baton Rouge, copyright renewed 1973, published by special arrangement Alfred A. Knopf, Inc. 2004 printing, 17

38 Sillers, ed., 135

39 Percy 231

(some of these families lived on the street). Many came to these prosperous lands farther north after a boll weevil disaster in South Mississippi. That is when the population of this hamlet increased from 520 in the first census of 1903 to 1,300 by 1920.[40] There were also a few Chinese.

Cypress trees continued to furnish the principal building material, for they flourished in these lowlands. There were no fire departments, so few old houses have survived. Notwithstanding the area's wealth, the houses were by and large featureless farmhouses. Early settlers in the Delta did not come with their highboys and lowboys, crystal and china; there were no fine French and English architects as in Natchez and New Orleans. I inherited one Limoges plate from my great- grandmother and a portrait of my great-grandfather as a young boy. The early settlers only brought their chattels, children, wives, slaves, and a library of leather bound volumes. The library that I inherited I notice when I remove the Christmas cards from the bookshelves. They include *Works of John C. Calhoun*, a second edition of Thomas Jefferson's notes on the *History of Virginia*, *Works of Daniel Webster*, Balzac, *Sparks's American Biography*, novels without the identity of the author (considered vulgar), *The Works of Lord Byron*, my great-grandfather Isaac's books in Greek, law books, medical books of his brother, (one mentioned that a healthy thing to do was to take a bath every day, and this was done with two pans, one above with a string, one below, and it was very refreshing), and a charming leather bound book (author undisclosed) of travels in the upper Nile. There were books on philosophy, two leather-bound volumes of Shakespeare, and a fat leather-bound Bible with deaths and births inscribed in a flourishing hand (observation is confirmed by William Alexander Percy).[41] Their civilization remained in the woodlands and within their souls.

The rich land produced all types of garden vegetables as well as soft fruits. The forest gave us possum, bear, deer, wild turkey, and duck, and the

---

40 Sillers, ed., 374

41 Percy 7

river gave fresh fish, but cotton remained the chief agricultural product. In 1880, when Mississippi ranked first among the States in the amount of cotton raised, the Delta was producing a large portion of this crop. The adventure appeared to have succeeded. Although the levee system protected one fourth of the four million acres of the Mississippi Delta, floods remained a threat until the 1930s, the penalty for this rich alluvial soil.

Sparsely populated, in 1880 the largest town in the state of Mississippi was Vicksburg, which had a recorded population of 11,814 inhabitants, and Jackson, the capital, 5,204 people.[42]

The first family to locate in the town of Shelby was that of Dr. A. P. Rose, who built a house on the other side of the street in 1885. He bought a dry goods establishment and added drugs to this stock. His son Willard came to own what we called a drug store on our street, although he sold no drugs for which a prescription was necessary. Dr. Rose was the first doctor in the town, the first postmaster and the first depot agent. The first school within the town's limit was organized in the back room of Dr. Rose's office. Five children attended; I note one of them was George B. Shelby. The first proper schoolhouse was a frame building on the lot donated by Mr. Godfrey Frank in 1887. There was one teacher, a Miss Annie Lusk. [43]If children were to receive any form of education beyond the most basic, they had to be sent away to schools. My relations were sent to schools in Tennessee (Christian Brothers in Memphis, Webb School in Bellbuckle and the University of the South at Sewanee.) After that it was considered a good idea to spend at least a year at the University of Mississippi in Oxford so that one would make local friends.

The children in my family and their Aunt Maggie Poitevent used their isolation to write letters to the New Orleans *Picayune* newspaper, which was owned by a cousin, the poetess Eliza Poitevent Nicholson (pen named, Pearl Rivers), who doubtless permitted the printing of these letters as a

---

42 *Encyclopedia Britannica*, 9th ed. 1898 522-523

43 Sillers, ed. 374

gesture of good will to her cousins who lived up country. Their main purpose was to tell the world and especially the people of New Orleans how we lived. Aunt Maggie sometimes used the *Picayune* to communicate with her relations who were spending their summers in cooler places.

One letter read: "Dear Pic, to my little nephew George Shelby, who is spending the summer in Monteagle, Tennessee, you have a surprise awaiting your return. I have procured a puppy from a little ragged colored boy in exchange for a bundle of clothes."

Another letter said: "Dear Pic, we have twelve pecan trees in our garden. My brothers George and Fred help gather these pecans in the fall and the women on the plantation crack them.
Janora Shelby 1885."[44]

A few months later Janora was dead.

Despite being educated elsewhere, all but one of the third generation returned to live on our street in Shelby. They had been orphans and family ties were considerably stronger than they are today. I believe that the motive was clear in a letter that my grandfather wrote to my grandmother in 1899, after he had been ill for fourteen days with a fever that he claimed left him scarcely recognizable, having lost fourteen pounds.

Our country is looking beautiful now. We can view from one of our upstairs windows 1200 acres of cotton in one field, about five feet high in full bloom, a carpet of green with immense forest trees surrounding the whole as a background. When I look at it I think of what I heard an old German woman say on the train last

---

44 I quote this letter to the *Picayune* from memory because I came across it in about 1962, after the death of my Aunt Mary Poitevent.

Darwin Poitevent Shelby about 1897.

*summer. She had never seen a cotton field before and early one
morning she looked out the window and turned to her husband in
surprise and exclaimed, 'Erste, look at the field of roses.'*

They had been pricked by the cotton rose and it seeped into the blood-
stream.

The street began to bustle with enterprises in the latter part of the
1890's, when several families who played an important part in this story
now came to live on the street. This was the beginning of the businessman
planter as described by James C. Cobb.[45] In 1897 William Connell and Dr.
J. C. Brooks opened a general merchandise store. Connell married my Aunt
Lula Poitevent and their colonial home remains one of the last houses on
the street. Dr. Brooks became a very wealthy Delta planter. Mr. Godfrey
Frank bought the plantation owned by Dr. Thomas Shelby and thereafter
donated lots for the Methodist and Baptist churches, the first school, and
the depot. Mr. William. T. Morrison, another merchant, had a house on
the other side of the street and his marriage to Miss Douglass Martin was
the first wedding in the newly erected Methodist church. They died in their
youths, shortly after the death of their baby daughter, and left one son,
Scott Morrison, an austere, handsome boy, who lived with his mother's twin
sister, Mrs. Smith from Merigold, a few miles down the road, and also in
Memphis. The Smith family had a son, Jimmie Smith, who was as wild and
witty as Scott was austere and they got on extremely well. Scott went away
to boarding schools and during the vacations made friends with the Memphis boys, among them my father. It was a close friendship for a lifetime.
Scott returned to Shelby and to our street and married Ruth Thomas. They
became an important part of my childhood. He served as mayor of the
town for many years, living in the Thomas house on our street.

Darwin Poitevent Shelby and Thomas Poitevent became prosper-

---

45 Cobb 93-5

ous quite early in their young lives. After his parents died of yellow fever, Thomas Poitevent moved to the Mississippi Gulf Coast region and worked for his relations in the Poitevent & Farve Lumber Company. He returned to the Delta in 1893 and bought an interest in the store that then became "Cornell & Poitevent".

Mr. J. W. Thomas came to the Delta selling fruit trees, according to his daughter Ruth. He also worked for Mr. Frank in a business similar to Cornell & Poitevent, until he acquired the major interest in this business and built a large house on our street.[46]

Thomas Poitevent built a gin in 1899 and a spoke factory the following year, established the Bank of Shelby, and in 1903 established an oil mill, for the processing of cottonseed oil. He also built some stores that were let to local merchants and bought some land.[47] All of his businesses were located on the street.

Darwin Shelby returned to Shelby after finishing Christian Brothers School in Memphis and working for Mr. Godfrey Frank for a year as a cotton buyer. He declared that he would rather have his own peanut stand than to work for another man, even his close friend. His good standing with Mr. Frank enabled him to buy the plantation called Lucknow from Mrs. Evans, one of the original settlers, which was located on the northern end of the street. He began buying other land (about 2000 acres) and built a cotton gin across the street from his house, which was the first house on our side of the street. I have a photograph of him sitting on bales of cotton at his gin, our house in the background and not a tree in sight. Darwin built a block of stores on the west side of the street, adjacent to the Bank of Shelby, and bought an interest in the bank. He then consolidated his holdings in farmland to Lucknow and the businesses, for he said that he only worked to put his feet on the fender all winter and read a good book. A debt on land was too great an impingement on his freedom. He was an avid reader of mainly

46 Sillers, ed. 372

47 Maynard 54

French literature, Balzac, Stendhal, Victor Hugo, and, always his favorite American writer, Mark Twain.

In 1997 William Washington Denton moved to Shelby from South Mississippi as the second Depot Agent and became partners with Thomas Poitevent in the spoke factory. He later bought the entire business, which became a cotton gin and afterwards formed the foundation for the Denton Manufacturing Company (which included many businesses to be described later when he went into partnership with his brother Charles.) Both brothers spent their lives on our street.

By 1895 the village was thriving enough to have a weekly newspaper, the *Shelby Exchange*. The town was largely destroyed by fire in 1896, but was quickly rebuilt, although a sewage system, sidewalks, a livestock law, and screens were slower to arrive. There was a most colorful law enforcement officer, called "Uncle Billy Wooten" (W. J.). He insisted that everyone observe the law, but reserved the right to break it himself when he felt so inclined. His many escapades and vigorous law enforcement methods formed a large part of local folklore and were a major factor in making sure that Shelby was not as wild as the river towns. I wish I could take his escapades further but that is impossible, as I find no document to record them. He deserves to be remembered, if only for one reason: the saloons were closed.[48]

The life of most African Americans, who continued to outnumber the white population of about ten to one in the period of about twenty-five years after the Civil War, had altered little between the War and 1890. They remained on the plantations, where they were given sufficient food and three-room shotgun cabins with outside toilets. I doubt if they had a school in Shelby at that time. The first African American school was placed on the other side of the street. It consisted of one large wooden room, located on the land of Mr. H. L. Wilkinson. It was painted red (schools should be red). A larger brick school was eventually built at the back of the town. There

48 Sillers, ed., 372-73

were separate, but not equal facilities. In the course of time (my time) there came a good and dedicated African American school principal, a Mr. Williams, who also owned a plantation and seemed to take a real interest in his people. The life of the Delta black was by necessity simple: birth, work, singing, propagating, church, and death.[49] *

Political discontent festered in the Delta at the end of the 1880s when a Farmer's Alliance Movement capitalized on the growing dissatisfaction of small farmers, black and white. The Alliance movement posed a threat of a biracial coalition of have-nots capable of ousting the Delta's planter-business elite from its dominant position in state and local politics. There was also a fear of a black majority seizing physical as well as political control. Rumors of riots swept across the counties in 1889 when anti-black sentiment erupted tragically in LeFlore County after a Colored Farmer's Alliance organizer, one Oliver Cromwell, received stern warnings and even death threats from local whites. Leflore County's blacks rallied to his defense, presenting a statement of defiance said to represent the feelings of "3,000 armed men." The Leflore County Sheriff called on the National Guard to keep the peace, but before they arrived, a posse of local whites

---

49 Attached as Appendix A is the honest, if unsettling account, of Senator W. B. Roberts of Rosedale as taken from the History of Bolivar County, Mississippi 161-165, which describes the activities of the Ku Klux Klan immediately after the Civil War, and how the white people through gerrymandering the ballot boxes retained political control of an area where they were out numbered 10 to 1. I never heard of any Klan activities in Shelby; the town may have been too small for it to have existed, or perhaps law and order were kept by "Uncle Billy Wooten." The Klan in later years became an organization to which no gentleman would belong, but this was not the case directly after the Civil War when former servants, numbering 10-1, had become the masters. This article by Senator Roberts was written factually, honestly, with some nostalgia of times practicing law along the Mississippi River.

apparently killed as many as twenty-five African American people; a number of those killed were involved with the Alliance. There were numerous reports of whites invading African American houses and even killing a little black girl.[50]

In the early 1890s a serious uprising took place in Shelby. The specific reason could have festered from the political discontent near to this time or the manipulations of the whites to disenfranchise the blacks, as both occurred within a short span of each other. In any event, black men obtained arms and barricaded themselves in the town hall, and for some reason, determined to shoot it out. They appeared to have trusted Darwin, who was put forward to try to talk to them through the door. He approached them calmly and unarmed. They allowed him to enter. He reasoned with them, conceding that they would succeed in winning this fight and kill many white people. After that he said that the State Militia would be called, whereupon most of them would be killed. "Hand me your guns. No harm will come to you." They came forward with their ammunition and the rebellion was quashed. There were no reprisals.[51]

A state constitution convention had been called in 1890 to consider disenfranchisement, and by 1895 their work was done with poll tax, literacy tests, and a secret ballot, incorporated into the 1895 gubernatorial election. By that time the Republican opposition (Republicans were then the party representing the black minority in contrast to today) was in disarray and the disenfranchisement provisions worked. The percentage of black males who did not vote rose from 71 percent to nearly 100 percent in 1895.[52] These troubles would appear to have lead to the uprising in Shelby.

*

Most of the earliest stores in the center of the town remain in situ, although today they are boarded. They were originally rented to the Jewish

---

50 Cobb 84-5.

51 Shelby 26

52 Cobb 86-7

merchants, the former peddlers, and the other side of the street remains to-day as it was photographed on the cover of this book. A Chinese merchant named Kuan Jon rented one of those stores. Kuan Jon returned to China in the 1890s and spent several years there. When he sought readmission to the United States, his appearance had altered from his last photograph and he was denied re-entry. Immigration authorities contacted Darwin, who identified him. This small favor seeded a crop of gratitude.

One year Darwin decided to conduct a test to determine his best friend. He never dressed in anything but the shabbiest of clothes. Dressed as he was, Darwin approached his uncles Thomas Poitevent, George Shelby, and William Cornell, shyly intimating that he was in a very bad shape financially. All sources met the hint with an embarrassed gentle stare over his shoulder, until his plight was made known to Kuan Jon, who responded enthusiasti-cally. "Mr. Shelby, here is my store. Everything in it is yours." Darwin then confessed that he was actually in good shape, but searching for his best friend.

At the turn of the century, Italian immigrants from Sicily came to the Delta in large numbers. They had originally been brought there by Sena-tor LeRoy Percy of Greenville to take the place of the African American labor.[53] They were excellent farmers and had no intention of replacing the black labor. Only machinery and chemicals did that. They farmed the land with their families and relied on very little outside help. The first genera-tion of Italians spoke only a few words of English and for some time re-mained semi-illiterate. Fortunate ones were given cabins upon their arrival, and others slept under paper and high grass on the riverside until they soon acquired plots of ground. Their small holdings came to be scattered around the town. A Roman Catholic Church eventually followed with church ba-zaars, selling spaghetti and homemade wine produced from the Muscatine vine, an ethnic treat. One Italian family, the DeMarcos, immigrated a bit earlier. The father had a tiny fruit vendor's store at the end of the shops on

---

53 Barry, John M., Rising Tide, Simon & Schuster, 1998, 109-13.

our street. Mr. DeMarco arrived with all of his belongings on his back and his son said that they were fed on rotten bananas. One son, called Sam, became a rich moneylender and built a large house on the street. His younger brother Jim, with Darwin's assistance, went to medical school and became a prominent doctor in Memphis. Jim and Darwin shared a young manhood. They took the train to Memphis and then to New York, where they walked down 5th Avenue at such a snails' pace that a stranger stopped them and said, "I know you are not from this city by the way that you walk."

It was a Shelby trait to impute noble birth to those for whom they cared and Darwin decided that the DeMarcos were different from the other Italians, because the De in front of their name meant that they had an aristocratic background, probably descendants of Marco Polo. He spread this myth.

After the railway came through the street, the most exotic of the visitors were the tramps. They arrived in boxcars, peeping from the sliding doors of moving trains to catch a glimpse of the countryside. Darwin was fascinated by these itinerants and ordered the night watchman of his cotton gin to invite them into a room in the gin for a warm retreat and a hot meal. They were bewildered. Today the idea would most certainly raise one's antennae. Many years later my mother ascribed this gesture to simple curiosity, the curiosity of a man born into a secure family on a frontier, coupled with generosity. The tramps were told to come to Darwin the following day, where they would be subjected to a number of personal questions to the tune of: "Why would a man want to live in a box car? Why does he choose to live a life, not knowing where he will sleep, carrying his belonging in a suitcase?" One weary tramp looked down. He did not have a suitcase. This search for an answer continued until after the First World War, when my mother remembers a polite tramp anxiously keeping an eye on his impending train while my grandfather cross-examined him about his lack of direction in life. Our house was put on the map of the hobo circuit. In the early 1950s tramps continued to stroll up the front walk in search of a hostel, interrupting Mother's afternoon nap. She spoke to them from behind a wrought iron grill over a double locked screen door surrounded by frenzied rat terriers that seemed to recognize the tramps by their clothes. They were discouraged or sent to my father for help.

There was a pasture of mules between the cotton gin and the oil mill in the early days, mules so sleek and fat they could hardly walk. They were another of Darwin's unique charities. He viewed a mule's life as nothing but drudgery with seldom a name or a pat or a rub. They lived by two simple commands, "Whoa mule," and "Get up mule." To compensate for this dreary life, Darwin turned them into pigs.

**

Darwin was thirty in 1897. He had had no serious girlfriends. Although fine-featured with a balding head, full lips, penetrating intelligent gray eyes that revealed a tender heart, he was essentially a man's man with no knowledge of the world that women inhabited. Both of his sisters had made their debuts in Memphis, where they lived with their Aunt Minnie Shelby Nelson. This had been financed in part by Darwin. Both sisters had married. It is doubtful if Darwin ever attended any of their parties. He didn't know how to dance. There was only a small equity in Monochonut after his father's death and the four younger children had to be educated. Darwin gave his share for his sisters' debuts and added more money. There was still much uncultivated land in the Delta, so that the price of a plantation was nowhere near $100 an acre or the $2000/$4000 an acre as it is today. The sizes were smaller as well, as everything had to be done manually.

Darwin's sisters were both beautiful women. The younger sister, Ellen, was a petite goddess, with her father's features, gray eyes, full lips, a classical nose, high color, and her mother's dark curly hair. Her eyes elongated and seemed to make an angle with the nose when she smiled, exhibiting a perfect set of slightly protruding white teeth. She fell in love (unwisely) with a young man from Grenada, Mississippi, when she was a girl. His name was Donald. He had no money and neither did she. Her father had died too soon to recover from the Civil War. The fruit of her debut was a rich widower from Nashville, Tennessee, a Mr. McEwen. He was a large and brilliant man, something of an inventor, but he was so large that when he went to the hospital on one occasion he had to have a special bed. Madia, her sister, also claimed that he had a peculiar odor. He came with full baggage of stepchildren almost Ellen's age, with whom she became most congenial. Nevertheless, he was a catch. When Ellen was eighteen a wedding took place at Monochonut. Madia, the bridesmaid, recalled that Ellen stood at the head of the stairway with Uncle George while friends and relations, having made their way over muddy roads, waited in the drawing room. Madia saw Ellen holding back her tears and turning trustingly to her kind old uncle. "If you say don't go, I won't go down the stairs." There was silence and the two proceeded.

What else was one to do with a girl in the Delta? There were not many eligible men, and marriage to a poor man could not be considered. The women were not trained to work. There was no health insurance, albeit doctors were cheap. They needed homes and someone to support babies.

The marriage lasted ten years, until his death. By the time that Ellen was twenty-eight, she was a rich and free widow, with three sons, Norman, Kennedy, and Donald (named for her first love), her youngest and favorite. The boys were sent away to boarding schools, and spent a large part of their holidays on our street. Ellen traveled almost constantly in Europe and America, accompanied by her husband's young daughter and his niece. She was never a happy woman. Most of Mr. McEwen's money was spent by those young ladies. Ellen even acquired an electric automobile. She is said to have had a scandalous affair with a Presbyterian minister in Nashville, during which she joined him in making calls upon his parishioners. One was late in answering the door. She kicked up her leg and rang the doorbell with her foot. Aunt Ellen never wanted to remarry. Her humor and sense of the absurd kept her going for a long time, until she committed suicide at age fifty-six in 1926.

Her older sister, Madia, had a much different life. She was beautiful as well, with a high bust, straight nose, elongated blue eyes, a charming smile and dark hair. The debut had not disposed of her. After one season she returned to Monochonut where life was tedious. Each weekend Darwin rode his horse over the mile and a half from Shelby to Monochonut to join his sister and fifteen or more relations in Aunt Janie and Uncle George's house. The table groaned with food. Men would ride out in the early mornings and inspect the crops and return to a breakfast that always included three kinds of meat, possum, ham and bear. How women remained slim is a secret worth knowing. Madia wrote letters to her sister in Nashville. "I have made candy, deserts, endeavored at needlepoint, and ride on my horse in the late afternoons."

Darwin shared his house in Shelby with a bachelor, an Irish doctor, Jim Murnan. He had red hair, twinkling eyes, and an impish sense of humor. He fell in love with Madia. That love was returned in full. There was a flaw, however. He came from very humble origins. She was twenty-six and met this impediment in a robust manner by consenting to the marriage on the terms of meeting his family after the wedding. The long marriage was all pipe and slippers and marvelous meals. Many friends came to their pleasant cottage on our street, with chintz slipcovers on the chairs and couches, cheerful pictures, and starched organdie curtains. Once she made this happy union she was very good to Jim's three plain spinster sisters and when she died the poor old ladies were provided for in her will. There were no children of this union. She didn't want any. Jim was enough. She must have secretly wondered what a beautiful woman would do with a daughter who looked like Miss Blanche or Miss Lizzie.

There were several doctors in the community; two in our family, for Fred Poitevent Shelby (the son of Uncle George and Aunt Janie) had recently qualified. Life of a young country doctor was one of struggle. House calls were made by horseback. Payments were sometimes made in chickens and eggs or not at all. The doctor was dependent on the planters to give them 'business,' as only planters could guarantee the care of their tenants.

Jim and Madia moved to Hillsboro, Texas, in 1896, where it was hoped that Jim would make a better living and Madia could benefit from a healthier climate. They nearly starved.

Darwin went to Hillsboro to visit Madia and Jim. He was accompanied by his black valet, Martin Pasco, whom he called "my pretty Martin" because he was so ugly. Martin had come into Darwin's service when the sheriff's posse was about to hang him, the rope already around Martin's neck. He was accused of killing his wife and mother-in-law. Darwin heard about Martin's impending doom and arrived on his horse just in time to release his neck from the noose by saying, "I'll stand for this man." He claimed that Martin's wife and mother-in-law were so mean that they needed killing and promised to take care of him for the rest of his life.

The two cut a figure in Texas. Martin lolled about Hillsboro and bragged to the other black people that in Mississippi his life was one of total ease. All that he was required to do was to polish Mr. Shelby's boots.

Darwin made a visit to a department store in Hillsboro, where he was riveted by the face in a mirror of a lady trying on a hat. He returned to his sister and said, "I have seen the most beautiful woman. I am going to marry her. She looks like my mother." Madia had to set about finding this vision. The description could fit only two people in the town, the Liner girls, but they looked so much alike that he and Madia had to call upon Mrs. Liner to pick the winner. They were Anna and Zula. His choice was Anna.

Anna, Frances and Zula
(1897-1903)

Anna looked nothing like the delicate and saintly Ellen, the mother whom the sixteen-year-old boy had lost. Her profile appeared to have been chiseled, complemented by an oval face, olive skin, Asian-black hair that had seldom been cut, brown eyes, an ample bosom and a determined chin. She was much more beautiful than his mother had been. Despite delicate health, Anna was a light and vivacious person, with no calling higher than the pleasures of life. She was artistic, a perfectionist in every thing that she did, and bursting with energy. Anna seemed to want few of the things that most women generally must have. She was neither loving nor maternal. If her choice had been wider, she would have been suited to a Bohemian life among artists in Paris, but her parents were genteel poor.

She was the poor relation of a rich Texas merchant family. They were as individual as Anna. The Grahams, her mother's family, were also early settlers of America and had immigrated to Augusta County, Virginia in 1773, after spending a few years in Belfast. They were known in America as the Scotch-Irish. A family genealogist, Thomas Graham Sinclair, has described in a recently published book, that the Graham, or Graeme, families descend from the Earls of Montrose, intermarrying on occasions with royalty, but for the most part were people of repute who accomplished important tasks and did not become embroiled in too many royal struggles. They were by and large lowlanders. The more immediate relations in the United States moved from Virginia and were found in buckskin trousers in a fort with Daniel Boone in Kentucky before moving on to Carroll County, Missouri, where Anna's grandfather married one Nancy Jane Minnis, the daughter of the local County Court judge and state representative.

William Harvey Graham (Anna's grandfather) tried to take a group of relations and friends from his town in Missouri to the Gold Rush in California. He became quite ill and spent most of his investment on staying alive. His physician advised him to return to Missouri, so he boarded a ship on the Pacific going to a point opposite Lake Nicaragua, where he crossed the Isthmus. He then boarded a vessel bound for New York. It was lost in a storm and by chance they came into the mouth of the Mississippi River, where they put in for relief. No one was allowed to leave the vessel, and after several days' waiting William Harvey Graham and a number of his followers deserted and ran ashore to reach New Orleans. There he took a steamer bound for St. Louis where he met his family. His devoted wife was still clutching a handkerchief with the $150 that he had left her two years before. He moved the family to Texas in 1871, acquired a farm, and took an agency to sell farm implements. He was the first to bring a harvester and cultivator to Texas soil. He produced a rather robust family of eight. Their two sons and a daughter (Aunt Jessie) developed a mercantile business when three railways came through the town of Hillsboro, Texas and oil was discovered. This was known as the Graham Syndicate, comprising 17 stores in Texas and Oklahoma. They would rise before the morning sun and sit on planks outside the main store until the country people began pouring into the town to buy their fabric. The family remained at work until half past ten in the evenings.

Anna's mother, Sarah Frances Graham, one of the Graham daughters, had married a dangerously handsome man named Jordan Taliferro Liner. He was from East Tennessee and university-educated. Although his anticipated education had been greatly diminished by the Civil War, he taught English for a while at a college in Louisville, Kentucky. That teacher's salary could not support his family, and they moved back to Texas where he became the bookkeeper for the Graham Syndicate. The whole family came to live in Hillsboro, Texas.[54] His salary with this new job could not support his

54 Sinclair, Thomas Graham, The William Graham and Harriet Forman family of Carroll County, Missouri, privately published by Thomas Graham

wife and three children in the custom to which the rest of her family lived. It was an unhappy household from which he was in partial banishment as a result of some infidelity. Anna's parents occupied opposite sides of their house and only spoke accidentally. Jordan took his meals at a local hotel for about fifty years. After his service to her family for probably forty years he was given a gold watch and chain, but no pension. He had to be supported by his children. There is a statute often seen in Hindu temples that touches me. It depicts a strong man carrying an amputee on his shoulders. Earlier societies were like this. The strong had to support the former generations, look after the orphans or those with no abilities to cope. Whites and blacks did this.

The Liner daughters worked in the family business. Anna, more delicate than her sister Zula, was consigned to making hats. That is why Darwin first saw her trying on a hat. At that time she was engaged to another man.

Darwin said that any man could get any woman he really wanted (politically quite incorrect). Letters poured through Anna's door, often delivered by Martin Pasco. Her parents could clearly see the advantage of this match for Darwin was well off and could give their daughter a life of ease. Anna was not sure she wanted to marry either man. A girl's honesty was no match against sensible parents and a man possessed. Anna and Darwin became engaged in the autumn of 1899. She had been stingy with her kisses, giving none until after the engagement was announced.

Darwin wrote euphorically from Shelby, Mississippi on 16th September 1899.

> Dearest,
>
> I will commence this to you by quoting a letter I have just received from my Aunt Janie in answer to a short letter I wrote her from Memphis.

Sinclair, St., printed by Anundsen Publishing Company, 2003 1-96 and 151-153 & 184, 180-183

'Darwin, you don't know how glad I am for you and I pray that you may realize your brightest dreams and enjoy a long life of happiness. I believe you have won a treasure (of course I have). I judge from what you tell me there must be few girls like her, a rare pearl and you must be careful of the jewel placed in your keeping. I know I shall love Anna very dearly and shall try to make our home pleasant to her and not let her miss her own people very much.'

You see my little lady my kinfolk are prepared to love you and are jumping on me in advance, as though I did not hold you above all jewels and have loved you since I first caught a glance from those bright eyes. What I have won no one knows better than I and while I can appreciate my victory, I greatly fear I do not deserve it. I know I am not good enough, but being of a persevering nature I will try and be a better and stronger man and become more deserving of the affections you have for me. In the days of my unbelief about this passion of love, I hooted and scoffed at the matter, thought it all imagination, a fancy set up by a brain diseased, an intangible something, with which the heart could not possibly have any connection. The heart to my mind was then only an engine to pump blood through the arteries, but lo, when I saw you my theories were scattered. I perceived that I had been blind, but now the scales have fallen from my eyes and the mists have cleared away. I am an unbeliever no more for I know when this passion gets possession of one it permeates one's entire being. A man to have never known a woman's love, to have never looked deep down into bright eyes and know that they shown for him, and him alone, poor fellow. He has never lived, only existed.

Now my sweetheart, when you answer this won't you tell me you love me? You do, I know you do, and you know so too. Just put that chin in the background and let your eyes say in words what I have read in their expression. Three words, isn't it so?

A country lad got on the train at Fort Worth and recogniz-
ing me as a man from the rural districts sat down by me. Within a
short while he gave me his confidence, telling me all about a love
affair he had on 'his hands', showed me the girl's picture, gave me
her name, address, and all the particulars of his first meeting, at a
'singing auxiliary' and said he was going to write to her while on
board the train and mail it at St. Louis and asked my advice as to
what he had best say (as if I know). I looked wise and pretended
as if I knew it all. If he followed my instructions he will break
himself buying stamps and stationary. A fellow feeling makes us a
wondrous kind, that boy and I, singing 'The Girl I left behind', or
rather he did as I can't sing. Of course, needless to say, I accepted
his confidence without giving anything in return save advice and
sympathy.
 Darwin

After this letter there must have been some expression of love on her part for he wrote.

 And so, my dear, you at last admit it, that in your heart you dearly love me. I believed it all along, 'the chin' had to give up, didn't it. I hope to prove worthy of the affection you have given me, but like all other mortals, I have plenty of faults and weaknesses. I hope you will overlook my shortcomings as much as possible. I feel you will do all you can to help me remedy them. I need help to do the things that are right, which is a hard struggle, especially when 'the right' is on one side, and self interest, habit, and inclination on the other, make it hard not to fall from grace.

 Arrangements were made. There were choices to consider between a Methodist or an Episcopal ceremony, a morning coat or a suit, the guest list, her traveling clothes. The dress she suggested sounded all right to him; he knew she would look sweet, although he preferred her in the white wrapper which she had made herself and wore one morning when she looked so beautiful that he had great trouble to keep from kissing her as he knew it would offend.

Uncle George Shelby, not Martin Pasco, accompanied Darwin on the next trip to Hillsboro, Texas. He and Anna were married in her parents' wooden Victorian house on Corsicana Street, on November 1, 1899. The house had been bought for her parents by her sister Zula from her weekly wages in the Graham department store. The newlyweds boarded the train for Mississippi, where they would begin their married life at Monochonut in Aunt Janie and Uncle George's house, as Darwin's bachelor house had been rented out to an Italian family for a short time. Anna said that when the minister asked, "Do you take this man?" he should have been made to say, "Do you take this man and all of his relations?" and also to be made to put the relations on parade for inspection. She was lucky to have been congenial with her in-laws.

The journey to Mississippi was not altogether happy. Anna's first fiancé happened to have boarded the same train. The couple was met at the station in Shelby by all of the laborers who worked on the plantation. After they moved into their own house in Shelby, it was not unusual for Anna to spend two weeks without seeing a white face other than that of her new husband. Anna's father wrote to her tenderly, recalling his own visits to the Mississippi Delta when he was a young soldier during the Civil War, and his memory of the loneliness, the bare cypress trees tracing a boundary across the limitless flat landscape. He sympathized by saying that of all illnesses he had experienced the greatest suffering was homesickness. Still, she was lucky to be surrounded by such a nice family.

Surrounded she was indeed. The sons of Aunt Janie and Uncle George Shelby remained at Monochonut. George Shelby languished before the fire, sucking an orange with a hole in the top between semesters at Sewanee, the University of the South, and gazed at Anna with the most beautiful pair of blue eyes she had ever seen. Fred Shelby still lived in his parents' house, as he had been unable to find lodgings in Deeson, a river town where he intended to set up his medical practice. Darwin's young brother Gerald (Fitzgerald) lived there as well during his breaks, where he too was a student at Sewanee, and before the end of the year Madia and Jim Murnan had returned to Monochonut, where they lived until their house could be built. Aunt Lula Poitevent Connell and her husband, Uncle Will Connell, with their second child, Thomas, were soon building a colonial house adjoining our orchard on the street. They had already lost their first child, Marguerite, to malaria, and Thomas would soon follow with one of the many diseases that swept away the children of those Delta years, leaving the couple childless with only ethereal portraits left behind.

Thomas Poitevent had married shortly before Darwin and Anna's marriage. He had chosen a wonderfully kind lady, Mary Maddox, the daughter of a country doctor, who lived about a mile from Monochonut near a tiny township called Perthshire. He had braced the mud and weather to court her throughout the year. Although she was large and no beauty, she radiated a comfortable presence, a generous heart and a down-to-earth personality to such a degree as to conquer even the trivial battle of love. She had a number of suitors. An old lady, Mrs. Hugh Connell, once told me of the evening that Aunt Mary accepted Uncle Tom's proposal. A group of young people had gathered on the veranda of her father's house near Perthshire (later in this story to be described as the Knowleton house, or Emma Lytle's house). Someone was singing a song. Mary appeared in the doorway, and said, "Tom, you know what we were talking about? Well, that will be all right with me." The moon reflected on his bald head and his face of absolute contentment. Aunt Mary said that she had received a proposal from another young man and could not decide between the two. Then she had an occasion to meet Tom in a city and he took her out to dinner. It was his elegance in ordering a meal that tipped the balance in his favor. Their marriage took place in 1898.

A newspaper clipping described the house as decorated with a profusion of holly and mistletoe. The bride was given away by her father, Dr. J. N. Maddox, attended by her ring bearer, little Gus Blanchard, a cousin of the bride whose mother had been a Blanchard. Gus later came to play an important part on our street. The bride and groom left on the noon train.[55]

Before Darwin's marriage in 1898, he wrote to Anna that his bald-headed uncle and bride had taken the train for St. Louis.

"The last I saw of him was that happy smile spreading and spreading over his bald head. He seemed to be happier than is ever allowed common mortals. May it ever be thus with him."

Darwin and Anna were soon expecting a baby. She returned to Hillsboro in May of 1900 so that the period of confinement could take place in a better climate and to be with her mother for the birth. Darwin continued to write loving letters, but he did not see her again until February 1901. Apart from planting and gathering a crop, he was remodeling their house to make it suitable for a family. There were troubles with builders who didn't show up and a paperhanger who showed up drunk. Only one letter showed any discontent with this arrangement, and that seemed to have been inspired by "gossipy hens."

> As to my not being with you when the little one came, if you and I are satisfied, the balance of the human family should be well pleased, as this was none of their business. You were the only one to have any say about that, and had you not been the sensible woman that you are, and willingly agreed to my absence during that period, I would have been with you at any sacrifice. Mean people are like gnat bites, so put on a brave face and cheer up.

> The first of November will be past when you receive this, and I hope my sweet Anna is as happy and content as she was twelve

---

55 Maynard 53

months ago. If I have done anything that has caused you to feel otherwise, just forgive and forget, and let's start over again. For myself I congratulate one D.P.S. on his good judgment or luck every day, in winning so good and fair a companion to cheer him through life's many journeys. You have been of great benefit to me, sweetheart, in a great many ways. While there is lots of room for improvement, I feel that I am a better man than I was a year ago, all through your influence and the love I know you bear for one unworthy bald headed man. So here is to the sweetest woman in Texas. I pledge to her good health in a glass of good Mississippi pump water. May she never know sorrow and may trouble be far from her.

Sarah Frances Shelby was born on November 1, 1900. A trunk beneath my Grandmother's bed contained her baby book, documenting little events, first steps, first cousins, first words, baby presents, and the first Christmas that she was able to appreciate in 1902.

Anna, Frances, and Darwin returned to their own house in February 1901. All of Darwin's letters were about the house plans. Anna was artistic, and her taste had inclined toward white linen slipcovers, small twinkling lights with silk shades, ivory furniture. When she arrived she entered room upon room of new, dark, Victorian wallpaper and brown oak furniture.

It was about that time that the street began to fill out. A lot between Aunt Lula's house and our house was bought by a Mr. Cogdill, a retired Methodist minister. With the advent of Aunt Janie and Uncle George building a house, and Madia and Jim and Tom and Mary moving on to the street, Anna no longer spent weeks without seeing a white face. Mr. and Mrs. J. W. Thomas also built a large Dutch colonial house next to the Connell house.

Darwin spent his entire day on a horse, as did all of the farmers. He and Anna would ride over Lucknow in the early mornings before breakfast. Her long straight black hair touched the saddle as she rode. After that she faced a long day of visiting relations and teaching the servants more about cooking.

The summers were relentless. There was a theory that malaria was caused by the miasma in the night air. The debate over the usefulness of screens continued. In one letter, written shortly before the marriage, Darwin closed by apologizing "I cannot continue as my hands are swollen by bites. People claim that screens will help, but I cannot see how they will prevent the little mites from crawling through the wires."

As a precaution against miasma, he insisted that the windows be closed at night. Anna flung open the windows and declared that she preferred to die rather than stay in that steaming box. Unlike Henry James' Daisy Miller, her impetuosity did not kill her.

They had a second daughter, Zula, named for Anna's sister, born at home in Shelby, Mississippi on March 8th, 1903. She was so tiny that Darwin called her "Dinky." Frances was called "Turk," because she was very brunette and looked like her mother's family.

Darwin had a premonition, which he confided only to Aunt Lula Connell. "I am going to lose Frances. She was sitting beneath me on the front steps, and she suddenly looked up at me in a way that reminded me so much of Marguerite (Aunt Lula's daughter who had died), that I know I shall lose her." Aunt Lula tried to dissuade him, but he continued. "Then she said to me, 'Daddy, you will soon not have a Turk, you will just have a Dinky.'"

Letter addressed to Mrs. J.T. Liner
315 Corsicana Street
Hillsboro, Texas
August 10th 1903
Shelby, Mississippi

  My dear friend,
It becomes my sad duty to write to you the details of our mu-

tual and irreparable loss. Precious little Frances was the picture of magnificent health and girlish beauty last Wednesday, a week ago, when she came to my house to bid her Aunt Janie goodbye. Anna with loving pride had dressed her more becomingly than ever before. Oh, how proud we were of her as she stepped daintily about the house, not touching a thing, but with her glorious eyes spread wide with an expression "Maybe Miss Lula had got something new since I was here last," until she spied the piano and asked permission to play, which was granted to her hearts content. She wasn't exactly well that day, yet looked so splendid.

On Saturday, she was more unwell. The actions from her bowels becoming very frequent, and changing color, until almost a cream color. The doctor prepared medicine, which she took at two hourly intervals and was very sick that night. The next evening she was so much better that she was dressed and playing about, giving all sorts of bright answers to any remarks made to her. She contended she wasn't sick, until Tuesday, at noon, when she became so dreadfully sick that she had to give in and plaintively said, "I believe I am sick." She grew worse and at midnight there was half an hour that there was almost no hope, but her strong constitution waged a fierce battle against that dread disease congestion, which was rapidly setting in bowels and kidneys, as they did not act any more after six o'clock Tuesday evening until three fifteen Wednesday afternoon, when the soul had taken its flight.

She rallied so often, and had so many good symptoms, at times lifting our hearts with such glad hopes for her recovery. She had closest attention, all that medical skill could do was done and repeated over and over. When the poison (malarial) attacked the nerve center, her sufferings appeared to be cruelly intense. Dr. Murnan assured us that it was not. She turned over and clasped her father's hands in both of her hands and shook like an ashen leaf.

How gladly would that father have laid down his life for his beautiful little daughter. Anna was too prostrated to remain with her precious darling except for a few minutes at a time. Dr. Murnan and Dr. Fred Shelby, Mrs. Murnan and Darwin worked with her for twenty hours, but to no avail.

No strange hands touched her. It fell to my sad lot to dress her. I accepted the duty with faithful old Mammy's assistance and with as reverent and gentle a touch as may be. I accepted the duty as work for the Master and felt honored in being permitted to clothe, for the last time on earth, that beautiful form in dainty garments, which her devoted mother through some mysterious presentment had placed to themselves, for that very occasion. When all was ready, Mammy's eager hands were held out to carry for the last time her baby to the little resting place in the parlor. But no, the father came in and taking her tenderly in his strong embrace, he lovingly bore the precious burden to the parlor and reverently laid her down. Oh dear friend, that was a sight to break a heart of stone!

Mr. Connell and Mr. Poitevent carried her to Memphis on the early train. Mr. Connell said that when they reached Memphis her lovely waxen hand still clasped undisturbed, some single orange flowers, tuberoses that had been placed there the night before. Her head, face, and all of her features shown out so beautifully, as if chiseled in marble, that even a stranger exclaimed in admiration, 'What a fine child.' Mr. and Mrs. George Shelby were already in Memphis and had ordered exquisite flowers, as did Mr. Godfrey Frank and others. Her little body reposed beside Darwin's mother's in beautiful old Elmwood Cemetery. There to await its resurrection. The minister read that beautiful ceremony beginning 'I am the resurrection and the life saith the Lord' and then paid a very touching tribute.

Anna and Darwin are bearing this bitterest of cruel blows with brave Christian fortitude. We are so glad dear Zula is with them and that the darling baby has appeared to cheer them through these days that would otherwise be black as the nights. I am sure that many earnest prayers offered up for them are strength to them. We are all so broken over this dreadful storm of sorrow.

I am afraid my letter isn't legible. I am so nervous and weak from continued use of quinine, which causes gastric trouble. However, I must write to let you know that my loving heart goes out to you, as does that of Mr. Connell and my brother. God bless you and help you to bear up bravely. Anna was feeling much better under Zula and Darwin's tender care on Saturday evening.

Lovingly your friend,

Lula P. Connell

(Lula's own children Marguerite and Thomas had died in 1897 and 1901, after which she was to remain childless)[56]

Neither Darwin nor Anna held the conviction that belonged to Aunt Lula and her sister Ellen. Darwin had been educated by monks, but also exposed too much goodness from a Jew, Mr. Godfrey Frank, and Buddhists, one of whom he allowed to be buried on his plantation because he had been refused an entry into a Christian cemetery. He was unable to view life as one straight line to heaven. His religion was based on charity and a broad spirit and he struggled with the fundamentalist perspective all of his life. Anna was somewhat allergic to the Methodist Church of her childhood in Texas. Life goes on with or without eternity. Mammy Lou placed a little fence around the garden that Frances had planted in the side yard. Anna

56 Maynard 38

soon visited her parents in Texas and upon her return Darwin bought a house in Memphis where his family lived for eight years until 1911. Frances was the last victim in our family to die of malaria, which had made the Delta an uninhabitable place for such a long time. Two more daughters were born to Anna and Darwin. May, my mother, was born on May 16, 1905 in Memphis, the day that the equestrian statute of the Confederate General Forrest was unveiled in one of the city's main squares. Eleanor was born two and a half years later.

Darwin rented out our house and lived with Aunt Janie and Uncle George Shelby during the weeks and his family in Memphis on weekends and during the rainy season. This was an expensive way to live and the family eventually returned to our street in 1911. They did not spend a dreaded summer in Mississippi for over seventeen years.

Anna Liner Shelby and her second daughter Zula Shelby; Sarah Frances Shelby with an umbrella about 1901.

Mammy Lou and Sarah Frances Shelby about 1901.

Part Two

May's Stories

(my mother - events
mainly from 1910-1940)

Children

I began life in Memphis on Bellevue Street with my sister Zula who was two years older. I called her La La, because I heard Mama say "Zu-la" and just got the last part. I adored her and followed her everywhere, saying, "La La, I sure do love you."

She would reply, "Well, *I just hate you.*" That didn't dampen my love at all. She was the leader and I the follower. Zula and my cousin Ruth Edwards played together. One day she said, "Let's play horse and buggy." They hitched me to a surrey in Cousin Evelyn Edward's back yard and both perched on the front seat and told me to pull. I pulled and pulled but I didn't move them one inch. In disgust they unhitched me and said that they would get another horse.

I went into the house feeling very dejected and said to Cousin Evelyn, "My side hurts." All the skin had been rubbed off.

"You poor little thing." She rubbed witch-hazel on me, but my wounds were in my heart and I still loved her.

Zula started to school two years before me. She decided that we would play school: "May, spell apple." Then she would spell it as fast as possible, so that I would not catch the letters. I tried to begin with "A," "P," but could not go further because she would slap me. I never told Mama, but at night we slept together in a trundle bed that pulled out near the floor beneath a proper bed. After going to bed I would think about all of the things that she had done to me during the day and how I had not retaliated. Then I would grab her arm and bite it.

Daddy came to Memphis every weekend. I thought that I was his favorite child. He would put me on the bed astride him and say, "How much

Three Shelby girls—Zula, May, and Eleanor—
at the time these stories took place.

to you love me?" I always replied, "A hundred dollars worth," which was the largest sum that I knew.

Then he asked, "What are you good for?" I answered, "To eat corn bread."

Sometimes he took me out alone and sat on a bench beside the graves of Frances and his mother, father, and brothers. I played over the graves and later I wrote a note to Mama and glued it to a penny in a box where she stored all of her memories of Frances. It said, "Dear Frances, this letter is to show that someone remembers you, May."

One weekend Daddy came home and Mama cried, "These children are driving me crazy." By that time my younger sister, Eleanor, was also troublesome.

Daddy said, "I will take one. Which one is the worst?"

To my delight I heard her reply, "I believe that May is the worst." That is how I came to Shelby for the first time, when I was about five to live at Aunt Janie's house, to have Daddy all to myself, and to be introduced to my roots.

The family that I went to live with in Shelby remained with me for the rest of their lives, while my sisters moved to Texas and California. We sat around a large oval dining table at Aunt Janie's house. By the time that I arrived, Uncle George had died. Aunt Janie lived with her son, Cousin Fred, a Mr. Coker who lived there to protect her when Cousin Fred was on house calls, and Daddy, between his visits to his family in Memphis. Numerous other relations appeared for dinner: Aunt Madia, called Aunt Deedee by us; Dr. Murnan, her husband; Cousin George and his wife, Cousin Joe, and their baby little George.

Nannie, the cook, always waited on the table. One evening was especially humiliating. They had chocolate cake for desert and I said, "Nannie, I want some more chocolate cake." Aunt Janie prompted me to say please. I refused. There was no more cake. When I went to bed in Daddy's room, beside my bed was a big piece of chocolate cake, placed there by Nannie.

My days were spent playing with the Poitevent girls, Uncle Tom and Aunt Mary's children. Isabel was almost eleven, Mary almost nine, and Janula was only three. I told all of my secrets to Isabel. After playing throughout the morning it was accepted that I came to their table for dinner (midday meal). They seated me next to Grandma Maddox, Aunt Mary's grandmother, who lived with them. I could not resist the temptation to look at what I knew would make me sick: Grandma Maddox's ears. They had wax in them. I promised myself at each meal that I would not look, but I was glued by the magnet, until finally I could no longer eat. After several weeks of this dilemma, I plucked up courage to decline the dinner invitations. A week went by with my boycotting the table, until Isabel pulled out the secret. The following day Aunt Mary said in her calm manner, "May, if you come back to dinner you won't have to sit next to Grandma Maddox." One would think they would have been glad to get rid of me, but I happily joined them again.

The sidewalks were made of wooden planks. I loved walking into town where Daddy introduced me to all the merchants who stood in front of their stores. Every day I passed a display of eggs. I kept thinking, "Wouldn't it be easy to steal one of those eggs? No one ever watches them." Finally I took one. I held it in one hand and then the other, put it into a puffed pocket and hoped I wouldn't smash it, then changed it to the other pocket. Daddy took no notice. I was all dressed up. We came to a store where Mrs. Joffee paced back and forth on her bandy legs looking for customers. She had stained teeth, probably caused by dipping snuff. When she saw me she exclaimed, "Mr. Shelby, oh what a pretty little girl!" then reached down and kissed me on the mouth.

Laden with guilt and humiliation, I returned to the Poitevent house in search of my confessor, Isabel. I made her come into the side yard where I unburdened my secrets. "Isabel, I have done something very bad, but you must not tell anyone."

"No, May, you know I won't."

"I have stolen an egg and I don't know what to do with it." She laughed and threw the egg onto the ground.

"That is not all. I have been kissed by Mrs. Joffee."

Isabel always told everything and after that I was known as May who stole an egg and was kissed by Mrs. Joffee.

I was supposed to return to Memphis after a month, until I heard with glee that Zula and Eleanor had come down with scarlet fever and were quarantined. I had Daddy and Shelby all to myself for most of the winter.

*

When I returned to Memphis Mammy Lou was still with us. She had worked for Daddy long before Frances was born. Then one day she announced that she was going to get married. Mama and Daddy didn't think she had ever met a man; she wasn't that type. We all begged her not to go, but what could we do? It was as if we had lost a mother. She got married. During the years that followed, Daddy would call on her when he was in Memphis, and kept telling her that she always had a home with us, but she stood fast, "This is my husband, and I am going to stay with him." Daddy would then give her some money, but she never returned.

**

I played with a little Jewish boy named Buck. He said, "May, let's get married." I said, "All right." He told me to come to his house on Sunday. I dressed up and told Daddy that I was going to the Boswich's house to marry Buck. In a short while I came back home, and Daddy said, "Well, did you get married?"

I replied, "No. Mr. Boswich said that the wedding bells hadn't come."

I continued to play with Buck and confided to him that I was very frightened about the prospect of going to school. Zula had told me that if you said a word when standing in line, they would take you out and switch you. Buck consoled me by saying "There is nothing to going to school. All you have to do is take a pencil." I thought that even I could take a pencil.

My first grade teacher at the Morris School on Bellevue would teach us to read by playing store. She would write the names of different items on the blackboard. The only word that I recognized was 'Apple'. I barely managed to walk to the blackboard and put a line under apple and repeated the word. I bought the same thing every day and remained terrified that someone else would buy apple first.

Shelby

In the middle of my sixth year Daddy said that Mama was spending too much money in Memphis and he no longer intended to keep up two households. We moved back to Shelby in 1911. Mama was furious. She pouted for the first year and didn't even hang curtains in the house. Then she adjusted, began to decorate, and cooked elaborate food. Dressed in her seal stole and muff with a silver pin clasping the stole and a fresh bunch of violets shipped from Memphis in a refrigerated freight car, she would walk down the wooden plank that substituted for a sidewalk, calling on all our relations.

I have a mental picture of the scene in our back yard the day we arrived in Shelby. There was a long table and lots of colored women were sewing up hams in white sacks. The hams had been cured and were placed in a concrete cellar beneath the smoke house in our service yard. Daddy had about forty hogs killed. He sent the fresh backbone and spare ribs to his neighbors, made sausages from the scraps, but the major portion of this pork was smoked or cured and used to feed the tenants on his plantation.

Shelby was a paradise. We had three terriers and three kittens. School was not in the least intimidating. We sat in double desks. I shared a desk with Rosa Bacareni. She brought me bright flowered handkerchiefs and picture postcards of Italy. I had never met an Italian except Dr. DeMarco, and he was quite unlike my new classmates. They were warm and friendly, but most of them disappeared from school after the sixth grade.

Discipline was ignored by many of the teachers, except one—Miss Bailey. She always made me stay in after school, and claimed that it was because I cut up. I would stay for a few minutes and then she would say, "You can go." I didn't see the point in this, but there was nothing I could do about it.

One day, while I was staying after school, Miss Bailey said, "May, I love you. Do you love me?"

"No, Ma'am, I don't."

"Don't you love me a little bit?"

"I sure don't."

After that she didn't keep me after school as much.

Her niece was Kathryn Henderson, the prettiest girl in the school. We shared a desk the following year. Kathryn didn't like Miss Bailey either, for she was masculine and mean. She tried to humiliate the boys in the class. There was one boy, Bruff Maum, to whom she was especially cruel. His family was poor. He indicated that he liked me and sent me a big valentine that stood two feet high. Zula put it in the door of the playhouse for the wind to blow it apart. He moved away from Shelby. Years later, when I was in my thirties, I made a purchase at Sterling's, the local dime store, and the manager asked about me. He told me that he was inquiring on behalf of Bruff Maum, who was the General Director of Sterling's. I was delighted to hear that he had done so well despite the humiliations of that awful teacher.

Our parents had different ideas about how we should be brought up. Mama was stricter with all, save Eleanor. Daddy spoiled us, and soon got us a pony. After a short time learning to ride in the service yard, Zula and I raced to the pony every day that we were not in school. Zula usually got there first, as I was slow to wake up; I had to ride on the back of her saddle. There were few automobiles so we had the run of the streets, playing cowboy and Indians with the little boys. During this time Mama invited our friend Regina Orpenhiemer from Memphis to visit. Her mother refused. She was afraid that Regina might step on a nail.

We were also free to ride into the fields. I used to ride to a house occupied by a family of Italians who rented a tiny holding from Daddy. They had a vine with a gourd and gave me water to drink from the gourd. Later they moved to Memphis and established an empire of supermarkets called "Montessi's." They seemed to have been related to all of the other Sicilian families in Bolivar County.

One day on my way to the Montessi's house my horse shied, and I almost fell off. Then I glanced at the spot where this had happened and saw a pair of human eyes peeping between the planks of a cotton house (tiny structures where cotton was placed if a bale had not been completed by the end of the day). I galloped home. This was the only time that I felt any apprehension.

In the side yard we had a large one-room playhouse. It had a real fireplace and a front porch with roses growing over it. We each had a corner of shelves for our toys, and the fourth corner was our guestroom. One day I decided to hire a nurse for my dolls, and found a little colored girl who was willing to nurse if I paid her a quarter. I went out onto the front porch and sat in a rocking chair. She came out as well. I told her that she was supposed to stay in the house and nurse the dolls while I composed stories. She replied, "You go outside, so I go outside."

I said, "You are impertinent. Here is your quarter. You are fired."

After that I sat on the porch of the playhouse alone, rocking and talking to myself. Mama would call, "May, what on earth are you doing?"

I always replied, "Telling myself a story."

Daddy believed in a childhood surrounded by animals. Of our three rat terriers, one was a female and produced lots of puppies. There was a cage of rabbits. Our pet rabbits were called Pretty and Beautiful. There was also a cat for each of us that did not impede the territory of the pet white rat. We called the white rat "Stinkpot." Our pony was so ugly that we called him "Buzzard."

Mama gave us beautiful clothes and imaginative birthday parties. A lady came to the house for a month each year to help Mama make our dresses. We were only allowed to wear white, as colors were not considered to be in good taste for children. Our dresses were white linen; hand embroidered by Mama with tucks and inset lace, worn over lace petticoats with white stockings and black shoes. The only time that we were allowed to wear a color was when we traveled. We each had a navy dress and a navy coat for travel. Finally Mama agreed to let us wear bloomers for riding.

We had a cow in the service yard, though none of us liked to drink milk. When electricity came in Mama bought an ice cream-freezer. In the winter we would have contests to see who could eat the most bowls of ice cream. I won. I ate eight. Uncle John, the hostler, had all that was left on the dasher, and there was plenty for everyone else in the house. Mama sold milk, cream and butter to the neighbors. She dressed in a white smock and a mop hat in the mornings, and went about her business. She made so much money off of butter and cream that she was able to reset all of her diamonds into platinum and buy a diamond studded wristwatch and a diamond brooch as well. Mississippi was a Garden of Eden compared to our life in the city.

*

Christmases in Shelby were in a different category from Christmas in Memphis. Zula and I no longer believed in Santa Claus by the time we moved to Shelby, but our little sister Eleanor still believed. I wrote her letters from Santa Claus. Our stockings were hung by the fireplace in Mama's bedroom. We were greedy and each hung two stockings, which were filled with small toys, nuts, and candy. Uncle John came early to build a fire so that we could get up at four in the morning to see the stockings. Trees were never sold in the town. Daddy would send a colored man with a team of mules into the country to dig up a cedar tree.

Two of these trees were planted in our side yard, where the playhouse stood. We were not allowed to go to see the Christmas tree until after breakfast. Then Mama would call the cook, the hostler, the house girl, the yardman, the ironing woman, and the milkman, and gave them all very nice presents. Our dolls were tied to the branches of the tree, and toys were placed all over the floor. As we had seven families of relations, as well as grandparents, an aunt and an uncle from the Texas side of our family, the opening of presents lasted a long time. Then the whole gathering had eggnog from a large cut glass-punch bowl. Colored people who worked for other families on the street knocked on the back door every few minutes saying, "Christmas gift," which meant a tot of whiskey. The big turkey dinner followed much later in the day. There was a large scrubbed table in the dairy room for all of the servants, and they each took home sacks of food, after receiving their gifts. At Christmas time Daddy said, "I feel sorry for people who don't have any children." Our world was so secure that it left little space for thoughts of any other existence. When life is that joyful, it can sow the seeds for future depression.

My Sister Zula

Zula originated all of our games and took the leading part. She was not pretty, but she had so much personality that one never noticed her lack of beauty. She invented the game of Town. She was the banker. I had the beauty parlor. We played Robbers and Jail. She was the policeman, and I was the robber. We played Hotel in Mr. and Mrs. Toler's barn, up the street. Mrs. Toler had a niece, Annie Mae Smith, who was our constant companion. Zula was the proprietor of the hotel, and I was the guest. The guest "borrowed" little children without telling their mothers we were taking them to a barn. Zula issued us play money. I chose the cheapest room in the hotel. We ate in the hotel on a table. Zula printed menus. I ordered peanut butter cake. It was a vanilla wafer with peanut butter on it.

Mr. and Mrs. Toler added much fun to our lives. They were an unusual couple. Mr. Toler was very good looking with red hair and was quite fond of the ladies. He was fifteen years younger than Mrs. Toler. They had no children, but their comfortable house was filled with relations whom they fostered for various periods. Together they must have reared about eleven children. Annie Mae Smith was Mrs. Toler's niece. Her mother had died, and she did not get on with her father's second wife, who owned a large colonial home in South Mississippi where children were prohibited from going into the parlor. Annie Mae came to live with the Tolers shortly after we arrived. She joined our family and played with us every day. Mr. Toler was very smart. He would sit on his front porch and add all the numbers on the boxcars of the passing train. There was no one to check his calculations.

Daddy gave us a meager allowance. As we lived extravagantly, he tried to teach us the value of the dollar. We each had ten cents a week to spend. Our vegetable garden comprised about an acre and there was a side garden of just onions. One day Daddy came in from riding over his fields and said, "The sparrows are eating my garden. I will give you a penny for every one that you kill." Zula devised a way of catching sparrows. By that time we no longer had any rabbits so she put chicken feed in the rabbit cage. Bricks were put under the corners to raise it and part of the floor was removed. When sparrows would go under the cage, we would go into the cage and perch on the few remaining planks that had been a floor. As the sparrows flew up, we would catch them. The girl sparrows were easier to catch than the boy ones; you can tell the difference as the boys have deeper marking on their heads. One time I prayed that when I went into the rabbit cage there would be three girl sparrows. My prayers were answered. Each of us had our own method of killing sparrows. I hit mine over the head with a stick. It was a cruel way to make money, and the only unkind thing I ever remember my father doing. We kept a list of the dead sparrows, and were paid on Saturdays. We drank many ice-cream sodas on the money we made from killing sparrows.

Then Zula made a discovery. One afternoon after school, she promised a string of children that she knew a magic word whereby she could buy whatever she wanted without paying. In an effort to prove her point, she took about fifteen children to the drug store. They all ordered sodas. Afterwards she blurted her word, "Charge-it." At the end of the month Daddy received an amazing bill.

When the magic word began to fail, we went into the scrap metal business. Boys picked scrap metal to sell to Mr. Henderson, Kathryn's father, who was the scrap metal dealer. The iron was then sold to the railway. We had a cotton gin, but we were never allowed to play there, as gins were notoriously dangerous for children. That was unfortunate for our business as it would have been an iron haven. There remained a great deal of iron in the cotton fields. Every Saturday we paid our hostler fifteen cents to hitch a mule to a wagon and take the iron to Mr. Henderson. When Mr. Henderson's man unloaded the wagon he threw the railway spikes out. If they were busy and our hostler unloaded our wagon, he put the railway spikes into the lot. We made about five dollars every Saturday.

Mr. Henderson also bought old brass and bones. For many years, we had brass lamps suspended from the ceiling. Then at last electricity appeared to be arriving. Mama said to the man who was preparing to install electricity, "I don't believe this. They have told us before that we were going to have electricity." He replied, "But this time we have the poles skint." The old brass fixtures were taken down. They were worth four times as much as the iron. We were getting rich.

I decided to gather bones to sell to Mr. Henderson. As our house was about twenty-five years old, there should have been treasure beneath. I crawled under the house all of one morning and took the discarded dog bones to Mr. Henderson with great expectations for a whole coal scuttle full of bones. My profit was sixty cents.

Then Zula had a bright idea, "Let's make some money that is not Daddy's money. Let's pick cotton." Henry Eaton was our favorite tenant farmer on the plantation. We asked him if we could pick cotton from his crop. He grinned and agreed. We put on sun hats and procured lace-trimmed pillowcases to use as cotton sacks. I picked from morning to evening and was told by Henry that it weighed seven pounds. My reward was seven cents. Labor picked an average of two and three hundred pounds a day. Later we discovered that Daddy had told Henry Eaton that he would give him the money to pay us and to weigh our cotton at twice the amount, so in reality I only picked three and a half pounds. When we found out about Daddy's intervention, we stopped picking cotton.

We also had rummage sales on Saturdays in our playhouse. We called to the people going into town to come and look at our things. Every time we sold a dress we gave them a pair of socks free. I don't remember us ever playing a game that we did not improvise, except that Zula played cards and always won. These enterprises that she inspired were the only money I ever made in my life, although I have always managed to live comfortably.

*

When I was about eleven, Daddy gave us some money to buy each other Christmas presents. Zula said, "Let's get up early and go Christmas shopping."

I never could wake up unless she awakened me. Just for meanness on this particular morning, Zula got up, dressed and did not call me. I happened to wake-up soon afterwards and was furious when I met Zula and Annie Mae already in town. I declared, "I am not going to give you a Christmas present because you have now seen everything."

Zula calmed me. "The stores have not even opened."

We then agreed that they would go to one part of town and I to the other. When the merchant came to open his store, he was surprised to see a little girl standing in the front freezing and waiting to do her Christmas shopping. I then went to a Chinese store that was owned by Daddy's friend Kuan Jon. After musing over the toys, I asked the price. He had one reply, "Not muchie."

Finally in exasperation I said, "Kuan, you must tell me the price before I can buy anything." He answered, "Aren't you Mr. Darwin Shelby's little girl?"

"Yes."

"Won't cost you a thing, won't cost you a thing."

I went about selecting everyone a Christmas present and returned with my money intact.

When Daddy found out about this bargain, he forbade us to shop with Kuan again.

We wrapped our presents, and Zula said, "I'll let you feel mine, if you will let me feel yours."

She put her hands on my present and said, "It's just an old alligator," for the tail was sticking out.

"No it isn't."

I then put my hands on her gift and said, "It's just an old shell box to put pins in."

She burst out crying and said, "I am not going to give you this present."

Daddy had to take her to the hardware store to select another present. She selected a wooden kitchen set with cabinets. It costs sixty cents. I was so worried that Daddy had to spend this extra money that I would rather have kept the old shell box.

I would never have had such fun as a child but for my sister Zula. She continued to boss my life. The last time that she visited me she told me that my pecan trees needed pruning, that I needed all new pots and pans, and that I needed some new bedroom slippers. I was fifty-nine years old. I can still see her expression as she boarded the train from Memphis to Dallas, her head tossed to the side in her usual perky manner. She sent me some bedroom slippers; two years after that visit she died. We shared an idyllic childhood, freedom without bounds.

Neighbors

Before we moved back to Shelby, we acquired neighbors too close for comfort, when Daddy sold the lot next to our house to a retired Methodist Minister, a Mr. Cogdill. His daughter married a Mr. Bullock and they had two children, Robert Cogdill and Martha Frances. He in turn divided the lot and sold one portion to the Henry family. Daddy was outraged. He said that he never intended to live so close to people. They might hear if he spanked his children.

Daddy's moans apart, they were perfect neighbors. Mrs. Henry was an elegant and miniature little lady. Mr. Henry claimed to descend from the Revolutionary Patrick Henry. They had two daughters, Flemma and Madge. Flemma already lived on the street and was married to Mr. Will Denton. Madge was a young lady in her teens. As Mr. and Mrs. Henry were considerably old to be Madge's parents, Mama became the chaperone for all of Madge's dances and other outings. Her young lady-hood was entwined with our life.

There was a gravel road on the north side of our house where our other neighbors, Mr. and Mrs. Joseph Yates lived. They were not quite so congenial. One summer we were in Hot Springs, Arkansas, and the manager of the Arlington Hotel placed Mrs. Yates at our table because we were all from the same town. She talked on and on about Tom, telling everyone at the table how many naps Tom needed and how long his naps lasted. Finally one polite man said, "How old is your little boy, Mrs. Yates?"

Zula piped up, "It's not a boy, it's a cat."

That was too much for Mrs. Yates, and when she returned to Shelby she found a little boy to adopt. We were elated to see an orphan. Gladys Wilkinson, fostered by Mr. and Mrs. H. L. Wilkinson, who lived on the west side of Holmes Lake, had already ripened our imaginations with stories of how her mother had kissed her goodbye at the steps of the orphanage, and how Mr. and Mrs. Wilkinson had saved her from this fate. True or false, as Gladys' stories may have been, it planted a seed of immense curiosity about orphans. Zula, Annie Mae and I called upon this child, who sat still with a straight string of a mouth, big solemn eyes, and a head full of curls. We belted him for details. "What does it feel like to be an orphan?" "Did your mother kiss you good-bye?" "Did you know your father?" "Are you glad you are here?" He endured this interrogation without answering. Finally he said, "You ask too many questions."

My Sister Eleanor

It took Eleanor two and a half years to grow hair. I was so embarrassed when we lived in Memphis that I decided to tell the world that she was not a boy but a girl. I stood her on a corner in the blazing sun where the streetcars stopped. Every time that anyone passed I shouted, "She's not a boy, she is a girl." I still remember one lady all dressed up and about to board the streetcar when I trumpeted my message. She was in a hurry, but she turned to me and it was the expression on her face that made me wonder if I sounded a bit silly. Finally Eleanor grew lots of curly black hair.

Zula didn't have the time of day for her. Eleanor was Mama's baby. She slept with Mama. That was the trouble. Whenever a word of correction was uttered such as "switch her," she fainted. Hence she never received any physical punishment.

I always felt sorry for her and hosted her puppy parties. We invited all of the children in town to bring their puppies to a party for Eleanor's puppy. I strung little doll bottles of milk on the ceiling of the playhouse for the owners to feed to their puppies. Zula wouldn't even attend.

We had to learn to ride a pony in the service yard, which was filled with guineas, a dove house, a cow, a plantation bell over a tower, the smoke house with its cellar for storage of hams, and a bed of cinders, contained in a concrete box. The plantation bell, used to call time for workers, rang. Eleanor was riding her pony, and one day he threw her into the cinder bed. The cook witnessed the accident, and was certain that she had broken her neck. She rushed out the back door to collect what appeared to be her dead body and found Eleanor alive, with no broken bones, but a face covered in blood and cinders. Dr. Murnan was called at once; Eleanor would not let him touch her. Instead she screamed for Cousin Fred, who arrived to no avail. He came closer to her, close enough to dab the wounds with antiseptic and cotton, but he was only able to extract a few cinders. Mama was away in Memphis at the time that this happened and when she returned Eleanor greeted her at the front door with a face full of coagulated blood and dabs of cotton. The cinders finally grew into her scalp, although the ones on her nose left a fine black line, which had to be covered with powder for the rest of her life.

She did everything her own way. Once I went into the bathroom and was scarcely able to see for the steam. Through a cloud, I deciphered the bright red face of Eleanor.

"What on earth are you doing taking such a hot bath?"

She answered, "Oh, I have been doing this for a long time. I got to thinking that I might die and go to the bad place, so I am trying to get used to it."

When Janula turned six, the usual age to begin school, Aunt Mary decided to keep her away from school for an extra year. Mama let no chance go by not to indulge Eleanor, so the child stayed at home until she was seven as well. Then she attended school for a day and declared that she did not like it and was not going back. Mama and Daddy were blasé about anything that she did and did not insist that she return to school. I grew desperate. The only solution was for me to teach her. I procured a Blue Back Spelling Book and other material from her first grade teacher, and played school every afternoon once I had been released from my own classes. In the midst of the lessons she would jump up and say that she was off to play with Robert Cogdill Bullock who lived two doors south of us. I would follow Eleanor across the Henrys' yard, with my speller and candy in my pockets to reward her should she reply. It all became too much of a strain. One day I broke down at the dining table crying. When Mama and Daddy asked what was the matter, I shook my head and sobbed, "Eleanor is never going to get an education."

It was so worrying that at the age of ten I sprouted a single gray hair. The following year, when Eleanor was eight, she began school, reluctantly. Thanks to my tutoring she was able to skip the first grade. Then they discovered that she was so smart that she could skip the second grade as well. She graduated as the valedictorian of her class.

When the time came for her to go to college, there was very little money. All that we could afford was a little women's college in Grenada and then there was Delta State Teacher's College in Cleveland, Mississippi, which had been formed in 1925. The Great Depression was to be a boon for Delta State. Three months before she was to graduate with honors, Eleanor dropped out of college and went to Aunt Zula's house in Texas. The logic: she had a great fear of becoming an old maid schoolteacher, so she nipped such a fate in the bud!

A Private School

In 1911, the year we returned to Shelby, Mr. Henry Cooper Carnes, his wife Lillian, and their four-year-old son, Hal, arrived. Mr. Carnes had purchased a plantation, and they built a house on the south end of the street, next door to Aunt Janie. They came from an old Scotch-Irish family who had settled in the Carolinas in the mid-eighteenth century and were quite prominent in the area around Memphis. Mr. Carnes's father had been an officer and scout in the Confederate Army of Tennessee under General Forrest during the Civil War, and his uncle, General Sam Carnes, was a general with the National Guard, and had been president of the Memphis Gas and Electrical Company, owned the first automobile in Memphis, and was president of the Memphis Country Club for more than two decades. They felt uneasy about the Shelby School for their only son.

Ruth and J. W. Thomas, who lived on the end of our part of the street, had a governess, Miss Duvall. When they outgrew the governess, Mrs. Hal Carnes decided to establish a little private school in her house, with Miss Duvall teaching their friends. This school was attended by Zula, Eleanor and me, the Poitevent girls, Isabel, Mary, and Janula, Aubrey Rowe, Hal Carnes, and Saul Bloom. J. W. Thomas continued to come for special tutorials in mathematics, before he could enter Culver Military Academy. Our ages varied from six to fifteen. All but J. W. Thomas were in the same classroom, presumably working on our separate lessons. Miss Duvall had grown up in Richmond, Virginia, and talked of nothing but Robert E. Lee. For three years he was the only hero in American history about whom we were taught. I hated mathematics, but didn't have to overcome my lack of interest because all I was required to do was to stand by the blackboard, write the formula on the board, and wait to be prompted by the other children. After much whispering I got the answer, and the class applauded. Then I would sit down.

One day a terrible odor permeated the parlor where the classes took place. Saul Bloom had had an accident in his pants. Zula, Eleanor, and I were told to go upstairs, where J. W. Thomas was awaiting his geometry lesson. He asked us why we were there and we held our noses. He held his nose and we all buried our heads and giggled.

The school was so silly that after three years Zula and I decided to boycott it. The one thing that we had been forbidden to do was to play with a girl named Rosa Shepherd, who lived on one of the back streets of town. The two of us went to Daddy and said that if we had to go to that private school any longer we were going to play with Rosa Shepherd. He relented and the following year we were back in the public school, where I remained hopeless in mathematics.

Other Playmates

Apart from Kathryn Henderson and Annie Mae, my other close friend was Flora Humphries. Our favorite game was Growing Up to be Ladies. We had many roles and many costumes, imagining what we would be when we became ladies.

Because of Frances's tragic death, the summers for my family were a time to go away. We put on our navy coats and navy dresses and in early May boarded a train to Texas to visit our relations and grandparents, and then to Boulder, Colorado, where we lived at the Boulderado Hotel; or San Francisco; or occasionally Hot Springs, Arkansas; and once the Mississippi Gulf Coast. We always stayed away until mid-September.

One summer, when I was about nine, we received a letter from Flora's father while we were in Colorado. The letter conveyed the sad news that

Sunday School class with Shelby girls and two friends,
Flora Humphries right and Catherine Henderson left.

both Flora and her brother had died that summer.

All my life I have driven past the Shelby Cemetery and looked upon their two concrete vaulted graves located near the road. I always turned my head away and remembered that Flora never got to be a lady.

When I was about fifty, someone rang my doorbell. There stood an old gentleman whom I did not recognize. He reintroduced himself to me as Mr. Humphries, returning to pay respects to his children's graves.

The Picture Show

The picture show was made of wooden posts with a tent for a top, wooden benches and a sawdust floor. It was called the Air Dome. Daddy loved it, and accompanied us most evenings to see a movie. Those were the days of silent movies, 1914-1921. A lady with large arms played a piano, scripted by the film, varying from melancholy to rapid for a raid by the posse. There was Gloria Swanson in *The High Life* with fancy bathrooms and later Cecil B. DeMille's *The Ten Commandments*. Daddy was dismayed to discover that Zula and I had crushes on Rudolph Valentino. He thought the man greasy and effeminate. Theta Bara also inspired us, but Daddy didn't know this. We watched *A Fool There Was* and tried to become "It" girls, buying flat brassieres that had the effect of flattening the muscles in our bosoms that were becoming ample. We wanted to look like her. Eleanor sat still as a mouse while she viewed Harold's Lloyd's *Grandma's Boy*, and even went to the matinee to see it twice. All of our hearts swelled to *The Birth of a Nation*, and the whole audience applauded.

These evenings were special to me, for I could walk home with Daddy and talk. Talk as if we were people, not a father and child. We often discussed the show. I remember one evening when the public endeavored to take up money for some charitable cause. A man had jumped to his feet and declared that he was pledging a substantial sum. On the way home Daddy said, "You heard that man. I am giving to that cause, but I would never tell the people in the picture show how much I was donating. In my opinion, that man was only demonstrating his generosity for the public. Christianity is a matter between man and God. Did not Christ say, 'Don't let your left hand know what your right hand is doing?'" These evenings provided treasured lessons.

The Air Dome had no restrooms. We had to go to the back of the building and stoop in a mass of weeds. Dressed in the white linen dresses covering our petticoats and a bodice and drawers that buttoned on to the bodice, it was an ordeal. On this particular night I developed a desperate urge and asked Eleanor to come with me. She was so intent upon the show that she refused.

I went out alone and encountered a very tough-looking boy lounging on the sidewalk. I experienced a sensation of fear as I passed him, so I covered my fear by smiling and saying "Hello." I was only ten, and thought that this would keep him from following me. I then proceeded to the back of the building. Just as I was arranging the buttons of my drawers he loomed up and grabbed me. I burst out crying and screamed, "Daddy!" Daddy was at home on that particular evening, but the word 'Daddy' produced the desired effect. He dropped me and I ran inside and cried throughout the rest of the film. The whole incident only lasted a minute. When I came back that evening I told Daddy about it and he replied, "Don't worry, I will fix Wallace Gentry."

A few weeks later Daddy and I were taking a walk and I nudged him and said, "Here comes Wallace Gentry."

He started to pass us, but Daddy caught him by the back of his coat, pulled out his knife and said to the boy, "If you ever so much as speak to one of my three little girls, I will cut you into pieces with this knife. Furthermore, when you pass any one of my little girls you are to get off the sidewalk."

After that, whenever he passed any of us he hung his head and got off the walk onto the grass. I have always wondered whether he went back there to kiss me, embrace me, or rape me. But that was all there was to it. He nearly scared me to death.

Big Fight

When I was twelve the boy who lived two doors from us, Robert Cogdill Bullock, had become a difficult child. He sat in a tree and threw rocks at colored cooks when they went to work. One day he made me mad about something. I don't even remember what it was, but I chased him up the street. He ran into his house. As the chase was over, I intended to go home.

His mother stood in their front yard and said, "You and Robert Cogdill are going to have a fight. I am not going to let him become a coward." Her idea of preventing him from becoming a coward was to have him fight a little girl. I was two years older, but we were the same height. He was a boy and the stronger one. I had no objection to fighting, so I stayed as his mother had told me to do. She then went into the house to get him. He was hiding under their dining table. She brought him out and stood him in front of me. He proceeded to fall to the ground. She stood him up again and he fell once more. The third time he stood on his feet and she said, "There he is, May."

I lit into him like a tigress. We fought as though we were little animals. He had the advantage in that he caught onto my hair and pulled my head back, pulling out handfuls full of hair. Finally I knocked him down and sat on him and asked, "Are you down?"

He said, "Yes."

Then I got up, and his mother said, "Now you two must kiss and make up."

I replied, "Do you think I am going to kiss that dirty little boy?"

Zula was watching. She liked Robert Cogdill and intervened, saying, "Oh, yes, you will."

She then jumped on me. I was completely exhausted by that time and began to cry. His mother separated us. When I told Daddy, he punished Zula by not allowing her to go anywhere for a week.

The news of the fight spread all over town. As I passed along the street I had to walk in front of a line of men sitting on planks by the stores. They stopped me and said, "Are you the little girl who beat up that Bullock boy?" I was very thrilled, for Daddy was proud of me.

In later life Robert Cogdill went away to Duke University. Then he came down with crippling arthritis, and spent the rest of his life in a bed in that house. All but three of his fingers became frozen into a closed position. His legs were clasped between two pillows. I procured the help of a well-known orthopedic surgeon in Memphis, Dr. Lipscomb, a friend of my husband's family. Within a few weeks Robert Cogdill's legs were straightened and he was improving. Then he went home and froze into the same position. Dr. Lipscomb said, "Too much mother."

Robert Cogdill used those three sad fingers to make animated figures from an acorn, pecan, and pipe cleaners. They depicted colored minstrel players, much in fashion at that time. He painted their faces and had them posed in many walks of life, gaining some local recognition from these figures. He made jewelry in the shape of bales of cotton, and his photograph was often in *The Commercial Appeal* newspaper because he was celebrated at the Cotton Carnival in Memphis. That was his lot.

The Poitevent Family

Uncle Tom and Aunt Mary were the happiest of couples. She grew ever larger and he would boast and say, "Look, I can still lift her!" He did and the children would applaud.

Grandma Maddox continued to live in a little apartment at the back of their house. She had a bedroom, a bathroom and a sunroom. Behind her bed were cardboard boxes that went to the ceiling. She would taunt us by saying, "You want me to die so that you can get into my boxes."

Then she died. Isabel and Mary led the pack, racing to her bedroom to get into the boxes. The younger children followed. The revelation was not as exciting as the race. We all tore into the boxes to discover nothing but rags, boxes and boxes of rags.

After that a very sad thing happened. Uncle Tom Poitevent developed a crippling disease. Suddenly he could not move anything but the lower parts of his arms. It was not polio. No one was sure what had happened to him. I used to sit on his stomach and say, "Uncle Tom, follow my hands, just move."

He always replied quite sweetly, "May, I would if I could, but it is not possible."

He then asked me to play my piece. I would go to the piano and produced something that I had memorized, and he even asked me to play it once more. He lived in that state for about six months before he died. One day I passed the house and saw Isabel and Mary sitting on the steps crying. Aunt Mary remained a widow for over fifty years, but it continued to be a very happy family.

*

The Methodist Church was two doors away from Aunt Mary's house, and we were sent to that church, as there was no Episcopal Church in Shelby. Daddy gave money to the Methodist and Catholic Churches and to the

Jewish Synagogue. Although my parents were broad-minded, neither was enthusiastic about climbing Jacob's Ladder and they did not attend church. On one occasion we all went to a program for children at the Methodist Church. Quite unexpectedly the Minister said, "Will Janula Poitevent now lead the prayer?"

Silence followed. The palms of all of our hands began to sweat. Finally after the longest pause that I can remember, Hal Carnes took up Janula's prayer. This gave us the chance to break rank, six girls tore down the isle of the Methodist Church with the minister in hot pursuit, shouting, "Wait, wait, please come back!"

We flew into Aunt Mary's house and hid beneath beds, inside closets, any space that we could find. Aunt Mary was perplexed, and we only replied, "Help, help, the Methodist minister is coming after us." Aunt Mary smoothed it over with the minister's wife and we all went back to church.

*

The Poitevent girls were all pretty. They had charming smiles, willowy figures, and an air of sophistication. While we were the girls for the horse shows, they were belles of the Delta.

Aunt Mary made sure that her house was the center of entertainment for young people. They danced on the front porch and in the living room. The rugs were rolled up and the furniture pushed against the wall. She was considerate enough to invite Zula and me to watch the dancing one evening, for we were four to six years younger than Isabel and Mary. That night I looked over my pink shoulder in the bathroom mirror and prayed that someone might dance with me. We were collected by Mary Poitevent and her beau, Hayes Carnes, the nephew of Mr. Hal Carnes. Hayes had come to Shelby to be the cashier of the Shelby Bank. As we walked down the street Mary sang a song, "Every body shimmies, even Hayes." For some reason, I felt sorry for Hayes, that he should be the butt of that song.

My moment of pathos vanished when Rance's Band started to play. This was a three-piece band, which played at all of the little dances in Shelby. To my amazement, J. W. Thomas asked me to dance. I replied, "I am sorry, I can't tickle toe."

He replied, "You are doing it."

Then a whole line of young men formed behind him to dance with me. It was the happiest of nights. The next day J. W. Thomas, who was by that time back from Culver Military Academy, and riding his horse, standing on top of the saddle, told everyone in town that he was going to wait for me to grow up.

The First World War and Our Hero

My Aunt Ellen had three sons: Norman, Kennedy, and Donald. They were sent away to boarding schools as early as they could be admitted. Kennedy and Donald spent a large part of their summers with Aunt Deedee (Madia) and later with my family on the street.

Norman became an inventor, inventing the time exposure on a camera when he was only seventeen. In his naivety, he took it to Eastman Kodak. They thanked him, praised his device, and he walked away, his schoolboy's heart filled with pride. The following year this was their feature. It meant that the whole family could be snapped without anyone sitting behind the camera. He returned to the company to collect his pile of money, only to be met with a cool reception. "You had no patent on this invention, Mr. McEwen." It was the first time that he had been called Mister.

Donald was his mother's favorite and a ladies' man. He was named for the man with whom she had been in love. But it was Kennedy who spent the larger amount of time with us. Aunt Ellen realized when he was a schoolboy that she could not handle him. Doctors diagnosed him with a

Kennedy Shelby McEwen in kilt of Canadian Black Watch,
World War I.

condition that they called 'dementia praecox,' a dividing of the brain.

Kennedy was the handsomest person in our family, with a perfect physique, magnificent teeth, a roman nose, and beautiful gray eyes. He had a heart too kind and a wit too cruel. The element of fear was absent from his brain. He was a powerful swimmer. I well remember one summer on the Sunflower River when limbs on a tree above my head began to break, and Kennedy flew down into the water.

World War I broke out and Kennedy volunteered! They would not have him in the United States Army or Navy, but the Canadian Black Watch took him. I have a photograph of Kennedy in his kilt.

The war did not help his nerves. He returned to us much more depressed. Everyone in the family said that he was in love with me. I knew it also, but even a sixteen-year-old girl could not respond to that slightly missing link. I was ill much of that year and had to go to bed once a month. While I was lying in the north bedroom, Kennedy burst into my room. He had heard that I was not well and had *walked* from Nashville to Shelby to see me. I asked him how he ate on the road.

"Oh, I went to houses and asked for food."

"Weren't you afraid?"

"No, I always carried my fraternity pin."

"But, Kennedy, you never went to college, how do you have a fraternity pin?"

He grinned, exposing those beautiful teeth, and pointed to his toothbrush, prominently displayed in his shirt pocket. "With this they know that I am not an ordinary tramp. I had a big breakfast this morning with a lady in Alligator. I had been to a party at her house, but didn't let on."

After he had served in the war, I suspected that he had been married and told the relations, because I heard him make a remark about a woman's cold feet in his back in the middle of the night.

When questioned, he acknowledged the marriage.

"What was her name?" I asked.

"Madeleine, and she was mad most of the time."

"Where did you meet her?"

"She sat down beside me in a park in Ontario and cried. I asked her what was the matter and she said that she had nowhere to go. So I said, 'Marry me.'"

Later I heard that the family had to pay her off.

After the long march he seemed to stay in Shelby. One day I walked into town and found Kennedy sitting in front of the drugstore with tears in his eyes and one of his beautiful teeth missing.

"What happened to you?"

"I tried to commit suicide and was hit by the train."

Apparently he had grabbed a clothes dummy from a shop and had thrown it in front of the train and then jumped after it, shouting, "I'll save the lady." The train hit him; he bounced into the air and landed like an acrobat with one tooth missing.

Kennedy buzzed around the Delta on his motorcycle with any young lady foolish enough to ride on the jump seat. Then he joined a carnival in Cleveland with his motorcycle, riding it in a shell with other cyclists. This job lasted only one night, for he drove the other cyclists out of the shell.

There followed another deep depression. He called his aunt into the garden to ask her if she heard voices. She despaired. "Look, look, on that clothes line, don't you hear them?" She saw three black birds, walking along a clothesline. "There they are, Mrs. Tom Yates talking to Dean Rowe about Ruth Edwards as she goes walking down the street in the rain." She appreciated the joke but after that he moved to her chicken house, where he perched on a shelf and cried and drank tins of Canned Heat, which contained pure alcohol.

It was during this time that Aunt Ellen committed suicide (1926). The night before she died, Kennedy was strangely agitated. He paced the floor at our house all night, and Mama wrapped him in a blanket.

One time everyone was talking about him in our living room. I said,

"No matter what, I like him, I even love him." Kennedy jumped up from behind the couch, where he had been listening.

Aunt Mary and Aunt Deedee got together and applied to have him admitted to the Veteran's Hospital in Gulfport. They obtained his military records, and were amazed to find a cardboard box containing numerous medals. In his effort to commit suicide, he would rush out onto No Man's Land and carry a wounded soldier on his strong shoulders to safety. He saved quite a few comrades and was never wounded. On one of these occasions he found a beautiful ebony cross with a silver crucifix attached to it. He brought this to Shelby and gave it to Aunt Lula because he thought she was the most religious person in the family. Despite his good war record the doctors did say that the effect of shell shock had exaggerated his preexisting condition. Kennedy had told the doctors that all that was wrong with him was "Shelbyitus from staying at the Murnanery (Aunt Deedee's house) too long."

The institution took him, and he remained there until his death in the late 1950's. I always sent him presents and visited him every few years when I was on the Gulf Coast. Once he wrote to me that he was swimming in the Gulf everyday to get into shape to swim the English Channel. He reasoned that this would make him so famous that the hospital would have to release him. That did not happen, but he did escape with two other patients, and they went as far as Mexico. There they were apprehended because they got drunk and hired musicians to follow them through the streets.

As the years went by, his brother Norman and I were his only visitors. By that time he was obsessively counting all of the objects in the room and could scarcely concentrate on anything else, but he remained strong. I wonder if there is not a bit of Kennedy in many heroes.

Transportation

I have a photograph of the passengers boarding one of the first trains that came to Shelby. It ran through our land. The train went from Vicksburg to Memphis. Daddy and Miss Lisa Whitworth were given a complimentary passage on the first train to Hushpuckena and back (eight miles round trip). The railway became the lifeline of the Mississippi Delta. Everything that Mama and Daddy missed most from Memphis was sent down once a month in an iced compartment of the train—violets for Mama and delicatessen food for Daddy.

Life was so safe that when I was seven I boarded the train alone and went to Cleveland, a distance of fifteen miles, to visit cousins George and Joe Shelby and their sons, little George and baby Gwin. It was thrilling to take this excursion by myself. The only other way to get about was on foot or by horseback. Motorcars were still too unreliable. At some stage during my childhood concrete sidewalks replaced the wooden planks. We were never allowed to have a car for Daddy despised cars. He had won one for shooting at a fair in Memphis, and tried to drive it on the muddy, rutted, road to Shelby. He drove it into a ditch and left it there. Mama's excuse for spending was that Mary Poitevent had an automobile and we didn't. As a result of this inverted snobbery, I have never been a good driver, and even my daughter became a bad driver. The roads were so bad and there were so few mechanics that for my first eight years in this town there were only a handful of automobiles. Then Hayes Carnes and a Mr. Rothrock built a Ford business on our street. Hayes's cousin from Memphis was Horace Hull, who owned the largest Ford dealership in the United States and was able to arrange the dealership. Our world quickly changed. All the planters who lived nearby spent their leisure time sitting around the Ford automobile building. Daddy found the automobile much too intrusive, and had speed bumps installed on the main street, so that cars passing our house

Gerald Shelby boarding the train to Huspuckana about 1893.

Rothrock-Carnes Ford Lincoln.

were forced to drive slowly, hence controlling the amount of dust delivered on to our front porch. The Ford Company was very paternal, so much so that Henry Ford gave each of his dealers a free trip to Detroit to meet him.

*

People lived in boxcars and worked on the railway. One year several families stayed most of the winter. They even had chickens in front of their boxcars and planted a few flowers beside the railway track. Zula decided that we should call upon one of these families. Theirs was a house like none that we had ever seen: one room, one woman, one rocking chair, many children, one on one breast, one on her lap, one on the side of the chair. They were white people. Zula immediately saw the opportunity, a feast of babies, and we each borrowed a child or baby to take to our playhouse and play 'Mama.' The poor woman didn't seem to mind at all.

*

When I was seventeen, I became very ill. After staying in bed for a week, the bleeding could not be stopped and Cousin Fred insisted that I be taken to Memphis to Dr. DeMarco. They carried me down the street on a stretcher to meet the train. The smell of blood caused a stray dog to jump onto the stretcher and attack me. Then I began to fade. The trip by train took several hours. Cousin Fred sat beside me as tender as a nurse and kept saying, "May don't fall asleep. Don't sleep."

At one point I could not help it and I slept. He took my pulse and mentally pronounced me dead. Then my heart began to beat again. Dr. De Marco found that I was a patient to be put on the medical records for having survived with so little blood left in my body. A month later, with the care of the Gartley Ramsey Hospital and their kind nurses, I was at home. My beautiful childhood was over.

Lovers

The first sign of spring was Henry Denton (Will Denton's brother) in his Roadster, scattering dust over the speed bumps that Daddy had so carefully installed. He was one of those attractive ugly men, tall, lean, and muscular, with a hooked nose, slightly crooked teeth, and eyes that protruded somewhat. I don't remember a woman who ever resisted him. I knew him from the time that I was a small child, when he romped with us at the Sunflower River Clubhouse, and later, when I was a young woman and a friend of his wife. I too became the recipient of one of his amorous advances. There was always a triangle that surrounded him, often a quadrangle. His finances were sound, but he bore the touch of a gambler, for he was known to play the commodities market, quite seriously. This was all the more incentive to make the rake appealing to women, who could then feel sorry for him.

It was the custom for young men to meet the night train on the off chance that someone exciting might alight. One evening Cousin Fred had stood around the depot until his conscience pricked him and he thought, "What is a busy doctor doing spending his time like this?"

He turned to go, but halted when he heard, "I wouldn't leave now. The wildest thing between Memphis and Vicksburg will get off this train." He stayed, and that was Ruth Benoit.

Ruth was not a beauty in the sense that Mama and Aunt Ellen were beauties. She was very petite, with vibrant blue eyes, light brown hair, bright red cheeks, not brightened by rouge, but later by alcohol. Her two front teeth had a little space that gave her an impish smile. It was her spirit that no man could resist. One of my earliest memories of her were of a lady all dressed up and walking in the rain, simply because she loved it. Although she drank and behaved in a way that was out of bounds for the time, she was well born. Her mother was a Foote from Greenville. She knew no conventions. Her life was a matter of intense merriment or intense sadness.

Uncle George Shelby had a gentle sister, Adelaide, who had married a wild redheaded man named Edwards. I never saw Mr. Edwards, because he died young, leaving her with four wild sons and one sweet daughter. Three of her sons were devastatingly good looking and they all had an ability to make money. Cousin Bob was the only ugly one, but he became the Sheriff of Bolivar County, which was a first step to becoming a serious millionaire, as Mississippi was a dry state and the sheriff received a stipend from every whiskey store and bootlegger in the county. When we lived in Memphis, he had already reached that peak, and he and his wife, Evelyn, nee Connell, lived down the street from us on Bellevue. It was in their yard that I was forced to play horse and buggy. The other Edwards brothers were Luscious, Ike and Shelby. Luscious and Ike were "shoot 'em up" wild. Shelby was simply the handsomest man I have ever seen. He had prematurely white hair, black eyes and eyebrows and the classical features which belonged to my grandfather's side of the family. He became a millionaire before he reached the age of thirty. Quite understandably he captured the heart of Ruth Benoit. They seemed destined for one another, although their marriage never bordered on the conventional. Much to their amusement, they had a darling baby boy, Shelby. They built a stylish green-shingled house at the south end of the street.

Cousin Ruth visited us in Memphis with her little cherub and Zula and I alternated kissing his feet. While we were playing with him one afternoon, I heard Cousin Ruth talking to Mama in the next room. Then she began to cry and cry and declared that she had discovered the most awful truth about herself. She was no longer in love with her husband, but was hopelessly in love with Henry Denton.

*

Madge Henry was only sixteen when she moved to Shelby to live next door to us. She soon became Henry Denton's fiancée *almost*. Her sister was happily married to his brother Will. Henry dangled Madge for nearly ten years until she was close to being on the shelf. Like Ruth, Madge was petite, delicate, highly intelligent, but she was somewhat prim. The threat of Ruth Edwards, who lived at the other end of the street, loomed throughout the love affair. Madge even succumbed to that temptation that sometimes befalls women who pretend that they are friends with the Other Woman. She began to smoke cigarettes in an effort to be as worldly as Ruth Edwards, although Ruth's appeal did not lie in tobacco. She did not even smoke.

Madge became desperate and even considered a proposal from ugly Mr. Meek, another rich man that lived three doors south of us on the street. He had divorced his wife because she had an affair with Cousin Fred. I knew all about it because I had to share a bedroom with the first Mrs. Meek on her last night in Shelby, when Aunt Lula and Uncle Will Connell were the only people to receive her. I happened to be spending the night at their house and was unfortunate enough to hear her cry all night in the bed next to mine. Cousin Fred settled some money on her and she went back to Nashville, Tennessee.

During this bleak time for Madge, she confided all of her troubles to Mama, for she was Mama's protégée. Most girls in those days had two choices: to marry and hopefully make a good marriage or to become an old maid schoolteacher. The choices were not hard ones to make.

Mr. Will Denton had a younger brother, Charles, who had completed his engineering degree at Georgia Institute of Technology in Atlanta, after serving in the First World War and in the Battle of the Marne. He was very handsome and sparklingly bright. The moment that he moved into town he fell in love with Madge, and they became engaged. She was off the shelf and married to the man who became the richest and, I might add, the most successful and attractive man in the region. Charles and his brother Will came to own a cotton gin, a flour mill, a dairy that also manufactured ice cream, an ice plant, a cotton de-linting plant, a company to sell chemicals to farmers, a lumber company, and thousands of acres of the best land in Bolivar County. Her diamonds became so heavy that it was hard for her to stand straight and balance their weight. Madge and Charles were a delightfully attractive couple and remained our neighbors for forty years, until their finances dictated that they build a grander house resembling Monticello, located on the back of her sister's lot on our street.

*

Henry's love life did not become simpler. Margaret Brooks, a belle who lived on a large plantation out from Shelby, drove her car into Holmes Lake in a plea for Henry's attention. Fortunately the car was the only thing that was lost in the lake.

Henry's affair with Ruth Edwards never subsided throughout her marriage to Shelby. Twenty years later, after I became a young lady, and after Shelby's death, I went to a dinner party at Ruth's house. Henry was seated at the other end of the table. I have never seen such fascination in the light of two people's eyes. They were meant for each other. Their love had lasted almost twenty years, but it never bore the test of living together every day.

Eventually Henry became involved with a beautiful, slim friend of Isabel and Mary Poitevent, Ouida Bland. She was a much younger woman and from a simple background; Ouida's father was the depot agent in Shelby. Henry proposed in a moment of passion and immediately regretted his rashness. He went to Ruth with his dilemma and asked her how he could get out of it. For all of her unconventionality, Ruth did not have a scheming bone in her body. She refused to assist him in getting off the hook, and declared that Ouida was a lovely girl, he had led her on, proposed, and now he must carry it through. Henry married.

It was never a happy marriage. Henry built Ouida a nice house, and then refused to let her buy any furniture. It was during this time in the empty house that he began to reach out for every woman who came to see Ouida, including me. It was rumored about that time that he was losing a considerable amount of money on the commodities market.

There was a fire at the oil mill, which was located across the street from our house. In those days people often attended fires for the excitement. Henry had been watching the fire when he decided that he had seen enough, and backed his car with a certain amount of thrust, killing a small boy who had been standing behind the car.

A few months after that, Henry shot himself in the head. He didn't die immediately. We all gathered at Dr. White's little clinic, located on the south side of the city hall on our street. I remember seeing Madge and Charles, Henry's brother. I wondered what Madge was thinking. Ouida was there. Ruth was out of town. He died later that night.

**

Ruth began to go downhill before that happened. Her marriage had long since gone downhill. Darling little Shelby would cry (like a dog) when he saw his mother put on certain garments and say, "Wed sippers, mama dance." She and Cousin Shelby once hit each other over the heads at a dance on our street in the City Hall. Kathryn Henderson took me there to see the blood.

After her husband Shelby's death, Ruth had a bad accident. The tornado that flattened Duncan, Mississippi, in 1929 demolished the City Hall at the moment that Ruth was there paying her taxes. The building collapsed and Ruth and a colored man were trapped under the building. Fortunately they were both retrieved, but her back had been broken and she always walked in a slightly bent fashion.

When she was drinking, there was no food in the house, and she gave her son some money saying, "Here, go to Shorty's and get a hamburger." That was the beginning of a modern mother. No one else had even heard of Shorty, or a hamburger for that matter. We were still eating off damask tablecloths with pads beneath and a servant passing four courses in silver bowls of homegrown vegetables, porterhouse steaks and biscuits for two meals a day plus a substantial breakfast. Shelby Edwards, their son, used to boast and say, "I am high powered, I was raised on Tabasco sauce." Years later my daughter called him 'Cousin High Power.'

One of the men in Ruth's circle was a Mr. Warren Meek, a friend of

William Faulkner. He commented to Ruth, "You know what your face reminds me of? A tin of chopped tomatoes." She went into peals of laughter and told everyone. That laughter is how she survived the loss of her looks and her bent back and the loss of her reputation. A much younger man was enamored with Ruth and in a moment of fervent passion said, "Ruth, I must kiss you." She replied, "All right, but for me it would mean no more than kissing a baby."

***

Another couple who was a very important part of our family was John and Lucia Gortner. Lucia was a niece by marriage of my aunt Ellen McEwen, who lived in Nashville. Aunt Ellen took Lucia out West as a traveling companion, where they met an attractive man named John Gortner. He showed Lucia some attention and would have forgotten her, but Aunt Ellen said, "Send him a postcard." That had more than the desired effect of rekindling his interest, and he married her. As a child, I first met them in Memphis when they were newlyweds living in the first apartment house in the city, located on Union Avenue. Then John bought a big plantation out from Shelby at a place called Honey Bayou. He was a horrible husband. It would appear that by the time that he and Lucia moved to Shelby, John had grown truly tired of Lucia, although she was an attractive and elegant lady. Men could treat women as they liked in those days, for women had nowhere to go and recourse to the courts was usually unsatisfactory. John left Lucia in the Mississippi mud, living in something like a commissary, although he was many times over a millionaire.

After Henry died, Ruth had a serious affair with John Gortner. Poor Cousin Lucia came quite close to losing her mind. There was a short period when she even went blind from depression.

Shelby Edwards, Sr., began to lose his money and his health. Ruth carried on with John and thought that he was actually going to marry her. She decided to divorce Shelby, and asked Lucille Patterson, a close younger friend of our family, who had lived on the street from time to time, to go with her to Cleveland on the day that she got her divorce from Shelby. Lucille told the story that when they returned Shelby said, "Did you get it?" as if he were talking about the purchase of a tin of beans.

She replied, "Yes."

Shelby didn't blink, but continued living in his house with Ruth as though nothing had happened. On another visit Lucille found them in a state of mad ecstasy. Their player piano was blasting forth with "Running Wild, Lost Control," and Ruth was dancing about the room with a roll of toilet paper, wrapping it about Shelby. It transpired that his brother Luscious had died, and Ruth loved him as well. That was her way of exhibiting grief.

During this period Mama asked Ruth how she got away with her outrageous behavior without being socially ostracized, reminding her that her neighbor was Lillian Carnes and two doors down the street was Julia Yates, the biggest gossip in town. Ruth replied, "When I go on a toot, the next day, I send all of the neighbors some sticky jam." Two years after Ruth purchased her "tin of beans" in Cleveland, Shelby died of cirrhosis of the liver.

When John Gortner died, in about 1942, the executor found mistresses all over the place, some of whom he had mentioned in his will (not Ruth), who by then had remarried. There were women upon whom he had bestowed gifts of property. No one knew who the mourners would be. Ruth said, "I hear they have John in cold storage." He remained in a freezer in Memphis for weeks before they could have a respectable funeral.

About eight years later Cousin Lucia hired a lawyer from California, who visited all of us and untangled the quagmire of John's estate where Lucia had signed documents at a time that she did not know what she was doing and could not see, as a result of depression. This included some bequests of property that were nullified. At last, Lucia was blessed with a prosperous and peaceful old age, having regained her sight. She never forgot the adopted relations who were loyal to her in Mississippi and quite often returned form California for celebrated visits. On one of those visits she made sure that Hayes and Carole and I had tickets to see "My Fair Lady." However, by that time Ruth and Lucia had become an exotic memory, and they were both old ladies.

****

Cousin Fred Shelby was the man who fulfilled most women's ambitions. He was very small in frame and looked like the Poitevent family, having inherited the sweet and sensitive face of his mother. His appeal for most women was considerable. Nor did he suffer from the curse of heavy drinking that afflicted many of the Shelby family. He had been educated at the Webb School in Bellbuckle, Tennessee, the University of the South at Sewanee, and had spent a year at the University of Mississippi to have a good time, where he had two sets of evening clothes, one to lend out and another for himself. After that frivolous year he went to a medical school in New York. Such bachelors were in short supply in the Mississippi Delta. No one made money as a doctor in those days, but he was a prudent investor and acquired several thousand acres of good sandy land, a fine herd of cattle, and together with Charles Denton was the richest man in town. It was his gentle manner that made women fall in love with him and know that they would never find someone better. Many had to make do with another suitor or become a spinster, as was the fate of sweet Alice Gardner, one of his girl friends. Women in the last pangs of labor would call for him, because the sight of his face enabled them to relax enough to have their babies naturally.

The years went by, and still he did not marry. He fell in love, gave women expensive gifts, took them to grand events, but continued to live at home with his mother, Aunt Janie. He treated women too well, and later dashed their hopes. He had two constant loves, Liza Gayneau, his colored Creole mistress, and Ruth Edwards, his cousin's wife. He noted the lady who alighted from the train that night, and never ceased to be fascinated by her, although he always remained gentle and kind to her husband, his first cousin, especially in his later years of troubles.

In 1938 Aunt Janie died. A few months later, Cousin Fred, who was then nearly sixty, married Ruth Edwards. He was devoted to her splendid son and treated him as his own, although he was clearly the son of Shelby Edwards, for they looked exactly alike.

Cousin George and his wife, Joe Shelby, moved into Aunt Janie's house with their two handsome sons Gwin and Fred and their brain damaged daughter, Jane, because before Aunt Janie's death, Cousin Fred was spending most nights with Ruth. Cousin Joe and George took care of Aunt Janie's domestic arrangements, and Cousin Fred deeded his share in her house and plantation to his brother, for by that time Cousin George's wife's fortune had been depleted.

There resembled a royal schism. Joe hated Ruth. The rift was never rectified until the late 1950's when Ruth died. They lived two doors apart, but Joe and George never received Ruth, who laughed it off as she had done everything else. It was Ruth's turn to become the richest Mrs. Shelby, and Madge's time to become the richest lady in the town.

Aunt Zula

Aunt Zula never lived on the street, but she visited every year. In Daddy's earliest letters to Mama he mentioned her attractions. She was not as beautiful as Mama, but equally appealing. When she was a young lady in Hillsboro, Texas, she and a man named Guy Armstrong fell deeply in love. For some reason unmentioned in family memorabilia he did not marry her at the ripe time. She was vibrant, with a full figure, although she lacked the clear-cut features that Mama had inherited from her father. Notwithstanding, there was a warmth and sensuality in her eyes that kept men falling in love with her for over fifty years.

Aunt Zula continued to work in her family's department store in Hillsboro, Texas, while Guy courted her. Then he went away for a while and did what young men often do—he found someone else, to whom he proposed. Shortly after that, he realized the disaster that he had made and came back to Aunt Zula, begging her to marry him. She agreed, but his father stepped in and used considerable influence to impress upon Guy that a man's word was his bond. He must honor his promise. I do not know why Guy's father's influence was so great, but it was.

She soon acquired another admirer, Dow Sawyer, who begged her to marry him. Her greatest failing was dithering. In her state of indecision she came to visit Mama and Daddy. Among Daddy's earliest letters to Mama, one letter mentioned his redheaded cousin, Ike Edwards (the brother of Shelby Edwards). Ten years later Ike and Zula were introduced, fell in love, and became engaged. Ike didn't have time to purchase a diamond ring before she returned to Texas, but as a token of his pledge, in Edwards' style, he gave her his pearl-handled pistol. She went home to clear up the matter of another engagement.

In Texas, she discovered that Dow Sawyer had become terminally ill with tuberculosis. She broke the engagement to Ike Edwards, mailed back his pearl- handled pistol and administered to the dying Dow Sawyer. He begged her to marry him. Although he was clearly on his deathbed, she could not take the plunge.

On the night that Halley's comet appeared, Aunt Zula and Dow's sisters sat in the yard beneath the clear Texas stars to watch it. Dow called to Aunt Zula and begged her once more to marry him. She squeezed his hand, kissed him, but avoided the pledge. He died that night. Aunt Zula put on black widow's weeds and mourned him as if she were in that position.

Mama and Daddy decided that it was time for another long visit. As Aunt Zula worked for members of her mother's rich family, her visits were not a matter of a two-week holiday. She came for the entire spring.

Aunt Zula Liner with the love of her life Guy Armstrong.

Before we left the Delta, our refuge in the late spring and early summer was a rustic clubhouse several miles out from Shelby on a tributary of the Sunflower River called the Hushpuckana Creek. This was where we learned to swim. There was even a sand bar for sun bathing, although girls were not so keen to tan as today. I would freckle. The clubhouse was a bucolic haven for city relations. We had a haystack. Mama's brother Sam Liner and his wife Catherine, who had been a minor silent film actress and a dancer, arrived from Chicago. Aunt Zula joined the merry band. Other people from the nearby towns in the Delta came and went, but we stayed at the clubhouse for a considerable period.

After we had been there for about ten days we ran out of supplies, and Mama gave Henry Denton a list to give to the hostler, Uncle John. He loaded Henry's car with everything Mama had ordered and added a feather duster and a Bible. Perhaps Uncle John had heard the rumor that a Bible was needed. Among our party was an attractive married man from Memphis who owned land in the Delta.

Mama was always slow to catch on to the essentials. Several months later, she mentioned to Lucille Patterson that she did not think that Sister Zula was making her usual good impression upon the relations this year. Was there something happening that she needed to stop? Lucille replied, "It's too late now." A big affair had developed between Aunt Zula and Bo Peep Turley.

Like most affairs with married men, it ended by their going separate ways, the man back to his comfortable surroundings, the woman to her hard and empty life.

Then Guy Armstrong's wife died, leaving him with a little boy, who became my childhood beau when I went to Hillsboro to visit. Guy returned immediately to the arms of Aunt Zula and asked her to marry him.

We were to be flower girls in the wedding and were very excited. Two years later we were to be junior bridesmaids, and later bridesmaids, but the wedding never happened. Guy suffered from syphilis. There was no cure at the time and his condition deteriorated until he died, leaving Aunt Zula in a much worse position than that of a widow.

Her life was a hard one. Mama and Uncle Sam did what they could to make it bearable. I remember one summer in Colorado when someone inadvertently described a person as an old maid. We were in a cafeteria and I was standing next to Aunt Zula when I saw tears fall from her eyes.

"What's the matter?" I begged.

"I am an old maid."

The three of us rushed to her, "But you are not." She was more of a woman than Mama, and we all loved her just as much.

She continued to live in Texas and came to own a dress shop with another lady. When she was in her fifties she acquired an attractive beau, Garland Rhodes. He owned an ophthalmology business and was quite rich. Aunt Zula was nine years older than Garland. They did not marry until she was seventy, but they spent nineteen happy years together as a married couple, dying only six months apart. She was eight-nine, and he was eighty. Aunt Zula continued to carry Garland's breakfast to his bed on a tray until a few months before she died. She was born to be a mistress.

The last time that I saw her was in 1958. She and Garland passed through Shelby and only had time to stop for dinner. The moment that she walked into the house she turned to me and said, "I want you to know that your father was the best man that I ever knew."

"Yes," I replied, "I always knew that. He married the wrong Liner girl."

Then she and Garland were on their way in a big car to Canada, while Uncle Sam was bravely holding his life together after two failed marriages and a bitter disappointment in his son. Mama was in a nursing home, blind from cataracts that she had refused to tell anyone about until it was too late to operate, because she had become a Christian Scientist. Aunt Zula was to have eleven more good years than her brother and sister.

Another Beautiful Lady Visited

Her name was Sarah Gwin. She was the sister of Cousin Joe, who had married George Shelby. Sarah was much prettier than Cousin Joe, for she had dark eyes accented by heavy eyebrows, curly black hair, an angular nose and a petite figure. The years went by, but she had not married. There could have been no shortage of proposals, for she had also been rich before Cousin George lost her money as well as his wife's money. She had been well educated by a good governess and graduated from Mary Baldwin Women's College in Virginia. Afterwards she studied music at a Conservatory in Paris. Mama asked Cousin Joe why Sarah remained a spinster, and Cousin Joe hinted that the only man Sarah had ever been in love with was Cousin Fred. This explanation begged questioning, for Cousin Fred had never paid any serious attention to Sarah Gwin.

When Sarah returned from studying music in Paris, she spoke of nothing but a Frenchman, Philippe, but he never crossed the ocean. It was now time for her to perform. Cousin Joe rented a concert hall in Memphis and sent out engraved invitations. All of my family made a special trip on the train to hear her play the piano. Sarah came onto the stage in a beautiful gray silk evening dress, sat down on her stool in front of a grand piano and failed to play a single note. After that she bought a silent piano and only exercised her fingers.

She did, however, obtain a job teaching music at a Catholic girls' school in Memphis. It was during this short foray into the real world that she met a fellow teacher, a nun. Her name was Caroline. They fell in love. Caroline decided to quit the convent, but the Church refused to release her from her vows. Sarah and Caroline ran away. They made an excuse that Caroline needed to attend some event pertaining to the school, and Sarah collected Caroline in a taxi, where Caroline changed from her habit into fashionable clothes. This was done on the back seat of the cab. Sarah had even thought to bring Caroline a wig, for in those days nuns had to shave their heads. They fled on the night train for El Paso, Texas, where they spent the rest of their lives together, often returning for long visits to our street. They were simply known as Cousin Sarah and Miss Caroline. Both were attractive, feminine women.

A Wedding

Isabel Poitevent was the first young lady to blossom in our family. She had a tall, willowy figure, big blue eyes, pearly teeth, and a good disposition. She could always make a joke about herself. Every relation with any resources supported her coming out. She had attended Brenau College in Gainesville, Georgia. This was a fashionable institution at that time, and she and Mary both went there.

Aunt Mary had grown up in the Mississippi Delta and knew everyone, for she was the favorite chaperone. Her disposition was so easy that young men would often fall asleep on her shoulder driving back in the early hours of the morning from a dance. The Poitevent house was the center for gatherings.

When Isabel came home from college she lost no time in choosing a good man, but not her mother's choice. He was Billy Barksdale from Grenada, Mississippi. Billy was attractive looking, and definitely his own man. He had a mean old widowed mother and a dead father. There was some money in the family, held tightly between his mother's fingers. He liked his liquor.

Zula and I were bridesmaids in the wedding. This was our first introduction into society. Isabel and Billy were Episcopalians, but there was no Episcopal Church in Shelby, so they borrowed the largest church in town for the occasion, the Baptist, and imported the Episcopal Minister from Clarksdale to officiate in front of the River Jordan.

Pre-nuptial parties lasted the entire summer. We stayed in Shelby longer than usual that year so that we could enjoy some of the events. The wedding took place in the days of Prohibition. Billy declared that everyone was going to "have a good time" at his wedding.

On the evening of the event, crates of corn liquor were procured for the groomsmen. They dressed at Hayes Carnes's lodgings and he said that they put on one sock and took a swig, then another sock and took another swig. Hayes never appeared at the wedding.

Candles were lit by the remaining core groomsmen. When the minister pronounced the couple man and wife, Aunt Mary slumped and Cousin Fred rushed forward with smelling salts. Then the wedding party made their exit down the isle. Everyone heard Isabel say, "Billy, you are stepping on my veil." They also heard Billy reply, "What's in a veil." There was a little rip, but the veil remained in place. Whatever the beginnings and misgivings, it was a happy marriage, producing two attractive daughters, and the couple gave much loyalty, warmth and merriment to their friends and relations throughout their long and successful lives.

Hayes Carnes revived for the reception and joined the line to greet the guests. One stalwart man came down the line shaking everyone's hand rather pompously. When he reached Hayes, Tal Thomas (Billy's cousin) leaned across others in the receiving line placing his face directly in front of the man and asked, "Hayes, who the devil is that son of a bitch?"

That was the Vicar, Mr. Deakin, the Episcopal minister from Clarksdale, the grandfather of Tennessee Williams.[1]

---

1 In the early 1950's Billy Barksdale was having dinner with us and commented, "It's no point in sending Mr. Deakin any muney any more because the boy is doing real well in New York." Later Billy said to me, "He made him a writer, told him about everybody in town."

A Summer of Madness

Daddy looked at me in the early spring of my tenth year (several years before Isabel's wedding) and said that I seemed run down. He suggested that Mama take me to Hot Springs, Arkansas for the baths. Zula and Eleanor remained in Shelby to finish most of the school year. Mama was always glad for an excuse for a trip, so we boarded the train in our navy dresses and went to this delightful resort, where we stayed at the Arlington Hotel. We both took the baths, which were exhausting, because no one told me that I should only stay for a short time. The first day, after an hour or more, I fainted.

Hot Springs collected a delightful group of young people from all over the South, who came on the pretext of health. Mama was soon the center of their group under the guise of being their chaperone. I was the only child at the resort; everyone else was in school. We went to a dance most nights, and I would fall asleep on a gilded chair, watching others dance. There was a charming redheaded man from New Orleans in our group, a Mr. Du Bois. He made a great to do over me and brought me a tiny baby doll. I am now looking at a photograph of the party, and it is clear that his real baby doll was Mama. They had fallen in love.

We extended our stay, which was originally to have lasted only a month. Zula and Eleanor finished most of the school year and were sent to Hillsboro, Texas, to escape the Delta summer. The round of parties continued and the baths continued. One night some men suddenly stepped out onto the street in front of me and I jumped and cried. I had never been a nervous child until that summer, but the combination of late nights and hot baths were not having the desired affect. From that time forward, I have always jumped if a person suddenly stepped out before me.

When we returned to Shelby, Daddy was appalled by my appearance. I had dark circles under my eyes, was thin and jittery. He admonished Mama,

*Anna Liner Shelby (2nd from left) with Mr. Du Bois (2nd from right)
and May (center), Hot Springs, Arkansas, 1915.*

"What have you done to this child? I sent her away because she was run down and now she looks worse than ever." Mama shrugged off the question and a few days later we joined the others in Texas for the rest of the summer. Mama received many letters that summer, supposedly from the young friends that she had made in Hot Springs.

When we returned to Shelby in the autumn, Mama found a go-between for her correspondence, Ruth Edwards. Somehow, in the middle of the school year, Daddy found out about these letters. We all heard them arguing behind closed doors, Mama crying, "They were only a few innocent letters."

Daddy said that he was going to divorce her. Ruth Edwards was banned from our house forevermore and we were all sent to Hillsboro, Texas for the rest of the year.

A divorce was serious in those days. If a woman offended, she could simply be cast out, without any alimony. Mama could have ended her life in Hillsboro, Texas, living with her parents and Aunt Zula and once more making hats in The Graham Department Store. All three of us wrote letters to Daddy, pleading with him to let us come home. It wore him down. He brought his heavy heart to Aunt Janie, who was almost his mother. "I have no reason to take her back," he declared.

Aunt Janie replied, "You have three reasons."

He began to thaw. We kept up the pressure. Finally Daddy wrote that we would be coming home.

Children have no shame. We then demanded a special gift to await our homecoming. The ransom was a new pony and a new cart.

I have always experienced a sense of blessed freedom when coming down into the Mississippi Delta from the small hills that surround Memphis. The wind swept through my hair from the open windows of the train. We gazed upon flat land and row upon row of a good stand of cotton about six inches high. This lasted from Tunica to Shelby. It was late May and the temperature was approaching eighty degrees Fahrenheit, perfect weather for our homecoming. The smell of newly cut grass by the side of the tracks permeated the train.

Uncle John, the hostler, met us at the station, sitting in a dark green cart with a prancing pony. Buzzard was a thing of the past. We fell over Uncle John with hugs and were driven down the muddy street to our house. There were more hugs from the cook and the house girl and the washwoman and the yardman. The playhouse was waiting and the terriers were yapping. Annie Mae and Kathryn Henderson were there to greet us. Even Hillsboro, Texas seemed like a dull suburb compared to this. Daddy was sitting on the front steps with a hat slouched over his face. I threw my arms around him and crawled into his lap and wouldn't let Zula or Eleanor near him. Mama and Daddy greeted each other frostily with a quick kiss on the cheek. She went to her bedroom on the south side of the house and from that time forward, Daddy's bedroom was on the north side of the house.

I slept that night dreaming that my parents were getting a divorce. We were in a courtroom. I thought that the Judge would let children decide which parent had custody. The Judge banged his gravel. Zula and Eleanor said, "Mama." I observed their pert faces on the other side of the courtroom, already on their ways back to Texas. There sat Daddy, alone, dejected with his hat pulled low.

The judge asked, "And May, who do you want?"

"Daddy!"

I watched his face break into an easy smile and we walked out of the courthouse hand and hand.

*

We were soon trying out the new pony and cart. Mama drove us to a birthday party. Before we arrived at our destination the pony bolted. Mama at best would never have been described as a horsewoman. She could do nothing with this pony. The cart had an extra seat on the back and I was in that place. Mama thought that she might save one child from this peril and said, "Jump, May! Jump, May!" I looked down at the wheels of the cart spinning over the bumpy ground and had no courage to jump. Finally she loosened the reins and the pony ran into a ditch. Mercifully we did not turn over.

We kept trying to ride the pony and drive the cart, but it was an ongoing struggle. One day Eleanor spotted a dot of red on the seat of the cart and pointed it out to Zula and me. We tied the pony to a post and rushed to Daddy. "This is not new pony and cart. We have seen a red mark. The cart has been painted."

"Well, that is so. It belonged to a little boy whose family was moving from Arlington, Tennessee, to Memphis, and they could not take him to Memphis. Furthermore, the boy had grown too big for the pony, so I bought the pony from his uncle."

We were never again as enthusiastic about that pony once we found out that he was secondhand, and he remained difficult. Finally he was sold to someone else.

Sixteen years later I married the little boy who had to sell that pony. He never understood our difficulty in controlling him and always declared that he was perfect. When Hayes put him on the steamboat *Kate Adams*, to go to Mississippi, the pony bayed for him until he could no longer hear the forlorn sounds as the steamboat rounded the bend of the Mississippi River.

The Heart Breaks

Zula and I had scarcely more than three years remaining of this happy childhood when we began to become young ladies. We learned to dance early in the Delta. Mama bought a Victrola and guided us around the living room, making sure that we always followed. "Now pretend that you are stepping on eggs," she would say.

We were soon practicing these golden rules of ballroom dancing on the front porch to Rance's three-piece band. Mama made us long taffeta dresses for the occasion. Mine was green with a plum-colored belt and Zula's dress was lilac. At intermission we had un-spiked punch and marguerites, which were vanilla wafers with peanut butter and toasted marshmallows. Zula and I were very popular because we could teach the others how to dance. It seemed that most of the people our age in the town were invited. One man, called "Skeet," arrived uninvited. He had come into town with a carnival and carried a monkey on his shoulder. This was the source of Mama's last moan about being forced to move from Memphis to Shelby. "In a small town people come to my house and dance with my daughters, who they would have never seen in a city, much less entertained." The party broke up at ten o'clock.

Everyone had such a good time that they begged us to have another dance the following Saturday night. This continued all spring until we left for California that summer. When we wanted to dance longer, the young boys often took up a collection to pay for the band to continue. Daddy would then give the band an extra twenty dollars. The most attractive boy in our group was C. V. Davis. He came from a poor family, but he was good looking, amusing, artistic, and a good dancer. This was the boy that I liked. Just before we left for California that May, he brought my cousin Janula Poitevent to a dance at our house. She was only thirteen. He then bade me farewell at the railway station, and I admonished him not to go off with Janula while I was away. That is exactly what happened. He never let go of her until they married, when she was in her early thirties. The marriage lasted only six years and they had one beautiful daughter. Their divorce was the third in our entire family.

That spring the pony went to another owner. The playhouse was abandoned for the front porch. In California Zula and I bought midi-blouses, and navy serge skirts, and our first pointed toe shoes with tiny heels, and silk stockings. We returned in the autumn, and the dances continued until the front porch became too cold and we moved into the dining room and rolled up the rug. Mrs. Joseph Yates, who continued to live next door, said that she had to grow a high hedge on the south side of her house to keep from seeing the 'goings on' in our house. The flapper age had arrived.

Our society quickly became divided between those who danced and those who did not, so that I never really knew people who might have been just one grade below me in school and acceptable, if they were not dancers. Zula and I began to develop more interests in common with Mama. Daddy's nicknames for us were Dinky, Chuck (for Chuckhead, my name) and Froggy, Eleanor's name. As a result of our growing to be young ladies, it was Froggy who remained behind and became closer to Daddy.

*

J. W. Thomas was at home from Culver Military Academy and a short stint at Sewanee, where he stayed long enough to join a good fraternity and then got bored with his classes, declaring that he had no interest in corn whiskey, and he neither whistled nor whittled, and there was nothing else to do on the mountain. He became the debonair bachelor about the Delta, and spent his daylight hours playing with a new invention, the radio. Telephones had been installed and he would call Zula and me and say that if we ran down the street we could hear the time from Washington D. C. We were out of breath when we reached the Thomas's house and climbed the stairs to his radio room, put on headphones and heard, "It is now ten o'clock in Washington D. C."

I found a new set of friends. Not only was J. W. most entertaining, but also his mother was a charmer. She was a good artist and painted a portrait of a gypsy girl that would have been recognized, had she been a known artist. She was the second cousin of Jefferson Davis. His sister, Ruth, had recently married Scott Morrison. Ruth played the piano, and we all tried to sing. Then Ruth taught us how to bake cakes. Why had we lived by this family for all of these years and never been friends? The answer was a dispute between gentle Uncle Will Connell and Mr. Thomas. Their houses were side by side and it seems that Aunt Lula and Uncle Will had sold part of their large lot to a Mr. and Mrs. Cruise, who were to build a tiny house right under the bedroom windows of the large Dutch Colonial home of Mr. and Mrs. Thomas. Tempers raged to stop this intrusion into the neighborhood. Eventually guns were drawn. Uncle Will drew on the support of some of his relations and Mr. Thomas massed his troops. Nothing came of it. Aunt Lula and Uncle Will sold the lot despite the protest and Mrs. Cruise opened a beauty parlor in her front room. Everyone went to the beauty parlor for it was the nicest one in town. Only Ruth and Mrs. Thomas had to frequent the less fashionable place. The seeds for Romeo and Juliet had been sown.

J. W. was too old for our dances, but he was not too old to collect me after school every afternoon. We rode in his father's Sedan. It was a grand car with curtains and a little vase for flowers on the side next to the passenger door. He told me one funny story after the other and I responded in kind with my best stories, which I had been saving since I had rocked on the front porch of the playhouse. I played the ukulele and we sang songs, boola boola, while driving all afternoon over country gravel and dirt roads. He began to take me to school in the mornings. Daddy was dismayed by the sight of this boy who had, in his opinion, nothing better to do than to drive his father's car all day and court a sixteen-year-old girl, seven years his junior. I scarcely appreciated that Daddy had grown up in the wilderness and his experience of women was limited to a colored mistress and Mama. In his opinion, to pay that much attention to a woman of honor meant marriage. He had been brought up to be a man of serious intentions.

Daddy's health was bad that year. He took more frequent trips to Hot Springs, Arkansas, for the baths. The moment that he left the house Mama's parties began. Ruth Edwards came back and announced, "I'm back from the cold."

There was a lively group of young married people: Lucille and Pat Patterson; Henry Denton and any pretty lady he might chose to bring; Cousin Lucia and Cousin John Gortner; Dean and Mike Rowe; Bo Peep Turley;

and Uncle Sam arrived from Chicago with his first wife Catherine. J. W. started attending Mama's parties. Eleanor and I passed trays at these parties. Zula had gone off to Gulf Park College on the Mississippi Coast. Mrs. Yates's hedge grew higher.

On one occasion while Uncle Sam and Catherine were visiting, Daddy returned earlier than expected. Mama had her group of glib friends on the front porch and Daddy sat down for an hour to join them. They were spellbound by his conversation. When he left, Catherine Liner exclaimed, "Why Anna, he is a knock out." Mama shrugged. I was so proud, for Catherine Liner was the most sophisticated person I knew.

That spring Daddy confined himself more and more to his bedroom, scarcely bothering to supervise the planting of his crops. He was a closet drinker and had been so for a considerable time, never getting drunk, but always nipping. But he did take enough pride in his plantation sausages to send a breakfast to Gulf Park College, where Zula was in school. Despite this endeavor, he continued to lack luster, his kidneys began to cause him considerable trouble.

I was still wearing my midi-blouses that were rolled and then pinned with large safety pins on either side of my hips. My hair was worn in buffs over each ear. These had to be teased to produce the desired effect. In the center of my forehead I grew one curl. It was called a 'beau catcher.' Daddy would look at me from his bed and say, "May, I will give you ten silver dollars if you will let that beau catcher grow out." Nothing changed my hairdo. I would tiptoe through his room, endeavoring not to disturb him, but he always knew when I was there.

"Say, May, I wish you would let that fiddle headed Thomas boy alone."

I skipped by, replying, "I'm not doing anything to him."

One afternoon Daddy ventured out onto the front steps and I sat down beside him as I had done in the old days. I suddenly said, "Daddy, do you believe in a hereafter? He replied, "I don't know. Let's make a pact, May. If I die before you, I will make every possible effort to get back to you, and if you die before me you will do the same."

A few weeks later Daddy was taken to the Gartley Ramsey Hospital in Memphis under the care of Dr. DeMarco. His kidneys had failed. After he had been in the hospital for a week, we were told to bring Zula home from college and she joined us in a hotel in Memphis. The man lying in that bed in the hospital did not seem like Daddy. When we arrived one of the nurses asked, "Which of you is May?"

"I am."

She called me into the hall. "You must be your father's favorite, for he talks about you all the time."

By that time, I felt that she was mistaken. It was Eleanor who had taken my place as his favorite. He talked about me because he was worried about me.

A few nights later we received a telephone call in our hotel room. Daddy had somehow got out of his bed and had taken strychnine and killed himself.

It was a small, sad funeral in Elmwood Cemetery, attended by family and Mr. Godfrey Frank and Dr. DeMarco. Daddy was only fifty-five. His short life had spanned the period between the aftermath of the Civil War from 1867 to the aftermath of the First World War in 1922, with all of the new inventions, changes in society, and the values, that that implied. It had seldom been an easy life, not because of personal failures or financial deprivation, but because of the loss of those whom he loved and the flaws in others he loved. This culminated in his despair.

I was only sixteen when this happened. For the rest of my life I have experienced something odd and wonderful. Whenever I was really worried I had a dream about Daddy. He appeared looking radiant and spoke to me in his calming manner. I awaken each time rested and positive.

Stuck on the Back of a Ford

Melissa Townsend: "You are often quoted as saying you can 'see a hundred years in history in twenty years in the Mississippi Delta.'

Shelby Foote: "Yes, things moved very fast there, especially personal fortunes. They went up and down. My two grandfathers were both very wealthy men at one point of their lives, but each died close to broke. But they died on schedule. That's quite common in the Delta. I didn't know of a single family that didn't have antecedents who were either on top or absolute bottom. And sometimes both." - Melissa Townsend ed., Delta Magazine, I, v, 20

In the autumn of 1922, after Daddy died, Zula and I went to Bristol, Virginia, to Sullins College. Well, it wasn't quite college for me, because I had been dreadfully ill that spring and nearly bled to death, so that I could not graduate from high school. I went to Sullins as a special student. We happened to go there because the President of the College, Dr. Martin, came to town recruiting students. Mama told him that she had heard that Sullins had a reputation for having wild girls. He promised her that if she enrolled her daughters that autumn he would give her a month's visit to check out this apprehension. He also knocked two hundred dollars off of each of our fees. Zula and I went to a fashionable college and our fees costs six hundred dollars a student.

We went on a big spending spree and charged a thousand dollars worth of dresses in one morning at Phil A. Halle in Memphis. Then we boarded the train with Mama and the Keeler girls, who lived in the country near

Shelby, and went to Bristol. Mama had thought to warn us that at boarding school we might encounter women who were different; they fell in love with other women. Although we had grown up with Sis Bland, who once told me that she had been in love with me, I had simply thought it odd and never considered the feeling. We had not even heard the word lesbian. Cousin Sarah and Miss Caroline were simply attractive relations who lived together and brightened our holidays. There were two such people that Mama had warned us about on the train in the compartment next to ours. We spotted them in the dining car.

Zula slipped a long stemmed wine glass from the table into her purse. We put it to the wall of our adjoining compartment and stayed up half the night listening. Then we whispered for the rest of the night about what we had heard. The real world was proving to be very entertaining.

After Mama spent a month at Sullins, she approved of the college so thoroughly that she persuaded Mr. and Mrs. Toler to send Annie Mae Smith to join us, and obtained a reduced fee for her as well. We all had a happy year, enjoyed our courses, and made great use of the extensive library.

There was not a man in sight. I have photographs of girls dancing with other girls with painted moustaches, dressed like boys. The only boys I saw were from the distance of a taxicab that we had taken to church. They were in an adjoining cab, and threw their cards into our window, giving us a flutter. Our social contacts centered on the mail. I had two fraternity pins, a Kappa Alpha pin from J. W. Thomas and a Sigma Chi pin from Warren Moore, whom I had met in Hillsboro, Texas the previous summer. I displayed the photograph of Warren Moore in my room, because he was the best looking, but I was in love with J. W. Thomas. His letters were the most entertaining, never failing to send me into peals of laughter. I wore the fraternity pins on two dresses, and anyone who borrowed the dresses became pinned. I now think of the solemn, faithful lives the girls my daughter's age are having, pure fidelity to a man who has given them a high school ring made of glass with a bandage around it covered in dark red nail polish, or

May Shelby, late 1920s.

worse, the pledge of a football jacket with a letter on the back. These poor young girls imagine they are being independent, because they are almost losing their virginities to these first loves. We dressed like flappers, but our flapper existences were a figment of our imaginations. We never had a glass of whiskey the whole year or saw a man. Instead we danced and danced. Dresses had suddenly dropped to ankle length and the girls looked very elegant.

At Thanksgiving Aunt Deedee (Madia) put a feast on the train in Shelby, but it spent two days reaching Bristol. The feast included oyster dressing. No one died or even got sick.

I was not so well again the following year and could not follow the Poitevent girls to Branau College in Georgia or to the University of Mississippi. Mary Poitevent was now at home, having graduated from college. We spent much time together, dabbling at the crafts that were popular, painting flowers and fruit on white porcelain plates that we baked in the oven. The older generation described us as "being young ladies."

*

Daddy had told me that I would not have to worry about finances; although I would not be rich, he would take care of me. He claimed to have a watertight will, the proceeds of which would be divided equally between Mama and his daughters and it would be tied up for the next generation so that no unworthy son-in-law could encroach upon his estate. When he died he left five hundred and sixty acres of farm land in a prime location for development unencumbered; a $50,000 life insurance policy; a block of stores in Shelby; some stocks in a gold mine, a bank, and a fan company; a house; and a considerable number of city lots next to the land that he had given for the Shelby High School. The Bank of Commerce in Memphis had been appointed our trustees and it was anticipated that they would dole out about three hundred dollars a month to each of us for the remainder of our lives. This was a comfortable sum in 1922 when Daddy died.

For some reason that no one understood, in the latter part of 1923, we seemed not to have as much money as we had had the previous year. Zula decided to go to Hillsboro, Texas, to work in Aunt Zula's dress shop, called the Betty Zula Shop. J. W. Thomas's father was killed when the train ran over him, while he sat in his Sedan on the crossing of the railway, looking in the opposite direction. J. W. discovered overnight that he was not as rich a young man as he had been in his eternal youth.

That year we had acquired a farm manager, a Mr. Bell. He came to live at our house and lived in Daddy's old room. Every evening he sat at our dinner table in Daddy's place and told a corny joke. He had jerky little mannerisms and put his napkin in front of his tie instead of on his lap. When he told these pathetic stories I smiled politely. Eleanor sat like a stone. Eventually he began to take this as more than a concession, and after a tedious story, he would cast his beady eyes across the table and say, "Watch May smile."

Eleanor glared straight ahead, and eventually I ceased to be polite. Only Mama seemed to enjoy his company. They listened to his radio together and went for drives in the automobile that we had now acquired.

Time lay heavy on my hands. Until the latter part of 1923 my life had been all joyous expectations. I anticipated that it would continue along a path of finishing schools, Delta dances, more summers at hotels in cool resorts, and a cruise, where I would meet someone very romantic, become engaged, have lots of parties, marry and have three little girls. Now I was sitting in Shelby, had been dropped by J. W. Thomas, was baking plates with Mary Poitevent, and playing croquet with Mel Powers, who lived at the north end of the street. There were afternoon naps followed by visitors who sat on a swing on the screened porch beneath a ceiling fan, telling stories and drinking fresh lemonade. They told their stories several times; that is why we in the Deep South have such total recall for stories. Then we went for a drive to look at the crops, which were bad. In the late evenings we stopped at the drugstore for a fountain coke. My friends were away at college, and I had already exhausted the supply of young men who lived in the town. Eleanor took a photograph of me at that time, poised on the back of a car and said, "There you are, May, stuck on the back of a Ford."

Kathryn's Story

Kathryn Henderson, my best friend from childhood, whose father bought our scrap metal, noticed that I was marooned in Shelby and invited me to a Saturday dance and a weekend at Ole Miss. She had remained the prettiest and sweetest girl that I knew. She had Germanic features inherited from her mother, who was related to the Weissengers, a German family who later came to live on our street. Even more praiseworthy than her beauty was her character. She was quite simply honest—different from the other coy women—and she was highly intelligent. I am proud to say that I recognized her value in the second grade, when we shared a double desk after Rosa Baccarina found another companion.

In 1923 Ole Miss had very few girls, as most young ladies went to girls' schools. Kathryn was the belle of Ole Miss, and was soon to be featured in their yearbook as one of their beauties.

I accepted the invitation immediately, and was to change trains in Holly Springs, Mississippi. Dressed in my best wine-colored suit with a gray fox collar and a navy felt hat, I was seated next to a respectable-looking elderly man, who bore a strong resemblance to Daddy's brother, Uncle Gerald (Fitzgerald). He introduced himself as Dr. Dell and began to talk to me. I saw no harm in responding. He asked where I was going to change trains and told me that he was a railway doctor, traveling on a pass. When the conductor came to collect our tickets, he looked at the doctor's pass. I had my ticket on my lap, but the conductor walked away without asking for it. I pointed this out to Dr. Dell and he replied that it didn't matter because the man would be coming through another time.

An hour later the conductor passed us again, and I stopped him and said that I was to change trains in Holly Springs, Mississippi. He looked perplexed. We had passed Holly Springs half an hour before. I would have to get off at the next stop and he would give me a pass to Holly Springs. He then admonished Dr. Dell, saying, "What did you mean holding up two fingers when I looked at your pass?"

As I departed the conductor said, "That man held up two fingers and he was going to take you to Birmingham, Alabama."

I can't imagine how he could have thought that I would have sat there into the night, waiting to alight at Holly Springs, Mississippi and arrive at Birmingham, Alabama. No doubt he had a smooth story up his sleeve.

I got off the train at an unheard-of stop with a dilapidated station, an iron stove, and a cat, and cried all over my kid gloves, ruining them with tears. I found a telephone and called Kathryn, telling her that I had almost been kidnapped and that I would not arrive at Ole Miss until eleven that evening.

Kathryn met me in Oxford with a group of young men, who were curious to see the girl that had almost been kidnapped. By that time I had somewhat forgotten the misadventure.

The dance was the following night, and I wore a flame-colored red cut-velvet evening dress with a rhinestone belt and rhinestone straps. My date was called Bootsie Barner, and I was the belle of the ball, which was held in the gymnasium. After a surprising number of glasses of bourbon, Bootsie tried to pitch me into a basketball net. When the dance was over, I caught a glimpse of myself in the mirror. A rhinestone strap had broken, my hair was in strings, and the silver band around my head had slipped down onto my forehead to become a headache band.

In the early hours of the morning, Kathryn and I exchanged confidences. She told me that both Bootsie Barner and Will Wells had proposed to her. What should she do? Will Wells was polished, clean cut, in law school, and Kathryn and Will were both active in the Marionettes, the dramatic club. Will had graduated from Virginia Military Institute and was to become the historian for his first year of law school. The Ole Miss Year Book of 1926 said, "Our Beau Brummel from Jackson formerly held world's record as ladies man at the Co-op." Those were the days that most women wanted a "ladies man." In the wee hours of one morning in the spring of 1923, my judgment, unaided by bourbon, was that Will Wells was the more suitable of Kathryn's two proposals because Bootsie Barner seemed to drink too much. Although Will was nice looking and polished, he did have a slightly weak chin. Two years later, in 1926, Kathryn was featured in the year book as the secretary of the Junior Class and described as having "Entrancing colors - graceful lines - a bit of fashion - a pleasing ensemble . . . She is the sort of girl who reminds us of dollars, champagne and limousines." (Hardly a fair comment.) By the time that Kathryn finished college her beauty had matured and her intelligence was evident in her face. Shortly after she graduated, she acted on my early morning advice. Kathryn and Will married, moved to Jackson, and had one daughter.

It soon became apparent that Will not only drank heavily but was also a serious gambler. Their marriage went downhill very quickly. Friends from Ole Miss brought groceries to their apartment, where they found Will either drunk or away from home. She was alone with a small daughter. Kathryn's behavior became increasingly bizarre. Her nerves were a wreck. They divorced.

We lost touch with each other for many years. Then in the early 1940's Kathryn came back to Shelby for prolonged visits with the Weissengers, her relations who lived on the street, and the Cowans. She was still beautiful, dressed in pleated slacks, which showed her good figure. But her behavior perplexed her relations. She was drinking seriously. The last straw from her family's points of view was that she hitchhiked, catching lifts with truck drivers on the street (now Highway 61). We watched her in front of our house. There had been nothing in her happy childhood that could have predicted this downfall. Her parents had been respectable, and she had a stable brother. By this stage her parents had moved to Florida.

I had been the nervous one. We would study for examinations together, and I was the one to lie in bed most of the nights worrying, while Kathryn went sound to sleep. In desperation her family had her committed to the State Lunatic Asylum at Whitfield, near Jackson, over a hundred and seventy miles south of Shelby.

Throughout the mid-forties and fifties Kathryn would come back to Shelby for short periods of leave from Whitfield. She often had to stay with her hated masculine aunt, Miss Bailey, our former teacher. Her parents were either dead or exhausted. She would always come to see me on these visits. My husband took the precaution of locking the liquor cabinet, but nothing deterred the fun that we continued to have together, sitting on the porch. Aided only by the stimulant of a coca-cola, we kept the swing moving and the wicker chairs rocking, while we giggled like the schoolgirls we would continue to be when we were together. She never described her present existence, I never asked about it, and after her visits I once again became immersed in my happy and seemingly normal life, but we continued to giggle into the past.

Towards the end of the 1950's miracle drugs meant that the doors of the asylums were opening and Kathryn was released. She had spent fifteen years at Whitfield. By this time she had nowhere to go, and again it was horrible old Miss Bailey who gave her a place to live. Then an old beau, someone she had known in her heyday at Ole Miss, looked her up and married her.

They did not live happily ever after. The marriage lasted only a few months, before he brought her back to Miss Bailey. She then moved to the town where her daughter lived, and was given an apartment a short distance from her daughter's house. She remained there for the rest of her days, which were not a long time.

In my memory she was simply my best friend, and the weekend that we spent together was one of the happiest of my youth.

The Noose Tightens

The next year the dwindling supply of money became more obvious. I couldn't afford cut-velvet evening dresses. Last year's editions were brought out once more. Zula remained in Texas and Eleanor went to a small women's college in Grenada, Mississippi, which was all we could afford. I continued improving my game of croquet in the front yard with Mel Powers, where time interspersed with a few bright breaks. Finally Aunt Mary Poitevent sought to divert me. When her daughter Mary got a job teaching at Gulfpark College on the Mississippi coast, Aunt Mary rented her house in Shelby and took Janula and me to Gulfport, where she rented another house. She hoped that in this move she could find someone new for Janula and that I would meet someone eligible, but Janula and I would sneak down the street to a local shop where she received C.V.'s telephone calls and I met no one.

Somehow Mama got together enough money for us to spend a month in Hot Springs, Arkansas, and there we met two delightful sisters from Pine Bluff: Hedy, a dark brunette divorcee, and her sister Vashtye, who was a platinum blond. That autumn they visited us in Shelby, and we had a supper-dance for them. The house was decorated with autumn leaves, and spiked punch was served in a cut glass bowl and placed into block of ice covered with ivy. Mama said that the most appreciative response she received from the many guests whom she invited was from Hayes Carnes, who said that he was so glad someone was doing something entertaining in Shelby.

Hayes had been in love with Mary Poitevent for a long time, but he was her second choice. She had fallen for a man named Johnny Redwine from Gainesville, Georgia, and was biding her time until he proposed.

I brought out last year's navy crepe dinner dress trimmed in silver leaves and Hayes paid me especial attention. After that evening he began to take me out to dinners and to plays in Memphis.

Hedy and Vashtye soon repaid our invitation and invited Zula and me to a dance in Pine Bluff. There I met a charming man named Jack Purdue. We were instantly congenial, for we had the same sense of humor. Jack was exactly the type of man that I wanted and he appeared to respond in kind. He made several trips to Shelby to see me. The following autumn he went Harvard Business College and kept my mail full of letters, which I later noticed were all about himself. He was also rich. In the spring he came to visit once more, and for some reason I ran out of conversation and told him about my bad health. His ardor cooled.

J. W. Thomas married a rich lady, Elizabeth Kirk. She was to become my second closest friend. We had been placed together on a bed when we were babies in Memphis and got along instantly.

Uncle Sam's first wife Catherine had committed suicide when he was about to leave her. His second, much younger, wife, Marie, gave many invitations to visit Chicago, but there was very little money to get there. When Eleanor was a child she had saved from her allowance. Every dime was given back to Daddy with the instructions, "Put this in the bank." She made quarterly enquiries as to her worth and he would deposit a five-dollar bill. By now this little sum had grown to a hundred and fifty dollars. I borrowed half of it to go to Chicago and never repaid her, but at least I had a good summer on Lake Michigan and acquired another beau.

I had no skills, and no money to develop skills, and my health was too bad to permit me to work, even in a ladies' dress shop. Ruth Edwards, always kind to a young lady, had her sister Dale Crosby invite me to visit in Greenville. I had a marvelous time at a dance and one young man said, "Where have you been? A flower wasted on the desert air."

A Watertight Will

I n 1926 Zula married a man from Texas, Thomas Brown, and moved to Dallas. Our own house became cluttered with a few lodgers. Apart from Mr. Bell, who remained in Daddy's room, bringing his obnoxious self to the dining table, we rented out a back bedroom, and even rented the playhouse to a bachelor, Carl Black from Rosedale. Mama's dinners, with a meat bill of forty dollars a month, continued to be somewhat lavish. We always had a cook, a house girl, and a yardman. Our situation was not quite as bad as that of a family friend Dotty Perkins from Clarksdale, where a cook carried a heavy silver platter into the dining room, carefully placing it on a padded damask cloth on a round table lined with relations, handed the silver serving spoon to her mother, and it was quickly depleted of its milk toast. There was another friend in Rosedale from a well-off family and during the depression they lost their bath stopper. There was no money to replace it and water had to be sealed by paper. However our Depression had begun before 1929.

Hayes Carnes came to be one of our boarders. I told him about our plight, and he took me to Memphis to the Bank of Commerce to see what had happened. The apologetic manager appeared with an account, endeavoring to give an explanation for the management of the estate. Hands up, it seemed that they had trusted Mr. Bell, the farm manager, who had claimed that he needed money to furnish the crops on the plantation and had in turn loaned the money to two men in town, neither of whom could repay their debts. The block of stores was now empty. The Bank of Shelby had failed. The insurance money and stocks had vanished. The farm was producing next to nothing in income and no real estate had been sold.

I took the case to a distant relation in Clarksdale, a lawyer, Mr. Fitzgerald. As soon as he received my brief and encouraged me to sue the Bank of Commerce for breach of trust, he died. I then took the case to Mr. Sillers in Rosedale. He was delighted with the potential lawsuit, so much so that he said that he needed nothing more than my summary to succeed in the claim. He told me that if I would go to the University of Mississippi to law school, he would give me a job in his office. There were no women lawyers in those days, so that his praise gave me a big boost and a dream of a life that might have been. Then Mr. Sillers died and the case was relegated to his son Walter Sillers, Jr., who was running in an election to become a Representative in the Mississippi House of Representatives (he later became Speaker of the House for about fifty years). Walter didn't have much time for the case, but before he had a chance to neglect it, the stock market crash of 1929 occurred and The Bank of Commerce also failed.

Mr. Bell had his immediate walking papers. I took over the management of the plantation. Zula's husband, Tom Brown, was appointed trustee. He made one visit to Shelby with a sleazy Texas lawyer, and they advised us to sell everything and live on the proceeds in 1929. I reminded them of the watertight will. Eleanor, Mama and I needed an income. This was not our land to sell; it belonged to our future children. The sleazy lawyer had missed the point.

The following year I rented the land to a blue-eyed Italian. I even had to furnish his crop. That is how hard times had become. I would ride over the farm and complain that I saw Johnson grass on the land and he replied, "Miz May, if you plant him six feet in the ground, he will still come up." He paid the rent and we each had a bit of income.

The second year he did not pay the rent and left. Mama could not bear depressing situations. She went on an extended visit to her rich Aunt Jessie

Graham in Denton, Texas. Eleanor and I were left in Shelby with seventy-five dollars a month to live on, the rent from the boarders. Mama sent us clippings of her photograph on the front of the society section of the Denton, Texas newspaper, "Mrs. Shelby of Shelby, Mississippi visits her Aunt Mrs. Jessie Graham. A Luncheon is given in her Honor." Then she returned with a breezy idea derived from her Uncle Charlie in Beaumont, Texas, who owned the White House Department Store. He said to his wife Etta, "Here Etta, take this money, put on your fur coat and diamonds and buy something from each of the merchants in the main part of town."

She replied, "Charles, they will throw eggs at me."

"No, Etta, they will be happy. You must go out and show confidence." So she did.

This jaunty approach fell on deaf ears in the Delta where some families did not have money for postage stamps. Two gentlemen called at the door each morning, one delivered *The Commercial Appeal* newspaper, and the other man brought the milk. They rode together in a wagon pulled by a horse. One was a doctor, the other a qualified surveyor.

J. W. Thomas got so depressed that he had to buy an airplane to take his mind off the Depression. We paid our cook $1.50 a week, and a house girl $1.00 a week. The bells that we rang for breakfast ceased to function, and we were left with a symbolic faded peach silk tassel over each bed. A T-bone steak cost ten cents. Somehow, I escaped on my half of the seventy-five dollars and went to Dallas to visit Zula, where a T-bone steak cost five cents.

In the evenings we listened to the radio. Roosevelt became our hero, repeating the same words over and over again, "You have nothing to fear but fear itself." He will always be deeply mourned by all classes in the South.

Hayes Carnes lost his Ford business. He had set up a Chrysler business in Greenwood, Mississippi, but with the crash of '29 that also failed. He returned to Memphis, where he lived with his father, who remained employed as a director of a rubber company. Mr. Carnes had two unemployed sons and a brother-in-law all living with him. Hayes's best friend was Buddy Tate. They had graduated from Memphis University School together. Buddy's family owned all of the Yellow Cabs in Memphis and Atlanta and a building in Memphis called the Tate Building. The cabs were empty, and so was the Tate Building. Hayes and Buddy would occupy empty offices in the Tate Building and simply put their feet on vacant desks. That was the Depression.

During this time I began to suffer from terrific migraine headaches. They occurred at the same time that I experienced the consoling dreams about Daddy, the dreams that would last for the rest of my life. In the early hours of the morning I would see Daddy. He appeared when I was especially worried. He always looked ebullient and would simply talk to me. The dreams ended by him saying, "May, I am all right, but I must go." Sometimes he wore an overcoat, but he always looked in good health and I would awaken better off.

A Bright Spot

Mr. and Mrs. Will Toler, who had fostered Annie Mae Smith and many other children on our street, sold their house in about 1920 to a large family from Hushpuckana, headed by Mr. and Mrs. Albert Daniel Murphree, who had ten children. No one had seen a white family of ten children since Zula and I had visited the people who lived in the boxcars. All of the Murphrees were as sweet as peaches. There were seven sisters (most of them pretty) and three brothers. They were in love with love, and if one word could describe them, they were compassionate. Although they were Baptist, they could dance! They filled our house with children. One of the cutest was the son Albert. The children seemed to run in pairs, looking after each other. Albert and his beautiful sister Christine frequented our house. The Murphrees moved to the street when Daddy was still alive, and Albert delighted him, for he had never had a son. Every afternoon Albert would appear on the front steps to visit. These visits were by way of a tutorial in farming. Albert would say, "Mr. Shelby, let's talk about pigs today." The next day it would be corn, and the following day mules. Albert predictably turned out to be one of the best farmers in the region.

The Tolers moved to a temporary accommodation, a garage apartment on a lot that Mrs. Toler thought beautiful. By that time they were down to only a few foster children. Mrs. Toler kept the train and the road to Memphis busy visiting architects who drew elaborate plans for a Spanish Colonial house with balconies and a tiled roof, facing the school house in Shelby, Mississippi. This folly was never to be, and except for a short interval renting Aunt Lula's old house in the 1940's, they remained in the garage apartment with Annie Mae and her three children for the next forty years. The garage apartment came to resemble a tree house, because it was eventually propped up by a small tree that seemed to have sprung into life to bear that burden. Mrs. Toler's niece was the cowgirl movie actress, Dale Evans. When my daughter was young, Dale Evans and her husband Roy Rogers came to town and had dinner at the tree house. My daughter went over there to meet them, full of dreams that they would put her into the movies. I believe that Roy Rogers got a traffic ticket for running a red light on this visit to Shelby. It was a long way from Los Angeles congestion.

During these bleak times of the late nineteen twenties when the Murphree children brightened our lives, the sweetest was Margaret. Their assets, too, were depleted. Margaret, who had a slight speech impediment, was known for hinting for things that she liked to eat. One day she said, "Mrs. Shelby, we've got no zelly nor zam or nothzing at our house." But they had merriment, which was in short supply, for they were the products of a devoted couple.

Mr. Murphree had been orphaned when he was young. He saw Mrs. Murphree at a church box supper when he was ten years old, and asked her to share his box. They remained sweethearts until they were old enough to marry. He looked like Abraham Lincoln and always farmed in a three-piece suit with a bow tie. He called his wife 'Mother' and everyone called him 'A.D.' Although they had the same cook for forty years and her husband who did the yard, Mrs. Murphree's hands were always busy, crocheting, knitting, sewing, making beds. All of the girls sewed beautifully tailored clothes. There were no bows on their heads to match the dresses that they had made. However, half the girls did not marry as well as they sewed, because they believed that love was all. Mr. Murphree said throughout his life, "Baby, come home." They did, one with three children and a mentally defective boy. The parents were happy to have them. A. D. farmed about a thousand acres of mediocre land and had an interest in Daddy's old gin. He managed to support the children in need, educate the ones who could take it, and set up his sons in farming. Mr. and Mrs. Murphree walked down the street in the late afternoons holding hands to the sound of the Baptist chimes until she died in the mid-1960s.

Married Men First

Hayes Carnes had got over being in love with Mary Poitevent for a long time by 1932, and Mary was happily married to Johnny Redwine and living in Gainesville, Georgia. Hayes was my constant beau and we talked about marriage, but this was interrupted when the crash came and his businesses were lost. I was almost as guilty of dithering as

Aunt Zula. I could not make up my mind. He telephoned me from Memphis in late September of 1932 with an ultimatum, and said quite simply that I had a few days to decide to marry. He had been offered a job auditing the plantations on which the Connecticut General Life Insurance Company was foreclosing. He was perfect for the job, and the salary was $275 a month with an expense account of $150 from which he could save. In view of the desperate times they could not hire a bachelor; family men came first. He had replied to the interviewers, "I will be a married man within one week." The deed was done.

I accepted the proposal and squeezed $150 out of Tom Brown (Zula's husband), now the trustee of our estate, took the train to Memphis, and once more shopped at Phil A. Halle and Levy's instead of the Three Sisters, to which Eleanor and I had of late been reduced. I bought a nice trousseau for that amount and we were married on the sixth of October 1932, in the living room of our house. Our only attendants were Hal Carnes (Hayes's first cousin), and Eleanor. The year before, Hal had married the Methodist minister's daughter, Anna Smoot, who lived on the street. Her father performed our ceremony. Eleanor turned the radio on to a good station for wedding music, and by some endeavor Hal had a bottle of champagne. We went on a short honeymoon to Arkansas and returned by Memphis, where I met Hayes's parents. His brother John said, "What a day, Papa stayed up after eight o'clock, Hayes smoked in front of Mama instead of going to the bathroom for his cigarette, and he brought home a wife." I asked Hayes why he had never told me about his charming father. He replied, "I didn't want to brag." The Great Depression was over for me, and so were my nine years of anxiety and gloom.

A year later, Hayes's brother John Carnes was married to Mildred Williams in the same house, with a similar ceremony. Mary Cornelia Murphree sang a song, and I hosted a dinner. Reverend Smoot again performed the ceremony. Hal brought more champagne. These marriages turned out to be much happier than those of most couples where a bride got to wear the big white dress and her father to spend tens of thousands of dollars.

When my daughter was in college, she took a course in psychology, and the professor quoted a study that said that the greatest factor in finding a mate was proximity. She and several of her friends decided that their next move would be to Cambridge, Massachusetts, so that they could marry Harvard men. This theory certainly seems to account for the clan system in the Delta. On our side of the street there were seven marriages between families, and three other people found a partner from the other side of the street or rather across Holmes Lake.

The Flood

Hayes rented our land, and looked after the farm in the evenings after his job. Daddy's former hostler, Zechariah Cook, became his straw boss. Zach rode a Tennessee Walking Horse from morning to evening, supervising the hourly functions of a plantation. Hayes also sold a few city lots that we owned in the area adjoining the schoolhouse, and a large city lot located across the street was sold to the cotton compress, for $10,000. This put us on our feet. Times were so desperate that I was able to employ Mr. Mann, a well-known architect from Memphis, to come to Shelby and remodel our house, taking off the dusty porches, reducing the size of the roof, and converting a portion of the house into an apartment so that Mama and Eleanor would have more income. Each of us now had a small independent income, and mine was put back into farming.

The levee of the Mississippi River came dangerously close to breaking for the last time in 1934. Water rose to the first levee, but a much higher levee had been built behind this one, after the big flood of 1927. The big flood of '27 never reached Shelby. Nevertheless, Hayes became anxious over the threat of rising water, and insisted that I evacuate to his parents' home in Memphis. In the event that the flooding should continue, he did not feel confident that he could rescue me and the mules.

Hayes's father was delightful, but he was away most of the week. His mother bored me and I bored her. After a tedious day visiting her many lady friends, we would sit together in utter silence. I felt obligated to try to entertain her and would endeavor to tell one of my best stories. She would put down her *Memphis Press Scimitar*, the evening paper, and pick it up again, without a word of comment. The telephone was in a corridor where conversations were easily heard from the living room. I made my call to Hayes, saying in a clear voice, "I look forward to you coming on Saturday." He would reply desperately, "You can't come home, the river is still rising."

"That is so nice, I look forward to seeing you on Saturday."

Young love works miracles, and on Saturday Hayes arrived to collect me. This was the last flood to threaten us, although the ghosts of floods always haunted people of my generation in the Mississippi Delta. Beneath our house rested a canoe that my great-grandparents had used in the first floods when they moved to the Delta.

Lizzie

By 1934 Hayes had acquired enough money to buy 375 acres, and he could now leave his job with the insurance company and devote his full time to farming this and our land. I had been the cook for the first two years of our marriage, taking lessons from my neighbor, Mrs. Henry, Madge Denton's mother. My whole cookbook is filled with

Mrs. Henry's recipes, as our former cooks could neither read nor write and Mama no longer had any interest in domestic activities. I spent hours preparing an evening meal.

Hayes was now at home about noon requiring a big dinner, and we tried to find a cook from the new labor, who had left the plantations foreclosed upon by the insurance company and come to us. One of these was a prize, Doc Osborn, in a white coat and a chef's white hat. Hayes hoped that no creditors saw him come to the door in that outfit. He was delightful, but he simply could not cook. I hesitated to complain. What was the point? The Depression had taught me not to be too complaisant, and I eventually mentioned this omission in his trade. Hayes discussed it with Doc, and the following day he sent his wife, Lizzie, whom he guaranteed was an excellent cook. Doc was as good as that word.

Lizzie was the child of intermarriage. Her mother had come from what she described as 'across the water', and arrived in Natchez, Mississippi with a planter family for whom she worked or to whom she may have belonged. They had told her that she was going on a holiday, but that was never to be, for they had no intention of returning whence they came (probably the West Indies). She looked half-white and the Natchez planter may have been her father. When I met Lizzie's very good-looking sister Willie Belle, I discovered that their father a large, strong black man had Native features and came from the area near Natchez. All three races came out in Lizzie, Willie Bell, and their brothers Anderson and Oscar, and in her little twelve-year-old daughter, Annie. Lizzie had golden skin and light brown eyes with brown specks in the irises. They were the kindest eyes I have ever seen. Her chin was strong and determined, indicative of her father's Native blood. Her hair was African and her forehead was high. She had a presence. Even if dressed in a faded uniform, her buttons were always tightly sewn, and the uniform was pressed and spotless. Her hands were a sculptor's dream.

She could cook. I tutored her in all Mrs. Henry's recipes and a few of Mama's. These dishes eventually became 'Lizzie's rolls' or 'Lizzie's pastry'

Lizzie on the left with another woman.

or 'Lizzie's dressing', eventually handed down to her little daughter Annie Giles, who became a cook in her own right.

Doc always seemed to be dissatisfied, and after one year on a plantation wanted to move. Lizzie was fed up with Doc's moving. She claimed that as soon as she got a crop into the ground he was ready to depart. Doc was Lizzie's third husband. The love of her life had been Annie's father, whose last name was Giles, but he 'didn't do right by her' so she had kicked him out. Lizzie had a strong foot, and was to kick out three more husbands. At this point in 1934 she decided to settle. She had found good white people with whom she wished to stay. A year later she brought her parents, her niece Idel, her brother Anderson, her sister Willie Bell, and her cousins the Wesbys to work for us and live in Shelby. These families and ours became intertwined for the rest of the twentieth century. Lizzie remained with us until she died in 1980 at the age of eighty-six. She and Hayes had been born only a few months apart and loved and respected each other deeply.

In those days the cook's job was second only to that of the straw boss. She had the second choice of houses or cabins and the first choice of the best plot of land if she or her family wanted to make a crop. We paid her doctor's bills and those of her family. Lizzie once told me that she had been 'apt in her books' but that her father took her out of school after the sixth grade and made her chop cotton. She always read our daily newspaper and often read a novel that I had finished. The opportunities were slim for the likes of Lizzie and her sister Willie Belle, and our umbrella was the best hope that they had.

In 1937 I had twin boys who died at birth. They were born in Memphis and my doctor was a well-known gynecologist whom I trusted. I returned from Memphis devastated with grief and depression. The twins were buried at Elmwood Cemetery beside my father and Frances. I walked into the house unsteadily. Lizzie simply put her arms around me and said, "I am so sorry you loosed out."

Losses

D r. Murnan died a few years after Daddy's death. Aunt Deedee nearly lost her mind from grief. Mama candidly told her that if she continued to talk about her sorrow it would only drive people away. This had a salutary effect. She pulled herself together, invited Uncle Gerald (Fitzgerald), her brother, to live in her house, began to entertain once more, making Italian dishes with homemade wine and acquired new and much younger acquaintances. Some were young bachelors. A favorite was a Dr. Bill McKenzie, a young dentist. Nothing was unseemly in her social life; she simply wanted to be stimulated. There is a life after becoming a widow. She lived until 1938 when she died of cancer.

Aunt Lula and Uncle Will Connell died in the 1930's. They had been an exemplary couple, pillars of Christian fortitude. Although they had lost their two beautiful children to the childhood diseases that had swept the Delta, they rose above gloom and tragedy, welcoming other children to spend as much time as possible in their home. Neither did they let one forget the lost children. Guests were always served a glass of elderberry wine and cake, and afterwards Aunt Lula would say, "Daddy, would you like to show the guests the children?" Their beautiful portraits were hung in the sun parlor, a cheerful room, and this visit was made without a hint of morbidity.

In 1938 Aunt Janie died. She was ninety. She had been a child during the Civil War, when shoes were in such short supply and her feet so small, that they had to be tied in rags.

During the worst of the Depression, I was despondent and said to Aunt Janie, "Don't you just hate farming?"

"No", she replied, "I have lived all of my life from the proceeds of farming and I have never so much as washed a pair of stockings. Now John," as she turned to her servant, "Would you please put another coal on

Janie Poitevent Shelby

the fire?"

Life had certainly not been that easy for her. She came to a plantation out post when she was in her mid-thirties to take over the five children of her sister who had died. It was an isolated existence, stuck in the mud in the winters and in intense heat in the summers.[2] By that time that she moved to Shelby, she had already lost one son and her daughter was soon to follow. She had outlived her parents and three of her sisters and was later to outlive two other sisters, her adored younger brother Thomas, her husband and first grandson (George Shelby). She had seen her only granddaughter born brain-damaged, a severe burden, and she also outlived three of her sister's children whom she fostered, (Isaac Jr., my father, and Aunt Ellen). Her life had spanned the Civil War to have the first electric Christmas lights in Shelby, which she placed over the shrubs in front of her house. Aunt Janie had walked on as if all had been easy. She never lost her looks or intelligence and was adored by every man who came into her house. She loved men and had a rather frosty relationship with her daughter-in-law, Joe, never acknowledged Ruth, and was somewhat frosty with my mother. The light of her life was her son Fred. He always had another adoring young man live at the house, to protect her when he was out on "house calls", usually with Ruth. Hayes was one of those young men. One might say that men and servants lined a very tough life.

---

2 Sillers, ed. 371

A Fortune Teller

Elizabeth Thomas and I encountered a fortuneteller in the Peabody Hotel in Memphis. We paid her a few dollars and had our fortunes told. The same question was on both of our minds: 'Will I have a baby?'

The lady knew nothing about us, but she drew a map and said to me, "I see two children that did not live. But I see a third child and all of the stars are right for this child."

She did not make out any such signs for Elizabeth, only saying, "There will be a child in your life."

Two years after the twins died, Hayes's old school friend, Dr. Gus Chrisler from Memphis, gently warned Hayes that I was not getting any younger. We decided to try to have another baby. This time I consulted a wonderful country doctor, Dr. O. J. Simmons, in Cleveland. It was hard for me to conceive and he gave me a hormone injection every week for a year until I was pregnant. After that he gave me another injection to prevent a miscarriage. I carried the baby to almost ten months, worrying all the time as to whether it would be normal, because I kept thinking about Jane Shelby, who we were told had a brain hemorrhage.

My baby was the second baby to be born in the new Cleveland Hospital. The first was a Chinese baby and the mother had brought eggs that she had buried for two years, and demanded that she be fed this delicacy after giving birth. The nurses fed her some fresh eggs and told that her they were the rotten ones. The third baby was Carolyn Laudig (Gaines), who became a friend of my daughter. The good ole boys played a trick on Mrs. Laudig and brought the Chinese baby to her. She never forgave them. All of the new babies were healthy.

The birth was natural and occurred on a Sunday morning on September 29th, 1940. I was exhausted, but I heard Dr. Simmons say, "It's a girl,

May Shelby Carnes and Carole, Autumn 1940.

May."

I replied feebly, "Is her head all right?"

"Yes, and she looks just like you."

I answered, "That will be a hardship."

We named her Carole Shelby Carnes. She was the product of two families who lived on this street.

I spent two weeks in the hospital being pampered. Then we returned to our house, where we hired a special nurse, Rena King, who specialized in looking after newborn babies. Carole was turned over to Lizzie six weeks later.

I nearly died when Carole was five months old. I had a blocked kidney where the baby had rested while in the womb. We were at the Carnes's house in Memphis, when my temperature rose to 106 degrees and I was rushed into the hospital. I became temporarily blind from fever. Before leaving their house I handed Carole to Lizzie with firm instructions, "This is your baby, yours and Mr. Hayes's. You and I have our method of looking after her, and I don't want Mrs. Carnes to impose any of her old-fashioned ideas upon us."

When I returned after several weeks in the hospital, I scarcely recognized the baby for she had gained so much weight. Lizzie said, "I just rounded the spoon."

"How did you cope with Mrs. Carnes?" I asked.

"You was right. She tried to tell me what to do and I jes picked up us baby and walked out." She had gone to another woman's house and sat there until she knew that Hayes had returned.

Bravo. A colored woman who did that in the South in 1940 had more than courage. No one could daunt Lizzie.

Part Three

Another Child

(Carole's stories,
1942-1958)

First Memories

In the early mornings I stood in a bed with bars on a sleeping porch adjacent to my parent's bedroom. A rooster crowed. I often heard Daddy get up and say, "That is Nee Nee's rooster," and then he would go back to sleep. I called Lizzie "Nee Nee" because I couldn't say Lizzie. The nickname stuck for many people. Nee Nee lived in a red cabin on the row of cabins on the other side of the railway track across from our house. Her yard contained many chickens and a vegetable garden that was ample for her family, where she grew something delicious called lady peas which I have never tasted in adult life.

I would look out onto the cedar trees, trees that had been my mother's Christmas trees when she first moved to Shelby. There was a terrifying sight, a nest of the ugliest creatures, baby birds, screaming and screaming and a feathered black thing that would flutter near and drop something to them, but the noise never seemed to stop, until I heard the comforting sound of two heavy feet on the back steps. Then I would pull my cotton bedspread over my head until I heard another consoling sound, the rhythm of pots and pans. After that there was the smell of bacon and then everyone was alive. Mother and Daddy had breakfast, I sat in my highchair and either Mother or Lizzie (Nee-Nee) fed me and very soon it was time to go out onto the street.

My mother read every contemporary document on child rearing and I was put into a sunbonnet and placed into a kiddy car and taken for a morning walk and after that there was a sunbath for ten minutes only. I looked like a brown boy. Another nurse, Rosalie, was obtained for me for Lizzie

Two friends for life - Carole and Ann Douglas Morrison.

was too busy cooking. Rosalie was the wife of Clarence Daniels. The Daniels, a family of ten children, had moved onto our land in the 1930's.

I talked all the time. That accounts for my early memories. I did not walk. Rosalie would sit on the floor and cross her legs and take the bottom out of the kiddy car to encourage me to walk towards my reflection in the mirror that was attached to a closet door. I did this with glee, and can still see the reflection. That is as far as I would go. Outside the kiddy car, I collapsed. Rosalie called me "Little Prophet", because my speech was somewhat advanced. She would say, "Little Prophet, when the Wah gonna be over?"[1] And then one day she was gone. Mother tried to teach me to walk. She would dress me in a pinafore with a sash, and put me on the sidewalk, that first and only sidewalk that the street ever knew. When I reached a spot between Miss Madge's house and our house, right by the vast oak tree that had been an acorn in the previous generation, Mother would say, "Go on, I will hold you." I trusted her to hold the tip of my sash with her fingers and walked. I walked as far as the boundary to Miss Madge's house by a hibiscus bush slightly beyond the oak tree, then I looked back and saw that she had let go. Seldom have I felt so betrayed. I sat and refused to walk again for some considerable time.

The next thing that I remember was that my parents took me to see Rosalie. She was in the hospital in Mound Bayou, an all-black town six miles south of Shelby on Highway 61. I saw Rosalie in the front room of the Taborian Hospital. I could not see her very well because Daddy held me to the window. I only saw her through a screen with the afternoon light pouring over my shoulder, but she waved a strong arm and I knew that it was Rosalie. Her bed was at the end of the ward. My parents would not take me into the ward because of diseases, as I was so young. But I waved and waved and made gleeful cries for Rosalie. After that I did not see her any more and was told that Rosalie had gone to heaven.

That was my first time to visit Mound Bayou, a unique town in Ameri-

---

1 I write in the dialect, which is the way I heard it, white and black.

ca. It continues to claim to be the largest all-black town in the United States, with a population of about three thousand people. The small town had been built by two black men, Isaiah T. Montgomery, and his first cousin, Benjamin T. Green, who were born into slavery as property of Joseph Emory Davis, the brother of Jefferson Davis (President of the Confederacy).[2] In 1942 the Taborians, along with Meharry Medical School, built the Taborian Hospital and Dr. T. R. M. Howard (a black doctor) opened this clinic.[3] It offered forty-two beds and operated until the 1960's when Medicare succeeded in forcing the integration of hospitals. That is where I found Rosalie.

Five months after Rosalie died, I was taken to my first movie. I was probably two and a half years old. The movie was Vincent Minelli's *Cabin In the Sky* with Lena Horne, Ethel Waters, and Eddie "Rochester" Anderson, an all-black cast. It was decidedly the most thrilling thing that had ever happened to me. In the last scene the dead Lena Horne climbs the steps into heaven with much singing. I clearly remember the bright lights in the vestibule of the picture show after the movie had finished. I turned to Mother and asked if what I had seen was heaven.

"No. Carole, it is only a picture. It only exists on the screen."

"How do I get on the screen?"

"Well, you have to work in the movies."

"When I grow up I am going to work in the movies."

I never swerved from this direction until I was about twenty and came face to face with some of the realities of the acting world. Throughout my early childhood, I simply thought that I had found the means of joining Rosalie.

---

2 For a brief history of this unique community see Appendix B which is my synopsis of an article written by Williams, Mark & Strub, Denise, complied for The Bolivar Commercial, called Reflex ions of Bolivar County and Surrounding Area Vol II, D-Books Publishing, 107 N. Kansas Ave. Marceline, Missouri, 2000, 22-3

3 Sillers, ed. 338

Continuity

This was a tree-lined street inhabited by genteel families. I acquired a tricycle, and my daily hurdle crossed every crack on the sidewalk. I knew them by heart and mother followed closely behind. If I got outside early, I could meet Rush, the milkman from the Denton's dairy, with his pony and green-painted wagon making his deliveries. Rush only had three fingers on each hand, which appeared to have suffered an accident, but these sufficed to handle the reins. His was the last horse on the road in Shelby.

I seldom ventured north of our house because the concrete was very broken at Mr. and Mrs. Yates' house and it was a mess in front of the Murphrees' house. If I rode in that direction, the last point was in front of Mr. and Mr. Powers', three houses north of ours. The sidewalk stopped beyond the Powers' house. After that there was the Texaco Station. Madge, Charles, and Madge's mother, Mrs. Henry, continued to live next door to us. Only one broken patch in front of their house impeded my way. Then I reached the Bullocks' house. That was interesting, because there were the handprints of Robert Cogdill and his sister Martha Frances embedded in the walk that led to their house. By that time Robert Cogdill was bedridden, attended by his mother, sister, and children on the street. I would stop on every occasion and measure my hand by their hands. The next house belonged to Mr. and Mrs. Meek (the second Mrs. Meek) and then one reached the big bump, the one that occurred in front of Mr. and Mrs. Will Denton's' house. Next to the Dentons were the Weissengers, of German origin, and every blade of grass seemed to be the same length. There were no broken patches in front of their house. This did not ease the burden of crossing no man's land, for the Weissengers had a fierce rat terrier, one who appeared to have green eyes and would come tearing off their porch, opening the screen door of his own accord and chasing my tricycle onto the next boundary. I did hear (but I can't remember who said this, certainly not my parents) that the dog was mean because Mr. Weissenger had German blood. Then I reached the most cracked portion of the walk. That occurred in front of the house that had formerly belonged to Uncle Will and Aunt Lula Connell. Now Mr. and Mrs. Gus Blanchard lived in that nice colonial house. It was later owned by George and Mabel Scherbaum.

Mother always stopped me at the next house, Mrs. Cruise's beauty parlor, as she was afraid of the many cars coming into the driveway. Then she let go of my tricycle when we reached the Thomas's house. There was an iron fence, behind which were several Yucca bushes. If I touched one, I pricked my finger, and blood came forth. Behind the Yucca bushes was a beautiful girl, one of the most beautiful children one would ever see. Her eyes were green and she had long blonde curls, a Roman nose, and full lips. What distinguished her looks were those eyes. She reminded me of a beauty in a prison. Ann was ten. I was three. I thought that ten was the most exciting word in the English language, because I had a friend who was ten. Ann had been my third word, after Mama and Daddy. She had played dolls with me every day from the time that I was born. She came to the house and fed me. Ann was the only daughter of Ruth and Scott Morrison, and the niece of J. W. Thomas.

I always turned around at the Thomas's house, making sure not to turn into their driveway where cars may not expect me, and negotiated the perilous journey past the beauty parlor and the Weissenger's dog before reaching my own front walk.

I was never allowed to ride my tricycle through the center of town, inhabited by businesses and men and stop lights, but should I have been able to do this, on the other side of the shops were more houses. Mr. and Mrs. Jim DeMarco lived in the first, a large gangly white frame house, and across the street from this bastion of Catholicism were the Methodist Church, the Methodist minister's house, a small rented house, and then Aunt Mary's house. Aunt Deedee (Madia) had died before I was born, but Uncle Gerald

(Fitzgerald) continued to live in her house next door to Aunt Mary. Then there was the house of Mike and Dean Rowe, old friends of my father and my grandmother, and their neighbors were Mr. and Mrs. Tom Yates with their six handsome children. Mrs. Rowe and Mrs. Yates did not speak to each other for some unknown reason, but they often collided, creating afternoon traffic jams in the long hall of Aunt Mary's house. Following that was the stucco colonial house that had belonged to Aunt Janie and Uncle George Shelby, where Cousins Joe and George, Gwin, Fred, and Jane now lived. Across the gravel street from them lived Hal and Anna Carnes and their two children Hal and Lura. Mrs. Lillian Carnes had been committed to the State Lunatic Asylum in Whitfield, Mississippi, after Uncle Hal Carnes had died. Cousin Fred and Cousin Ruth (formerly Edwards) lived next to the Carnes's house, where they were not received by Cousins Joe and George, who lived two doors away. Their house was followed by two rented houses. Then one reached the Gulf Station.

Cousins

Shortly after Rosalie died I was taken on the first trip that I can remember, to the Memphis Zoo. The most impressive sight in my estimation were the monkeys on the monkey mound, mamas and babies, grooming each other. Some were swinging from the bars or looking at themselves in mirrors.

Immediately after this trip I was taken to see a new cousin. Cousin Janula had married C. V. Davis and they had a baby. Her name was Janula Poitevent Davis and they called her Jan. I had never seen a newborn baby; the only babies with whom I was familiar were big fat ones in kiddy cars.

Daddy held me over the bed waiting for me to catch my breath. I looked down in disbelief and simply proclaimed, "It's a monkey." Mother was embarrassed for Janula's sake because a mother is sensitive, irrespective of the source of the comment.

Mother said, "No, Carole, it is Cousin Janula's new baby." I shook my head firmly, "It's a monkey."

The monkey grew to be a pretty pink little girl with curly brown hair and big blue eyes. She became my constant playmate. Janula and C. V. eventually divorced, and Jan and her mother moved back into Aunt Mary's house, so that the memories encased in that house became an important part of my childhood as well.

*

To my great relief Lura and Hal Carnes, the children of my cousin Hal Carnes, moved with their parents to Charlotte, North Carolina, when I was five, leaving me to savor my roots without much intrusion. I was happy about their departure because I was quite simply jealous. Mother and Daddy had a tinted photograph of Hal III on the dressing table in their bedroom. When I enquired as to why it was there, Mother replied, "Before we thought that we could have a baby, Hal was just like our own little boy." I slid the photograph into a drawer, but it reappeared again and again. Then Hal began to play the piano by ear. One would have thought that he was destined for Carnegie Hall the way they all carried on. He sat on his stool in the music room of their house and played. The adults applauded. One evening I had had enough and as we were about to depart, my coat safely in my hand, I kicked him off his stool. My excuse was that it was sissy for a boy to play the piano.

There came the forced apology, the apology after the switching. "Now you must call Hal and apologize."

"I won't do it."

"Well, I shall get out the switch again. He did nothing to you; you are only jealous."

With the greatest reluctance I dialed 52.

"Hal," came a voice as brisk as any four year old could manage, "This is Carole, I am sorry I kicked you off your stool. Bye."

The switch dangled from the mantle.

Then there was Lura. She not only sang, but once she sang on the Clarksdale radio station. Her song was "Dance with the Dolly with a Hole in her Stocking." I tried to sing. My mother encouraged me at the faintest hint of any talent, but she quickly shut my mouth if I attempted to sing. I lived in terror that Lura would get to Hollywood before I had a chance.

One day she came to play with me accompanied by an older girl, Nan Neblett. They said that they were bigger than I was. I stood against them, but they said it was so because their mothers had said they were the biggest. It ruined the afternoon. I wasn't in the habit of carrying my woes to my mother, but that was hard to take. Mother told me to tell them on their next visit that I was bigger than they were because my mother said that I was.

I invited them back the following afternoon and was relieved that they were free to accept the invitation. They were scarcely given a cookie and a glass of Coca Cola before I announced, "I am bigger than you are, because my mother said I am."

Lura shrugged and replied, "Well, I am prettier than you are because my mother said that I am."

Attempted Reproduction

Mother had enjoyed such a glorious childhood that she worked to give me everything within reason which she had enjoyed, notwithstanding that times had changed. The side yard with the former Christmas cedar trees, where her playhouse had once stood, now had to be fenced because of the highway. This became my play yard, with swings attached to her former Christmas trees, a sand pile, flowers in which to hide Easter eggs, canvas and wicker chairs for mothers and nurses to sit and a little rat terrier called Ziggie, just as she and her sisters had. I also had two rabbits and two ducks. One afternoon Mother and I were sitting in the play yard when she pointed to something creeping between the hedges that bordered the back fence. She exclaimed, "Stinkpot!" Here was a white rat, thirty years on, a descendant of their pet white rat. All the pets had been assimilated.

Grandmother eventually took up residence in the Boulderado Hotel in Boulder, Colorado. Lucky for her, it seemed that as her means descended so did the Boulderado. She was a bohemian in spirit and when she left Shelby she wanted nothing that she could not carry in one large suitcase. She kept her diamonds in a silk purse inside her girdle, and for about eight years before she moved to Colorado, Grandmother and Aunt Eleanor traveled the United States, Cuba, and parts of Central America with about fifty thousand dollars of jewelry (1940's valuation) on her person. This was supplemented by spending two months a year with each of her married daughters and two months with her rich Aunt Jessie in Denton, Texas. Then she discovered the Greyhound buses. I used to call these Grandmother's Greyhound Buses. She always alighted and regaled us with stories of the passengers. On one occasion two men sitting in front of her had an argument over the weather. Should the window be opened or closed? They went on a bit and then there was a silence. She looked up. One had pulled out his pistol and pointed it towards the other. The window was closed.

Grandmother stepped off the bus, rushing the season with spring clothes in February, cherries on her navy coat and a navy straw hat. She was in her sixties and had a fat stomach, but the loss of her beauty never seemed to bother her, apart from always wearing a girdle and dark clothes. She retained a presence because she was enchanted with life. When she walked into a room everyone had gathered and with her effortless interest in life, she was the room. Grandmother had found a new means of living well and cheaply: the first motels or efficiency apartments in the United States. She and Aunt Eleanor chose ones as near as possible to the grand hotels where they had summered in better times, and spent their evenings with more stimulating guests, occasionally dining. During these travels, Eleanor met her husband, Ray Booth, and moved to California in 1943. Now, relieved of her daughters, Grandmother was free to return to her beloved state of Colorado and occupy herself with crafts, many of which formed the elaborate decor of my birthday parties to replicate the parties she had given for her daughters.

Twenty boxes of theme decorations would arrive. The first was a Caribbean party, with crepe-paper umbrellas and a large one covering the table. Ruth Morrison made a special coconut cake. French pastries were sent to Shelby from a bakery in Memphis for all of the mothers and nurses and there was brick ice cream from Denton's ice cream company. When the cake was served I reached out and grabbed a big portion and smeared it all over my face. It was *my* birthday.

The following year grandmother produced a Native American party. The big present was a tent. Headbands with feathers and dyed macaroni stitched on to the headbands were given to all of the children. The boys had tomahawks and engaged in races, the girls had crepe-paper beads and Indian dolls. In the center of the table was a glass lake surrounded by ivy, with canoes. Never again have I been so lavishly feted.

Gussie McLean Phillips, a friend of mother's, brought her nephew Bill Causey. She had taken him to Sterling's dime store to select my gift. He insisted on a big doll. She tried to discourage him, as she knew that I had many dolls, but he bought it anyway. When the party was over, my twin beds were strewn with presents. Mother decided to give me a Biblical lesson.

"You have all of these presents and you don't need any of them. Don't you think that you should give some to the little colored children across the street?"

I agreed immediately. Then she continued, "Remember what John the Baptist said, 'If a man asks you for his coat, give him two coats.' That means that you don't give people things that you don't want yourself, you give away something you like very much. Now look at your gifts and find some of the things that you like very much."

The first item that I picked was the doll that Bill Causey had given me, not because I didn't like it, but because the doll had been my favorite gift. There followed many more items and which we loaded into the car and took across the road to three barefoot and happy little girls. One was named Odessa. I called her 'Dresser Drawer.'

After that symbol of generosity I came to mother in a dress that Aunt Zula had sent to me from Neiman Marcus in Dallas. The dress had two puffed pockets. "Should I cut off one pocket and give it away like John the Baptist said to do?"

Pets

Black people had replaced a large family for me. On Christmas Day they flooded the house. The first to arrive was Benny, the husband of the Murphrees' cook, Pearly. Benny was a veteran of the Spanish American War and received a pension for about fifty years after that service. Thus he only worked for a few special people. He knocked on the back door at eight with the words, "Christmas Gift." Daddy had a bottle of whiskey handy and the morning proceeded in bibulous friendliness.

After I emptied my stocking and we had breakfast, everyone gathered around the tree where Santa Claus's presents were waiting for me and all the other presents under the tree were dispersed. Every black person who had worked for us at the house was there. Mother was good about never giving cheap gifts. All had nice presents from Lowenstein's or Goldsmith's department Stores in Memphis. There followed eggnog and much later the Christmas dinner attended by friends and relations.

None of this satisfied me. When I walked into the living room to get my Santa Claus gifts, one casual eye was always turned to the front window and a certain pecan tree, where I expected to see the pony with his lead tied to the tree. There was no consolation for my longing for a horse, but the front yard remained empty. An only child was not going to break her neck on a horse.

I didn't have very good luck with animals. Ziggie, my rat terrier, dug her way out of the play yard and ran on to the highway and was killed. The next pet was a bird dog, which I named Carmel for a little Mexican girl who lived on the farm. Carmel died of worms a few weeks after we acquired her. Then a turtle lived in a pan on a rock in the bathroom, until the sight finally irritated my father so much that he said that the turtle needed a bigger pool and it was sent to the rice farm, which my father had acquired by that time. This was our farm on the highway north of our house of about six hundred acres between Shelby and Hushpuckana. The turtle was supposed to be living in the mules' trough. I would inspect that trough every time I went to the rice farm, but it was far too deep for me to ever catch sight of the turtle again. Cousin Ruth got drunk and bought me a baby deer. He never made it to the play yard, for he would have jumped straight across the fence. I cried for him, but my parents stood firm.

Puff was a kitten given to me by Annie Mae Price (nee Smith). It was a beautiful marmalade kitten, but absolutely wild. Puff was always in the air, jumping from curtain to curtain, clawing all of the furniture and faces. Mother couldn't stand Puff. I had just started to school when I acquired Puff. One day I came home for dinner and as usual called for Puff immediately.

"Puff, Puff," I called, but she was nowhere to be seen. Mother said, "You don't have to go back to school this afternoon."

I attended the Methodist Sunday School. It provided an excuse to dress in my best clothes and I was so dressed one March morning when Mother announced, "You can stay home from Sunday school today." I was quite happy not to go, once I had donned my pretty dress with puffed sleeves and pockets. Shortly thereafter, Daddy arrived at the front door. He was wearing a leather jacket and said, "Which pocket do you take?" I reached for the right pocket and there was a Rat Terrier puppy. Her body was white and her face was black, white, and brown. She was only six weeks old. I named her Prissy and she remained with me, producing three litters of puppies before she died when I was a sophomore in college.

The War

Pearl Harbor was attacked when I was almost fifteen months old. We lived in a protected industry—cotton—for it not only produced uniforms but also medical supplies. Very few people who worked for us went to war. Nevertheless, the South produced good fighters and fifteen men came from our side of the street when most could have been exempt as the farm labor, an indication of the fighting roots of the South. Gwin and Fred Shelby enlisted as well as Shelby Edwards who rose rapidly in the ranks in Europe. Fred Shelby wrote to me from England about victory gardens, planted by the civilian population in order to have food. There was Paul Murphree; three of the Yates family at the south end of the street; a son and son in-law of the Blanchard family; Billy, Joe, David, and

Jack Denton; and Joseph Yates, who was stationed in Tennessee, working on electronics. J. W. Thomas became a major and lived on Park Avenue and worked on films. The farm laborers were resigned to remain in their jobs until the end of the War when the South changed. This was a small price to pay compared to being shipped to the foreign country as infantry to be killed or wounded for a cause that bore scant connection to their lives. Daddy was flooded with "I will never leave you, Mr. Hayes," expressions of gratitude. My father was over forty-five, too old to serve and had a heart murmur that had saved him from the First World War.

Some of my earliest photographic memories were of Mr. Chamberlain with an umbrella and Mr. Churchill giving the sign for victory, pointed out to me by my mother from pictures in *The Commercial Appeal*. I asked where the war was and was told that it was over the water in Japan. The water was Holmes Lake for me and I drew a mental picture of two soldiers in helmets boxing in a wash pan on the other side of Holmes Lake.

We didn't need a victory garden for gardens abounded. Although there were rations, the black people on our land scarcely used their ration books, as they grew their own produce. They gave Mother many of their coupons. Rubber was in short supply and Daddy drove the same Ford for five years because cars were no longer being manufactured. I was promised balloons at my birthday parties when the war was over. But when they arrived, I was terrified of the rubber balloons.

There was a Camp Shelby in southern Mississippi, three hundred miles south of Shelby. The army often got their directions wrong so that exhausted, disappointed soldiers arrived in Shelby only to camp by the side of the railway track before embarking on another day's journey. Mother and I would see them when I went out for a walk. Germs were very much on my mother's mind. She would say, "Wave to the soldiers, wave sweetly, don't go over there, you can never tell what germs nest in groups." I waved a hand covered by a knitted mitten and walked on.

We had one soldier from the farm, Tucker, a private who saw action

J.W. Thomas and Elizabeth Kirk Thomas
working on war films on Park Avenue, NYC.

in Europe. Lizzie wrote to him throughout the war. He was our contact with the ground forces. We sent him date-nut cakes drenched in port and parched pecans (a Southern favorite; pecans toasted with a little butter and salt on a low heat for a very long time). When the war was over and he returned, Daddy invited Tucker into the living room and congratulated him and gave him a glass of whiskey. This was the first time I that remember seeing a black man received as a white person in the segregated South, although he did remain standing in the foyer. We assumed that he was Lizzie's boyfriend, but shortly afterwards Tucker married Lizzie's young daughter, Annie.

Despite the shortage of gasoline, as soon as the war was over Daddy said that I must have Jewish friends because they were loyal. (I presume that because of their history of being outsiders, they were staunch in their friendships to the gentiles whom they made into real friends.) He drove me fifteen miles to Cleveland and fifteen miles back to play with Sue Davidow. I later came to like Sue very much for we went to college together, but at age five she was not my favorite. We had both been hands on a clock in Mrs. Hart's theatrical ballet class, and her mother made her wear an undershirt beneath her ballet costume, so that she would not catch a cold. I despised undershirts, but this friendship was Daddy's choice of a way to spend his new gasoline rations.

On the journeys to Cleveland, Daddy would call in at Mound Bayou to visit his friend Benjamin T. Green (the son of the founder of Mound Bayou, called Judge Green.) His red brick house was not like that of other black people. It had two stories. We were given iced tea on his front porch and then to Merigold, a very small town a few miles south of Mound Bayou on highway 61. Here was a German prisoner-of-war camp, acres of tents near the highway with good-looking prisoners. They worked on the farms and seemed relatively content to be in sunny Mississippi and not on the Russian front. A friend of my mother's ran away from her husband and married a German prisoner as soon as he was released. I have no idea how they met. Mother didn't flinch. She said that the lady's husband was ugly, boring, and often drunk. The camp must have been a gold mine for unhappy women.

After that there was VE day. I was a patient in Dr. Montgomery's office in Greenville, following a tonsillectomy. We heard the news and he took me by the hand and went into the waiting room and shook hands with all of the patients. The next event was VJ day when flyers were dropped into our yard from planes announcing the event. Then the *Pres Semitar* arrived in the late afternoon. I remember hearing Mother and Annie Mae talking about the atomic bomb. The paper said they (the Japanese) had been warned (not quite true). Soon after the war was over they talked about this new device: plastic. It could be dropped and not break. A few years later, ladies became excited by The New Look. Mother rushed to Levy's to get a long suit. It was designed by a company called Lilly and had a tightly fitted coat with two beautiful crystal button and a double peplum over her hips and then came the long skirt. Those were my memories of world events.

The black flight to Chicago occurred the moment that peace was declared. They followed the river north to rumors of jobs, wages unheard of in the South, and indoor plumbing. Many succeeded, many others stayed to receive bigger sounding welfare checks than they could get in Mississippi, cold weather and crime. Of the younger black men on our farm, most except Freddie Hall and James Daniels joined the exodus. Freddie had lived on our farm since he was a small child, and James Daniels came from the large Daniels family who joined us in the 1930's, after they had been mistreated by another planter for twenty years. Tucker never returned except for visits. Even Pappy, Daddy's favorite tractor driver, left the morning after he gave Daddy a testimonial that he was the best white man he had ever known and he would never forget him.

The only alternatives for labor in the Delta were Mexican illegal seasonal laborers who swam across the Rio Grande without papers. Two men in cowboy boots bearing crates of grapefruit from McAllen, Texas, brought truckloads of Mexicans to the Delta. The black people who had been loyal and had remained on the land despised them, for Mexicans worked harder for less pay. I sided with the black people, who by that time were my surrogate family. They would complain, "They sleeps out in the open, under a truck and eats raw meat, and when they talks, they talks jibber jabber, jibber jabber all the time."

Daddy began driving into the fields with his English/Spanish dictionary. Zachariah Cook, our straw boss, was near to retirement age. He had been my grandfather's hostler and paced our farms for years on his Tennessee walking horse, Duke. I rode with him on the front of the saddle. Now he left the big white house on the rice farm and moved to the black addition in Shelby, to a house he shared with his horrid wife Selena, who remained unfaithful to the man from whom all her blessings flowed. A Mexican family, Joe Gonzalez, and his children moved into this house. Zach died of a stroke a few years later, and within a few more years, Joe and his family packed their pick-up truck and went back to Mexico, after which Freddie Hall and his wife Mary Lee took Zach's job. Freddie could not read or write, but was an excellent worker, and had taken Pappy's place as the top tractor driver. He was prime for this job, as long as it was shared with his wife, who had finished high school. After that the cotton picker and the combine machines arrived, gradually reducing a work force of fifty families on a twelve hundred acre plantation to four tractor drivers. We came to rely upon day laborers who were loaded onto trucks to chop the grass and pick cotton, but expensive machines did the main work. As most black people no longer lived on the farms and had seasonal work only, the plantation community disintegrated. World War II changed the South immeasurably. It gave many an experience of an integrated world and others who did not serve could look on and see the possibilities. The full implications of the war were not to be felt for another twenty years ending in the Civil Rights movements of the 1960's.

Fred Shelby

Gwin and Fred Shelby, the sons of Cousins George and Joe, were jewel sons who had grown up to be very close after the death of their brother George to a stomach infection, which they claimed was from eating mulberries from a tree; and later their sister Jane had been brain damaged by what was believed to have been a cerebral hemorrhage when she was a baby in the hospital. Both were handsome. Perhaps Gwin was the handsomest, but Fred had warm brown eyes, a straight nose, full lips and a nice physique. He also had an enquiring mind and when he was young read a book each night. Then he lost interest in studies and began to be a prankster, as boys often do, once making a fire with some boys that demolished a building at Mississippi State College. Cousin Sarah Gwin described this as "a little tragedy in the family." Always approachable by young and old, he would spend many evenings with my parents, although they were between ten and twenty years older.

Fred was considerate enough to write to me from England about the war. There were stamps with King George's picture. I was keen to dig up every petunia and plant onions for victory, but we didn't need victory gardens in Mississippi. Fred had made nice friends with one family in England, and Cousin Joe organized boxes to be sent to them, with cured ham, silk stockings, and always parched pecans.

Then Cousin George broke his hip and could not manage his plantation. Fred's parents leaned upon the draft board to release him and they succeeded, for managing a cotton plantation was more important to the war effort than one soldier.

We were all delighted to have Fred at home, but I wouldn't go near him, because I had a phobia. I would not get close to anything that was torn or ragged. The phobia was so perverse that one day, when I was walking into the middle of town, I discovered that a seam in my panties had come undone. I sat down on the street, kicked my legs into the air, and pulled them off for all to see me. By such contorted reasoning, I thought that anyone fighting must have torn clothes and I refused to go into the sun parlor to sit with Fred who was still wearing a uniform. I would not divulge my phobia to a soul, but simply scuttled beneath the piano whenever I saw Fred in his uniform.

Fred took on the job of farming cheerfully and fell in love with a tall, beautiful young lady from Rosedale who came from a family of old friends. Then sadly she received a proposal from someone else, perhaps taller, more suited to her ambitions, the man of her dreams, and she broke the news to Fred that she had accepted this proposal. He was cast into a spell of gloom.

In the early hours of the morning Cousin George received a telephone call from the Mississippi Highway Patrol. "Are you the owner of a green Buick, 1939 model?"

"Yes".

"And is the license plate number MXL5206?"

"I have no idea of the number of the license plate."

Cousin George put down the receiver, hobbled across the floor on his wooden crutches to his desk, rolled down the top and found some papers. That was his license number.

"That car has been found in the bottom of the Bogue, near Leland. We believe that someone is in the car." (The Bogue Falia is a watershed that starts near Perthshire and runs into the Sunflower River around Darlor and Estill, Mississippi.)

The news proved to be as bad as anticipated. Fred had been out with a group of young men in Greenville. He was depressed and drank a considerable amount of beer. The turn in the road had not been clearly marked and there had been other accidents on the same spot. Men dived into the winter water and found the body. He had tried to kick his way out but failed. Fred was the only war casualty on our street.

After his death I stacked dominos on the black and white tiles of the sun porch where I had scorned Fred. Mother and Daddy tried to visit two rigid, grief-stricken parents. The cold afternoon light covered my dominos and settled onto Jane's empty blue eyes. I was bored with the frozen atmosphere and thought that Cousins Joe and George were old people, and yet they were only in their late fifties. Twenty-five years before they had been rich and blessed with three handsome sons, then their first son died and later there came an afflicted daughter. Now they were left with one son who was still in the Navy and they had the constant care of Jane.

I banged on the piano, but it was out of tune. I announced to Cousin Joe that her piano only played old Boogie Woogie, while Cousin Ruth's piano played pretty church music. She stiffened. It was inconceivable to me that thirty-five years before that time, William Alexander Percy had described Cousin George as "the wildest boy on the mountain" (The University of the South). He was also purported to have said that he knew that when George married he would marry a lady, not an especially astute prediction, for few gentlemen did otherwise in those days.

George and Joe Gwin had been a match planned by their parents. Her mother's family, an old English Catholic one named Hughes, had known the Shelby's since colonial times, co-lateral descendants of Cardinal Hughes, the founder of St. Patrick's Cathedral in New York. She came from Grenada, as did the Poitivents (Cousin George's mother's family). Her Christened name was Willie Joe Gwin, because her father had wanted a boy. Her parents were rich, but they had died young, leaving Joe and her sister, Sarah, with a governess. When George and Joe first met, he had chased the elegant but somewhat prim Joe around the dining table. They were in their early teens. She had been thrilled and never let a chance go by without reminding one that our Cousin George had been the handsomest man in the Delta and the best dancer. Now he hobbled on his walking stick to the kitchen to make some strong black French coffee, his specialty after he gave up drinking. He struggled to make hopeful conversation about crops. Whatever his shortcomings as a businessman, he was brave, kind and manly. Cousin Joe eventually got up from her bed of grief and resumed the position that she had come to inherit, as the matriarch of our family.

Gwin Shelby

About a year after Fred's death Gwin married an attractive widow, Nan Wilkinson Brettell, whom he had known as a neighbor throughout their childhood. She lived on the west side of Holmes Lake and was the daughter of Mr. and Mrs. Hiram Lee Wilkinson. Nan was very petite with the prettiest green eyes I have ever seen and was sparklingly bright, although she came with baggage. There were two robust little girls, Bobbie Lou and Becky, her daughters of her first marriage to Herbert Brettell, whom she had met while they were both attending Duke University. Herbert had been killed in a car crash only a few weeks before, Becky, the second daughter, was born in 1941.

Throughout my childhood I alternated between each one as my best friend. At first I was in awe of Bobbie Lou because she was known for biting people, whereas I did not get much chance to bite for I had to attend birthday parties with both Mother and Lizzie watching me and scarcely had a chance to play, much less bite. I had also heard the most glorious story about her. Two groups of boys were having a fight at the Denton's house and Will Denton said, "Let's call Bobbie Lou to sort it out." It was simply too intimidating for me to even be envious.

We had not played together, as my friends had been rather confined to cousins and people on the street. Herbert Brettell's parents moved to Mississippi from Boston so that they could know their grandchildren. One wonderful afternoon Mr. and Mrs. Brettell invited me to play at their house.

I had seldom had so much fun with two children. Their grandfather had recently celebrated a birthday and Bobbie Lou suggested that we put his after-shave gift on Buttons, their bulldog.

Then we played outdoors in our bare feet. I had only been allowed to take off my shoes and socks if walking on a rug. Mr. Brettell had a hobby in the back of the house where he made things with wood and nails. While we were playing, Becky stepped on a nail. I had never been free enough to step on a nail. I thought that she was lucky, to be free to step upon a nail and to have Bobbie Lou for an older sister.

As the August sun was moving into the west, Mother and Daddy came to collect me. They brought the news that Bobbie Lou and Becky had a new baby sister, Jo Gwin Shelby. It had been a bumper day. This little girl gave Cousins Joe and George infinite pleasure and certainly assisted in easing their pain after Fred's death.

For the rest of my childhood and early youth, Bobbie Lou and Becky were my constant companions. Becky and I would have a contest to see how many nights we could spend together without having a fight. We managed four, and then hit each other over the heads with broomsticks, requiring a separation for a few days.

La Belle Mimi

I first saw her in Mike Rowe's drugstore on the other side of the street, when the men pointed to the man behind the soda fountain and asked her, "Who is that?"

She swished her hips from side to side and said, "Mr. Tuppatini."

All the men laughed, but I didn't see what was so funny about that response from such a little sissy. Then my father called her Alberta, for her father Albert Murphree. I wanted more than anything to have had a boy's name, and why was she getting one?

My old demon jealousy arose once more when I was invited to a birthday party on a farm near Hushpuckana (the hamlet of three houses, four miles north of Shelby). It was no surprise that Mimi Murphree (Albert and Dot's daughter) was to get a Shetland pony, and the guests had been invited to share in her celebration! I could barely attend, such was my misery, watching the pony come to their side porch, everyone clapping while Mimi was placed onto the saddle. An elaborate party, just as elaborate as the ones that grandmother had inspired for me, only intensified the pain. I returned home to my artwork, and every picture that I drew was of Mimi on her pony. I made Mimi as much a witch as possible. When I grew tired of drawing a witch, I simply drew a girl on a pony and scribbled all over her face.

Then a wonderful thing happened. Albert and Dot moved to Shelby and had to sell the pony. Another good omen was that Mimi never rode very well, so that the pony didn't matter to her. After that I found her to be fun.

Mimi was game to do anything mischievous. As she was a year and a half younger, she sometimes agreed to be the dunce while I dressed as the fairy queen. She was no pushover, although we never seemed to quarrel now that the pony had been resolved.

We mimicked people and cornered the telephone, calling the undertaker, crying, waiting for the perplexed driver of the burial car from the black part of town to come into the driveway. Once we telephoned Mimi's Aunt Julia and pretended first to be the operator and then Mrs. Murphree, to say that another aunt, Doris, had given birth to a ten-pound baby boy. To our delight, Aunt Julia believed us and wasted money on many long distance calls in order to be the first one to deliver the news. Then she called Albert. We were at the dinner table when we heard him say, "That's those children." He warned us not to pass the store where Aunt Julia worked.

Poor old Mrs. Powers lived with her daughter and son-in-law, Lillian and Aubrey Rowe, next door to Mr. and Mrs. Murphree, the last house on the street. Mr. Powers claimed that when he was a small boy in Virginia, he had visited his uncle's farm, when Federal soldiers arrived to search their barn. There they had found John Wilkes Booth, the man who had assassinated Abraham Lincoln.

Mr. Powers, now dead, left Mrs. Powers' days quite long while her daughter worked. She had poor eyesight. Mimi and I decided to dress as ladies and to call upon her, pretending to be our grandmothers. There were plenty of clothes about the Murphrees' house, as they had so many daughters. We were soon into high heels, hats, bags, gloves and ankle length dresses. Mrs. Powers opened the door and Mimi said, "Lillian, this is Verna. I have a surprise. Anna Shelby is here from Colorado."

"Hello Lillian," I chanted.

"Won't you have a seat?" She seated us on the swing on her porch and somewhat apologized for her eyesight, much to our relief. Our visit lasted for nearly an hour, while I tried to carry the conversation, babbling anything that I could remember from grandmother's letters. Then we bade her goodbye. We had pulled it off once more.

We were both as skinny as twigs and it worried us. The ideal was to look like Betty Grable. Audrey Hepburn had yet to make her mark. We lived in dream worlds. Mimi subscribed to a bride's magazine and planned wedding after wedding. I subscribed to Photoplay Magazine with the excuse that I needed to know more about Hollywood, as I was to become a famous actress. This fascination for Hollywood made my parents uneasy. Aunt Mary consoled everyone and replied to my announcement that I would become a famous actress, "You will get married and have babies."

I answered, "I will get married, but I will have a career because I will have twin beds."

Aunt Mary congenially agreed, "Well, if you have twin beds, you will succeed."

While Mimi and I were pouring through our preferred reading late one Friday night in her four-poster bed, we discovered the answer to our anxiety in Photoplay Magazine. It was Weight On. There was a photograph of someone looking exactly like us, with thighs that one could see through and knife-edged shoulder blades over twigs for arms. Next to that photograph were thighs that touched and rounded arms. There was a guarantee: If one took the whole bottle one would gain this perfect amount of weight. The miracle drug costs $3.98 and postage was included. We had to save for several weeks from our weekly allowances of 50 cents. Eventually, the money was scraped together and two bottles of Weight On, with the guarantee, arrived. We went to the kitchen sink, found two big silver plated Milk of Magnesia spoons and filled them with Weight On. Only quinine had ever tasted worse. There was no possibility of anyone finishing the bottle.

Mimi didn't need Weight On. She had a way of moving that sent young boys crazy with love. When she walked, one knee knocked into the other; it made her tiny behind swish. She was born with a heart too soft and emotions too intense, only protected by her wicked humor. Her eyes were big, hazel brown, and very soft, and her blond hair complemented her tanned skin. Her mood swings were intense from nice to naughty. Children crossed the side yard of their house on their way to and from school. Mimi chased them, running with her strange skip, and spit at them to leave the yard. Her Mother decided to consult a child psychiatrist in Memphis. He carefully interviewed Mimi and then prescribed Peach Tree Salve (a switch from a peach tree).

When she danced the Charleston at dancing recitals, she brought down the house. Later there was the Jive, the Bop, the Twist, even the Foxtrot. Little boys begged their mothers for money to put an orchid on to her arm, and the stag line reached half way across the Rosedale courthouse, where most of the good dances were held. At the end of the dance when Rufus McKay of the Red Tops, the favorite band who came from Vicksburg, sang "Danny Boy," it was always the handsomest boy in the Delta from a far away school, who chose to sway and cuddle with Mimi to this song. When she went away to school in Virginia in the tenth grade and came home for Christmas, the boys were desperate. While the rest of us were scraping to go to five dances, and some of us had to endure dates that talked about the Seminoles, Mimi went to fifteen dances. It was a man's world and Mimi knew how to manage them.

The dances ended at one or two in the morning, and before the dances there were buffet suppers. They weren't very elaborate: ham, tinned peas in a cream sauce, a fruit congealed salad, and no alcohol, as we were all under age. The suppers were laid out on a dining room table beneath long portraits, embellished by Chantilly, Buttercup, or Francis I silver and served on Limoges. These parties were awkward, because we were only given forks and had to cut the ham without a knife. Mine would scatter and I kicked ham beneath many a chair. But the light supper before the dance afforded a preview of the young men to come. Both hurdles were difficult for Mimi and me because our glasses had been deposited on a bathroom mantle and we got by for ten hours with 20/450 vision. We danced for two hours, followed by numerous intermission parties, especially in Rosedale, then danced two more hours. After the dances we drove twenty or thirty miles across the Delta to a breakfast at either Mimi's house or Bill Eggleston's house on a plantation located across the road from the State Penal Farm at Parchman, where we danced to a record player until five in the morning. Across the gravel road from the Eggleston's plantation, convicts in their black and white striped uniforms were on their tractors as we departed in our evening clothes and the boys got ready to go hunting. The following afternoon cars filled Mimi's driveway. It was filled with the most eligible boys, exhausted from dancing and shooting and longing once more for Coca-Colas, cakes, and girls. I usually went to her house for the lemon cake and hopefully to catch any of the spares. Sometimes she stole one or two of my boyfriends, but it never really mattered, only a slight alteration to the ego. She fell in and out of love like a yo-yo, while I imagined love for four years.

We found another advertisement in a movie magazine when we were about fifteen; this was "An Illustrated Encyclopedia of Sex." It was much more expensive than Weight On had been, $15.98, but our allowances had increased to $2.00 a week. It was guaranteed to come in a plain brown paper wrapper, and we only needed one copy. We decided that Mimi's mailbox was the safer hole, and for six weeks she volunteered to collect her parents' mail. One Thursday, she telephoned me in her husky voice. "It's here. It's in the wrapper. No one suspects." We arranged to spend that Friday night together. I rushed down the street and ran though Mabel Scherbaum's side yard (formerly Aunt Lula's) to Dot and Albert's house that had been built on the back of Mabel's lot. After supper we went to bed as early as we could excuse ourselves without creating suspicion. There we tore off the wrapper. It looked like a biology book. I drooped at the thought of biology, for I was a romantic. The decision was made right then. I wanted to be surprised. The encyclopedia was consigned to the garbage can, which their cook no doubt found in the morning. When Mimi got married she sent me a postcard from her honeymoon with as tiny and fine a print as she could manage. It said, "Ouch!"

None of these experiences prepared Mimi for life. The love of her life appeared at the University of Mississippi. He was a law student and a friend of William Faulkner. But he did not marry her. There followed three unsuccessful marriages. I spoke to her recently and she said, "No one can buy me. My first and third husbands were two of the richest men in the South, and the second had nothing." She had divorced the first very nice husband before he came into his fortune and had a pre-nuptial agreement with the third husband, by which she received enough money for a tummy tuck and a trip to Italy. She was thereafter lumbered with a diamond ring too large to sell and a fur coat too pretentious to wear. Mimi worked hard in a world that the writers of bride's books had never contemplated for their readers. Her children once complained that other mothers did not work on Sundays. Mimi jerked them up, took them to a shopping mall, marched them up and down and said, "Look at these people. Don't you think that some of them might have children? What day is this?"

She became a real estate agent, managing large apartment buildings in Atlanta, often living precariously and frequently changing addresses and jobs because her employers had big ideas and shallow pockets. But her standard of living seldom went down. In true Delta tradition the Kossmans from Cleveland continued to deliver to Mimi a new Buick and there was always a long coat trimmed in fur. Her apartments were always sophisticated, if on a short lease.

When we were both almost forty-five, we converged in Shelby at the same time. Mimi told me of her early morning visitors. Boys were hooting in the driveway. She put on her lacy bedroom slippers, tiptoed down the stairs hoping that Dot and Albert would not hear her, and made a tiny opening in the red and green checked curtains of her parents' pine kitchen to peer at her admirers. They looked rather young. Then the penny dropped. They were hooting for her daughter, Ellen.

There have been many times when she has turned her face against the wall, but she never succumbed to defeat or jealously. She would have aspired to look like Grace Kelly, but she was simply Mimi, with her own indelible stamp. Mother Courage goes on, despite broken marriages, financial reverses, the loss of her brother with a tragic illness, and the deaths of her supportive parents, as well as her own terrible health. In 2003 Mimi was in a coma for three months. When she began to revive, I told her son to ask her if she needed some Peach Tree Salve. She smiled and I knew that she would come through. Now she skips on with a vast diamond ring on her finger, dragging her fur coat behind, as mischievous as if life had been a breeze. Her fortune has been in her children, Ellen Sanders Vokel and Rob Wilson, and the splendid relationship she has with them. Of course her grandchildren think that she is a fairy godmother.

Ann, Jan, Bobbie Lou, Becky, and Mimi formed the nucleus of my friends and they were constantly in my house on that street.

Babies

Everyone's mother seemed to be expecting a baby. Miss Dot (Mimi's mother) and Miss Laurie Alice (the mother of Will and Gus Denton) sat on a swing together and took up the whole seat and then they walked pigeon-toed. After that Charles Denton and Dan Murphree were born. Dorothy Wilkinson, who lived in the apartment of our house, was expecting a baby. That one I had been told about. Despite observing Laurie Alice, Dot, and Dorothy, I clung to the belief that babies were delivered by angels from heaven.

On a hot summer at noon we were having our dinner with the front door open, only protected by a screen door, in order to stimulate more cross ventilation. Suddenly Daddy jumped from the dining room table and rushed out into the yard, too late to catch Rowdy, Mr. Charlie Denton's bird dog, who was making his way into the Denton's yard with my baby trap in his mouth. It was to be the baby's bed, a ruffled pillow and blanket, which I had placed in our flowerbed to deceive the angels and make them deliver Dorothy Wilkinson's baby to us.

One afternoon I heard Mother crying to Cousin Joe on our side porch. She talked about an operation, the hospital in Memphis, and that she didn't want to die. Cousin Joe tried her best to make Mother brave, but her fear persisted. I thought she was utterly silly and that I now had a second hope. The baby nest had failed, but I knew that other babies were procured from the hospital. I spread the good news; my Mother was also going to have a baby.

Nanette Jacobs, an effusive lady, telephoned mother to congratulate her on "expecting". Mother then had to announce to one and all that she had a tumor, gulping, as she did not know what kind of a tumor. I was elated when she went into the hospital and counted the moments until the telephone rang to say whether it was a boy or a girl.

Dr. Gus Chrisler operated on mother and mercifully she was all right. The time arrived for me to visit her in the hospital. She was proud of the only child she would ever have, for her womb had been removed. She wanted Dr. Chrisler (who had encouraged her to have me) and the nurses to see her little girl, and she had instructed Ruth Morrison to fix my hair for the occasion. I told Ruth that I wanted it plaited and then make the plaits into round biscuits on either side of my head. Ruth obliged. Lizzie packed a special skirt and blouse for me to wear and Daddy drove me to Memphis to his parents' house to get dressed.

On the way to Memphis, he gave a young man from Shelby a lift. I was grateful to have been playing on the back seat, as I could not believe Daddy's rashness. I spent ninety miles hiding as much as possible, trying to get beneath the car seats, because I had heard that hitchhikers committed crimes, even murder.

When we reached Memphis, my face was gritty and red from the car floor. Granny had to scrub it, making it redder, and put me into the carefully selected skirt and blouse. She sat me before the mirror with five reflections over the tile dressing table in her bathroom. I smiled and said, "Now for the hair." The hairdo had been my inspiration for I knew the effect of overnight plaiting on hair. It made hair beautiful and wavy. I was somewhat less than thrilled when I saw the five reflections, but went on to the Methodist Hospital to greet my Mother after her ordeal.

Mother was dismayed. Her doll had wild hair that resembled a bad Afro wig. What had Ruth done? Mother had a large incision with metal staples instead of stitches. Operations were far from keyhole in those days. I entered the room and rushed to her bedside and asked about the baby. She assured me once more that she was not going to have a baby. I beamed. "You will be here ten more days, just wait and see, you will have a baby."

We collected her and Daddy took us to the Venetian Room at the Peabody Hotel. This was my favorite treat. I always ordered the same thing, turkey and dressing. The selection meant that I could get a tiny paper container of cranberry sauce and listen to a sometimes famous big band that played in the Venetian Room at noon and at the Skyway in the evening. After the sauce and before the dessert, I sulked over the rest of my food. Despite a selection from the cart of French pastries, I hung my head all the way to Shelby because there was no baby.

A few months following Mother's operation, Annie, Lizzie's daughter, produced twin girls in her cabin across the street. They were premature, but alive. She named one Cathryn (for my first cousin in Memphis) and the other Carole.

I was nearly six and had never been inside a cabin before. There was a front porch with a swing, where Lizzie's parents sat, then a bedroom, followed by another bedroom, then a kitchen. The house was spotless, for the floor had been scrubbed every day. At five in the afternoon, the sun produced considerable heat. In the kitchen, next to a burning stove, were two tiny red babies on a tray. They were covered in dabs of sterilized cotton and blankets, to give the effect of an incubator. They both had lots of hair. I had never seen anything so wonderful. Annie lay in the bed and waved. Willie Bell, Lizzie's sister, gave her sensual smile over the babies.

Three days later, Cathryn died. (One wonders what the outcome may have been today). The doctor had warned Annie that they both might not live. Carole lived. All of my equipment for sterilizing, play pens, and pretty clothes now made its way across the road. As soon as Carole was old enough to go out, she came to our living room where I put her on a blanket and kissed and kissed her. I too now had a baby.

Horse Shows

No one ever made money from horses, but it provided a focal point of exercise and social life for the Delta, second only to dances. Shelby was the center for the horse shows, while Rosedale, Greenville and Clarksdale were centers for the dances. The first horse show in the Delta was held in Shelby in 1927 in connection with a county fair.[4] They became a custom and Mr. Gus Blanchard finally gave up farming and did what he was best at, training Tennessee Walking Horses. His stables were across the street from our house, next to the cotton gin. The horses were trained in large red barn across the street, with a ring next to the barn. People came from Tennessee, Kentucky, Louisiana, and Missouri to these shows.

The shows were not limited to Tennessee Walking Horses, although they were the main emphasis. There were gaiter horses, workhorses, and a pony and carriage event. The Maid of Cotton (a college girl who had won a talent/beauty contest, second only to Miss America) always appeared, safely ensconced in a carriage. Daddy had about twelve walking horses, but the pair that never failed to win a prize was the two gray work horses that he had viciously named Zula and May, ladies who had never worked.

The dandies were at the stables every morning making sure that their horses were properly shod and paced. I was there every morning as well. Mr. Blanchard's son, Bill, had been born prematurely and was brain damaged. He wore thick glasses. The dandy of dandies was Rabun Jones from Leland. His sister, Alice Belle, had married my cousin Shelby Edwards (Ruth's son). Rabun dressed like no other planter, much less a farmer. He always wore high leather riding boots that glistened with polish. One day he felt something warm running down his leg. Bill had mistaken his boot for a tree.

---

4 Sillers, ed.374-75

Some people are born on horseback, and that was the case with Julia Mae. She was the daughter of Lizzie's niece, Idel. A sturdy little black girl with no inhibitions, she was only a year or so older than I, but much more advanced. She would mount anything, with or without a saddle, with or without shoes, and ride like a professional. I would have sacrificed all toys to have been Julia Mae.

Under the auspices of Mr. Blanchard, two very pretty girls stayed at our house, Ruth Buford and Betty Tatum. We were all instantly congenial, and although I was nearly seven in 1947, I was old enough to eavesdrop on gossipy adult conversations on the porch after dinner when my parents and the girls talked about various people in the horse world. One had knowingly sold a bad horse. Another refused to pay Daddy five hundred dollars for a horse that he had sold for him. When Daddy finally approached the man with much embarrassment for the money, his only excuse was that of a Delta gentleman, "Oh, Hayes, I spent that money a long time ago." It was a gentleman's sport.

I watched with awe when Ruth put on her jodhpurs, coat, hairnet, hat, tie, riding shoes and jacket. Betty was only the friend who watched her ride. A grandstand stood beside the Shelby country club where most people sat. A few boxes were reserved for the very prominent members of the horse show. The first box was always reserved for Miss Laurie Blanchard, wearing a feathered hat and matching pastel suit with a long strand of pearls. There were other boxes reserved for the entourage from the Memphis Cotton Carnival. Daddy and I went every evening, and Mother attended most evenings.

Ruth came out. It was so thrilling to watch her, but she didn't win any prizes. Mr. Blanchard won most of the prizes. On one particular evening Mother had to stay at home because of a migraine, and I attended with Daddy. He didn't bother with his seat and we stood by the sidelines with the men. I was dressed in another Nieman Marcus skirt and blouse, compliments of Aunt Zula. I had to go to the bathroom and nudged Daddy.

Grumpily he hurried me out before the events had got under way, but when I reached the country club the ladies room was well occupied. Daddy insisted, insisted with vengeance, that I stoop between two cars. Although it was now dark, there were plenty of spotlights, and this was humiliating. I could hear couples, ladies in high heeled shoes sinking into the mud, ice tinkling, men talking behind me, while Daddy stood guard and I was exposed to the gentry of the Delta!

We resumed our post by a white fence near the back of the show, when I had to go once more. Forget Daddy, I was not going to do that. I stood in my starched skirt and ruffled panties and put one leg at one end of the fence and one on the other and managed a perpendicular stream that hit the ground. This maneuver had been quite successful until I turned around and saw Hugh Allen Barclay, a boy from my first grade class, who was selling peanuts. He walked past me and stared in a perplexed manner. I gazed directly ahead and was confident that he failed to appreciate what he was seeing.

Mr. Blanchard won again. He rode up to the judge and took the ribbon, put it in his mouth, and rode away. As I was my mother's germ-guarded child, I could not stand there and see my dear Mr. Blanchard put something dirty into his mouth, so I belted out at the top of my lungs, "Take it out of your mouth, Mr. Blanchard. Take it out of your mouth." He survived, even though he didn't hear me.

When the shows were over and the guests had gone, I found a bit of mascara in our guest bathroom, left by Ruth Buford, and it emitted a glow that lasted for some time. This was the final horseshow for Mr. Blanchard moved to greener pastures in south Mississippi. The barn was pulled down. Daddy sold most of his walking horses. The last horse to go was Melody, a gray mare in foal, sold to a man in California. Several years later, he sent Daddy a photograph of the foal, a bay with a white tail and mane that resembled Roy Rogers's Trigger and was called Carnes Junior. The letter said that ten thousand dollars had been turned down for Carnes Junior. Once the sum was mentioned, I only needed someone to pay. Ten thousand dollars in 1949 was the average price for a house in Chickasaw Gardens, the most expensive new residential development in Memphis. My grandmother Carnes had died and I heard that Grandpapa had some retirement money. As soon as he came to visit, the photograph of Carnes Junior came out. "It's only ten thousand dollars," I pleaded, but was left for consolation with the empty tube of mascara and an annual calendar from Wartrace, Tennessee with a cover depicting Midnight Sun, a famous Tennessee Walking Horse stallion.

Malaria

Some of my earliest memories were of malaria. I often went to sleep in a paisley print nightgown, to awaken vomiting, with hands full of muck. My parents got into a frightful state and sprayed me with an orange hose attached to a tap in the bathtub. Sheets were changed and I was put into something ugly, a nightgown resembling an undershirt, in case I was sick once more.

No one seemed to suffer from cerebral malaria, or at least I remember no one dying, but there was a recurrence of malaria every summer. This meant trips to Mr. Waggle, the technician in Dr. Simmons's office in Cleveland. He was a vastly tall man with oily black hair, who worked in a dingy room up a flight of brown linoleum-covered stairs where he pricked my finger. Then he brought forth an orange rubber tube and sucked blood. After that ordeal, the blood was put onto a small glass plate and I was released to Owens' drug store, where I had a Coca Cola, before returning to hear the results, always 'positive.' My favorite season of the year had a daily ending in quinine.

Quinine came in two dreaded forms from the same silver plated tablespoon, the one also used for Milk of Magnesia, so large that, had it contained spring water, one would have gagged. Before I went to bed the spoon was produced over the kitchen sink. I stood on a chair and bent over the sink. In case the first spoon did not hit its destination, there would always be another. The initial dose was brown and bitter. I am now seventy-three and cannot remember having had to swallow anything so vile. A few years produced a new version. Mother tried to assure me that this one was better. It looked better, not so thick; it was white, clear and sugary. When tasted, one almost wished for the brown.

I would hear the ladies talking to each other on the telephone as soon as June arrived; "Elizabeth, May, Ruth, Annie Mae, Janula."

"I have malaria again." Dark circles appeared under their eyes. The summers progressed, eased by afternoon naps.

On one of these trips we sat in Dr. Simmons' treatment office waiting for the results. We could easily hear a patient in the other room, a country woman, who appeared to have had consulted him on many visits. She wanted to pay her bill. Dr. Simmons replied, "Your bill is one dollar." Then we heard her say, "Thank you, Dr. Simmons, I always want to pay my bills on time."

In the car, on the way back to Shelby, mother said, "You must have heard that conversation. That lady had consulted Dr. Simmons on many occasions, but he gave her the treatment without embarrassing her. Now, remember, Carole, when you do something nice for someone, just pretend that it is not much."

When the war ended, an army tank came into town. Every afternoon at half-past five, just as I was about to sit on the back steps with my dog, Prissy, and listen to the Baptist chimes, the neighborhood was sprayed with DDT. Prissy and I were made to evacuate into the house until the air settled. As I liked the smell of DDT, I often went out on the back porch before it had settled. Children ran down the street following the DDT truck.

Another bonus of the end of the war was the sale of army pontoons. I learned to swim in a pontoon. They were deep enough for adult swimming and my parents often did so, for the length was about fifty feet. My pontoon had a drain and a man came twice a week with a broom and Ajax to wash it, replacing the water with a hose until it was full and children could jump from the rubber sides. There were, however, many afternoons when the "safe" spray of DDT settled over the pontoon and we all swam the next day.

Many things have been said about the harmful effects of DDT. I lived in the spray for about five years. All of my friends did the same and are alive, and all except me have had children. DDT eradicated malaria in the Deep South and the Delta became a vast area for planting rice. Concrete swimming pools sprung up in most towns. It is hard to find anyone who grew up in this part of the States who takes the threat of DDT as seriously as they should. I lived in New Orleans in 1980 and my friend Fred Preaus and I were so dismissive of its dangers that we considered going to a country store in North Louisiana to get DDT (then outlawed) to spray the bugs in the French Quarter.

School

It was 1946 and most of my friends were already attending our first year of school. The cotton gin across the street began to chug and there was a smell of fire in the air. Friends passed me on their way to school and waved. I remained with Lizzie on the street. Then the air became crisper and I donned a brown corduroy suit and continued to walk the street and wave to the children. Not until I was into a winter coat and leggings did I attend classes. The reason was that there was an epidemic of measles in the town and Mother didn't want me to catch anything. When I finally arrived I must have resembled China's last empress. I sat in Miss Mattie's big pastel pink and green chair and two girls removed my leggings, then my coat. After that I stooped down for them to remove my little beret as well.

Even later than I arrived, the children of tenant farmers entered school. They had to wait until the cotton had been picked; they came in bare feet with long dresses. Many were very tall and looked too old for our class.

The lessons were not of much interest. I already knew how to add and subtract; it was common sense. We did begin reading a big book about Dick, Sally and Baby Jane, whose grandmother wore a dress that buttoned down the front and baked pies that she put onto the window ledge to cool. They also had devoted parents. It inspired me to dictate a letter to my grandmother and tell her that she did not look like a grandmother because she wore black silk lounging pajamas and smoked a cigarette on a holder.

The second grade was more interesting. My teacher was my pretty cousin Janula Poitevent Davis, who had recently been divorced. Before Janula was given the job, there had been a protocol of only hiring single women as teachers, based on the belief that teaching was a vocation and a woman with a family would not be dedicated enough for the vocation. Daddy had to speak to a few friends on the school board to get Janula the job, although she was far better educated than the other teachers and she assured the board that she was getting a divorce. Janula wore very fashionable clothes in keeping with her new release. Each of us was treated as special. If one wanted to be the Fairy Queen, the part was there. She either wrote or re-wrote her own version of plays. A poor boy was given the role of Jack-in-the-Box and she made his costume. He was able to make the audience laugh, perhaps for the only time in his life. She took a silent notice of children from very deprived backgrounds and made sure they had food and shoes. She was so natural in her job that there was no need for her to retire. She taught until she was seventy, finally in a well-paid expensive school in Texas.

We began spelling and the first word that she taught us was ME. We wrote sentences with the other words that we learned to spell and all of my sentences were about Mr. Blanchard. "Mr. Blanchard is a *kind* man." "Mr. Blanchard is a *good* man." I remember the perplexed expression on the face of his grandson, Gus Denton, who evidently wondered why I should be making all of my sentences about his grandfather. I was the one who missed him, for he had gone to South Mississippi with the walking horses.

The third grade was fire and brimstone. Miss Fern Patty read to us from the Old Testament about witchcraft. When I asked her to explain, she seemed to say that some people were witches even though they had done nothing to justify this label. I could not sleep all winter without a light in my room, clearly seeing a witch with a pointed hat who lived in the corner.

After Christmas we were all asked to recite what Santa Claus had brought to us. The middle class children sprang to their feet and recited a confident list. Then Miss Patty came to a little boy who sat in the back of the class. "Frank, what did Santa Claus bring to you for Christmas?"

"A gun."

That upset me and I got mad at Santa Claus and asked Mother why he did not bring much to poor people. As Mother enjoyed Santa Claus, she replied, "That is because they live so far out in the country that he can't find their houses."

The following year Frank's face and neck were severely scarred in a fire caused by the use of kerosene. He crouched even further into the back of the class.Spring released me from the third grade. I had chicken pox and then there occurred an epidemic of measles in the school. I had a mild case of German measles. Mother saw no point in my going back to catch the red measles. I finished that year by taking an achievement test on Miss Patty's front porch.

There followed a serious teacher in the fourth grade, Miss Speaks. She expected us to work. Used to impressing and unaccustomed to application, I told my family a big lie: that I had done extremely well on the new achievement tests, and that my spelling was on the level of a seventh or eighth grader. I thought that the word 'achievement tests' was a breeze. Mother went up and down the street telling everyone. Cousin Janula was so pleased that she approached Miss Speaks, "Why haven't I been told how well Carole did on her achievement tests? You know how interested I am in Carole."

"Well, let me see," answered the puzzled Miss Speaks. She brought out her files.

"I don't think that she has done anything exceptional on any of her tests." There were spankings and apologies to be endured and the only time that I saw a glimmer of upper grades was when Ann knocked on the door of my class to give me a message.

In the fifth grade I had a big fight. Maybelle Shrugs, a very poor girl in my class, had already failed several grades. This only aggravated her propensity to bully. She came from a large family who lived by the side of a public road in a shack. Everyone could see them sitting all over the steps. Even Santa Claus couldn't have missed them, had he chosen to glance in that direction. My mother had given me instructions to be very careful about unfortunate poor white people, that the slightest offence could trigger them or their families to burn my house down. I understood this, but there was another emotion that ran too deep. I knew that they hated "colored people", called them "niggers." One morning at recess, Maybelle challenged one and all in the fifth grade to fight her. I calmly announced, in the most aristocratic tone that I could manage, that I was not afraid of her. Pale blue eyes shot red darts of hatred. I sauntered home to dinner, ate my salmon croquettes, squash, butter beans, biscuits, washed down with iced tea and a peach cobbler as quickly as I could manage and announced that I would walk back to school that day. I arrived early, a first in my record, and was ready for the fight. The word went out among the children in the playground and they quickly found the enraged Maybelle.

The fight was encircled by everyone free during the lunch hour and they were all cheering for me. This was a new experience! I gave the most punches and her face grew redder. Then she grabbed my hair and pulled with all of her might. I heard myself saying, "That is not fair; that is not the way you fight." Tally Ho, the rules of the hunt, were not quite Maybelle Shrugs' criteria. Mercifully, Mr. Jimmie Anderson, the head of the agricultural department, broke us up and sent us to our rooms to put heads on desks until classes started.

After about ten steaming minutes, her older sister, Minnie Jo arrived at the door, saying, "I've heard you've been in a fight?" Maybelle raised her smoldering head.

"Did you win?"

Maybelle replied in the affirmative.

I burst into their conversation, "No, she didn't. I was beating her up until she fought unfairly and we were simply broken up."

Minnie Jo then said to her sister, "You did right, because she lives in town and has electric lights and thinks she's better'n you."

*

From that time on I simply ticked off the years of school as if I were in a prison. We acquired a new building which more closely resembled a prison than the old one, for it had metal windows. The prayer and the Pledge of Allegiance 'to the republic' were now announced over an intercom system from the superintendent's office instead of students going to chapel, which I had enjoyed.

Plays were the only bit that inspired me, as I always had the lead part. After the class play, which occurred in the springtime, the smells of summer began to permeate the air. I would come home at noon and the kitchen floor smelled of bare dark feet on scrubbed linoleum and starch on summer dresses. I could scarcely bring myself to go back and sometimes I would pretend to walk and never arrive. Soon I would be free with Prissy, the new swimming pool at the country club, and to play with Jan.

I daydreamed throughout school. The pleasant moments were always during recess, where the black janitor, Hal, loaded the Coca-Cola machine and those who had a nickel bought a drink. I liked this time best, because Hal reminded me of the consoling figures in my own home. I had two good English teachers, Mrs. Garrett from Cleveland, and Mrs. Elizabeth Alford from Gunnison, but this was not enough. There was one entertaining biology teacher, Lee McCarty (now a famous potter in Mississippi), who told us of a world that most people were not to inherit, while the principal shuffled down the corridor in his pleated trousers and gabardine shirt, buttoned at the top with no tie and peeped through the tiny glass hole in the door at Lee sitting in the window with his leg wrapped around his neck in a yoga position and the students convulsed with laughter. Then Lee decided to take his wife to Mexico for three weeks in the middle of the winter, "for my nerves." The school could not fire him, for where else would they find a science teacher with a Masters Degree from Columbia. There was a football coach who taught Mississippi History in the seventh grade and spent seven months on the Civil War, and one good American History teacher, Mr. Button (later the principal). I had four years of an excellent mathematics teacher, Miss Ora Bizzell. By far the best teacher in the school, she was also the librarian. If one checked out a sexy book, Miss Bizzell took it out of the locker with a simple note, "unsuitable." She appeared to have lived a monastic life, renting a room in Shelby during the week and staying with her brother and his family in Pace on the weekends. Her brother had two daughters who suffered from a muscular wasting disease and a nephew who became a very good County Court Judge. She once lived at Aunt Mary's house and would pass down the hall to her room declining any invitation to join the rest of us in the living room. She ate her evening meals alone at the only café in town. Her whole life seemed to be her job, which she performed as if it were a vocation. She knew what each student was about and the extent of their potential. At first we were all frightened by being taught by her, but when she entered the classroom, only interest was aroused. She made solid geometry and trigonometry my most interesting subjects. When she finally retired, she worked another ten years as librarian at Peabody College in Nashville. As she had read every book in our library, she should have been given a special assignment of teaching the more gifted students English. She compared with any teacher I have ever had at university. It was an impossible task to teach students from such diverse backgrounds and ambitions in one school and often one class.

Team sports seemed ridiculous to me. Hopscotch with Becky was the limit of my competitive spirit and even then we were both more interested in watering our lollypops over the drinking fountain than the square in which the trick had landed. We all learned to drive a car several years before gaining a license and drove on the back streets of Shelby. One hot August afternoon Becky and I were making our circles; I was driving my father's red Mercury and we were smoking. I spied the football team practicing behind the school. The very idea that "our boys will shine tonight" (a line from a football song) suddenly inspired me to go after them. I turned into the field and tore through the line of boys who were running laps in unison, dressed in full gear in the August afternoon heat. Becky was so embarrassed that she and her cigarette took a dive to the floor of the car, because she had ambitions for boyfriends and to reign as a football queen. I was the only one visible. After that I wondered why I was never asked to be a maid in the homecoming court, much less the football queen. When they nominated people for cheerleader, Mimi and I were the only reasonably attractive girls in school not mentioned. We went back to Mimi's house and consoled ourselves with Cokes and cakes and took an honest look. We tried to do a yell. Then we knew, and fell into a heap of giggles at the thought of yelling slogans about a team.

Ann married when I was twelve and she and her husband, Gene Coopwood, and their baby Betsy, lived in a small house behind her parents' house. I acquired another hideout for playing truant, which I did every ten days. My parents would leave me with Ann when they went out of town. It was almost as good as being a young married woman. After lunch I would hide in her car and she would go into the school and collect my books from my locker. Then I became one of the big girls, spending the afternoons with Ann and her friend Betty Harlow from Clarksdale. They gave me an unlimited supply of Pall Mall cigarettes.

I drifted through school with Bs and Cs and one A in history, a deportment card that said, Neat, Polite-1, Pays Attention in Class-4, Co-operates with the Group-5. A change occurred in 1957 when the Russians launched Sputnik I. American education was assaulted for lagging behind in space exploration. It became apparent that checks, matching luggage, dyed-to-match cashmere skirts and sweaters would not be enough to put me onto a train for a good college in Virginia or New Orleans or Nashville. I would have to compete with Sputnik and the baby boomers.

Polio

Polio invaded the hot sections of the States with a vengeance in the late 1940's and early 1950's. There was no cure; no one knew what caused this disease that attacked muscles and maimed lives. It seemed to appear after exercising, so swimming pools were quickly closed. There was some evidence that it was more common in the poorer parts of the country, but it swept across every strata of society. When the long-awaited summers appeared, we rushed to the pool for a few days and then two cases were reported in Chambers (now Winstonville), four cases in Clarksdale, three in Cleveland, and one in Shelby. The noose tightened.

Money Luckett from Clarksdale was two years older than I and had been attacked just after she had come home from Camp Kittywake on the

Mississippi Gulf Coast. Polly Schas from Memphis came down with the illness after she had been participating in many high-school sorority activities. They shared a room together for a year in the Isolation Hospital in Memphis. Money was a member of Mensa. She wrote to important people all over the world and was an avid reader. She could possibly have become a high-powered trial lawyer, like her father. Polly was artistic and musical. If one visited her for the first time because she was disabled, one continued to call upon her because of her radiant charm. After polio, Money was consigned to an iron lung for most of the day and night until she died at sixty. Polly spent most of her life between a wheel chair and an iron lung until she died in her late thirties as a result of the strain on her lungs.

Mothers did not know what to do. Flies were thought to be carriers. When a case of polio was reported in our area, Mother packed our bags to go to Colorado. A few days later she unpacked the bags, because another theory developed. Should one move from a hot climate to a cooler one, the disease could be stimulated. Some said the word "virus." Viruses were a new word. In desperation parents reduced their children's world to one of afternoon naps, no more swimming, and carefully selected companions who had mothers equally terrified of flies. Even the picture show, my pastime for four or five nights a week, was prohibited.

One summer afternoon I was riding in our car with Mother and Daddy and begged to go into Sterling's dime store. Just as I was about to alight, we met a stricken Janula holding Jan's hand and hastily retreating from Sterling's. She said one word: "Children". The back car doors swung open, Janula and Jan piled inside, and we were off. Polio did not seem to invade cousins, so that Jan and I were left to our own devices for many summers, eating bananas that had been scalded, peeled and dropped onto a plate so that no germ on the outside of the skin had a chance to move inside through a crack. We had home-baked bread, which no undetected fly had touched while it cooled in the bakery. I was deeply embarrassed over this delicious bread for fear someone would suspect that my mother was afraid of Wonder Bread. If a housefly got into the dining room it ignited a panic.

Our isolation caused us to invent games and lasting memories. Aunt Mary's house was a treasure trove. She had a finished attic with trunks going back for three generations and even let us skate there on a rainy day. We played Civil War and wore Aunt Lula's blue velvet coat with long tapered sleeves that were puffed above the shoulders. Aunt Lula had also left a black silk coat with black beads. This was saved for when we were in mourning. Then we became flappers. By the time that we reached the Twenties trunk the heat was over 120 degrees Fahrenheit in the attic. I looked upon a bright red Jan in Isabel's fringe-encircled black crepe dress with rhinestone straps and a rhinestone headband. Jan even learned to drive a car on the sidewalk from the Methodist Church to her grandmother's house during this time (four doors).[5]

When the heat drove us from the attic, we decided to play "poor people" and brought down ragged cotton dresses. For days we lived in an abandoned hen house and swept the hen yard, as poor people did. The next game was "night club." Jan knew where some liquor was kept, but we had to wait until Aunt Mary was deep into her afternoon nap. Then Jan crawled on her stomach past her bed, opened her closet door and procured a bottle of New York State Port that Mother and Daddy had given Aunt Mary for Christmas. I had seen people serving champagne in a silver bucket surrounded by crushed ice. We found a white enamel pan and scooped up some blocks of ice. Jan then put a dining chair next to the china cabinet, found the key and brought down two dusty crystal wine glasses. We first considered drinking out of these, but I thought that in nightclubs the glasses should be clean. It sounds odd today, but growing up in the Deep South, two reasonably intelligent girls had never washed a glass and weren't sure how it was done. We ran a cold tap over the crystal glasses, and scraped out the dust, now turned to mud, with our fingers. We then hid behind the

---

5 A German friend read this version of my story, and said, "Wasn't there a law against this?" I replied, "A law in Mississippi?"

cook's house, squatting on opposite sides of the pan and rang our glasses together with the word, "Toast." After emptying the bottle of Port, we collapsed into fits of giggles, became sleepy and asked Sophie, the cook, to allow us to take a nap on her bed. I can still see Sophie's man rocking in a chair, while Jan and I quietly passed out.

When we started to play in Sophie's house, we made a serious discovery. Sophie's house faced the back street that was parallel to the front street. This was a gravel street with some small houses leading to the black part of town. There were hedges bordering this street in which we had hideouts. One Saturday afternoon we found about six bottles of some sort of spirits in the ivy that grew around these hedges. We took them and placed them in another hideout in the side yard. We tried to taste one, but it smelled like urine. The following Saturday afternoon there were more bottles bearing the same scent and all were in half-pint bottles labeled, 'Old Kentucky.' We noticed that if we made a search at three in the afternoon there were no bottles, but when we returned at half past four there were many. Mississippi was a dry state, so we were on to something. We made solemn promises not to tell our mothers. Our stock had risen to twenty-seven bottles, when Jan broke down and told Janula. After that Mr. Stafford, the town sheriff, drove down the street at the strategic hour and our adventure in bootlegging was over.

During this period I remember that race relations were so easy that strange black people deposited their groceries each Saturday evening on Aunt Mary's front porch. The screen door was never locked. After going to town in the early hours of the morning, they collected their groceries, and Jan and I would hear people cross the side yard as we nestled on an adjoining sleeping porch. One could have sprung the lock on the front door with a butter knife. No man or pistol had lived in the house for fifty years. Twelve years later, Jan was at home from Ole Miss for a weekend. She and Janula went to bed rather late and somehow remembered to lock the bedroom doors. A man came into the long hall, high on something and

Jan Davis sitting on the lap of her Grandmother Aunt Mary
Poitevent, quarantined against polio.

laughing. He tried to enter the bedrooms, but as the doors were locked, he waited for a short time. Gwin had given Janula a pistol, but neither knew how to use it. The telephone directory was in the hall, although they had an extension phone in the bedroom. Jan pulled the wire of the extension phone into the bathroom and crawled on her stomach into the bathroom to make a call. They were afraid to turn on a light and Jan tried to dial the only number that she could remember, that of Margaret Rose Reeves, with whom she had been out that evening. All the time the man was pushing at the bedroom door. Mr. Reeves answered and the police were there within minutes. The intruder was armed. Shortly after that Janula moved away and remarried, to Mr. Jimmie Anderson, the teacher who had separated me in my grand fight. In the 1990's Nan Shelby's house was broken into twice. By that time she was a widow and living alone. One man was found hiding in her shower with a large butcher knife. Afterwards, she moved to Cleveland.[6]

*

I chose a dirty spot to tell Jan about the facts of life, which I had learned from older girls when I was eight. I took her to my back lot and sat Jan between two garbage cans. She squatted on her little pink legs with her trusting blue eyes looking up at me. "Jan, they all do it, even the Methodist minister does it. It happens down there. They put it together. That's how babies are born." I watched her disbelief and added, "It's in the Bible. It is called committing adultery." This encompassed all whom she had loved and trusted, but she acknowledged that my reference was good. Suspicious, she asked Aunt Mary what committing adultery meant. "It is in the Bible."

Aunt Mary replied, "Oh Jan, there are so many big words in the Bible, I don't know the meaning of everything." Jan began to doubt her beloved grandmother.

We were still free to carefully cross the highway to Denton's ice cream plant, carrying two nickels to buy an ice cream cone, safe from polio be-

---

6 Shelby, Nan Wilkinson, *A Portrait In Words* New York, New York, 2005 p. 131

cause the ice cream was frozen, the cone protected in a paper container, and there were no children at the plant.

After all games had been exhausted we played "cars." We would sit on a wicker swing on the front porch and count the cars coming from the north and the south. The one who got the most cars won the game.

As autumn arrived, school started, polio subsided, and on a Saturday Jan and I had a rummage sale. We erected a clothesline on the street. Then it occurred to me that we could move the line a bit north and have our sale in front of the Methodist Church. "We are not telling a story, we are not saying anything, but more people will buy from us because they will think it is for the Church." We made about sixty dollars. Mother insisted that I give my share to Aunt Mary, as the clothes had belonged to Jan and Janula. I didn't mind; the fun was in the sale.

When I was about twelve I visited my cousin Cathryn Carnes in Memphis. She opened a large closet with neatly stacked games on shelves and asked me what I wanted to play. "Nothing." Then she said, "What are the fads in Shelby?" I had never heard the word and mispronounced it, enquiring, "What are fades?"

"Fads. They are something that everyone does for no reason, like turning up your socks and then turning them down one inch."

"I would never do anything that everyone did, especially for no reason." As a child, the city had no attraction apart from buying clothes and going to the Peabody Hotel.

We went back to the picture shows in the winters where there was always a polio appeal before the main feature. One saw a darling little boy on crutches, and Howard Keel sang "Walk on, walk on, with hope in your heart and you'll never walk alone." After that song there was a collection. It was my job and Becky's to pass the corrugated cardboard box. Howard Keel had us reduced to tears by the time that we reached the second row.

Every February, to coincide with the March of Dimes (established by President Roosevelt), towns throughout the Delta held an annual, if incongruously named, "Polio Ball." These were far more democratic than the other Delta dances, for one paid to attend. Every white person in town was encouraged to dance for polio.

At last there came the first ray of hope, the gamma globulin injection. These were given if one had been exposed to polio. I took it once. Kate Hollingsworth, the new doctor's wife, put me into a room in the Shelby Clinic (not air-conditioned) and told me to kneel by the bed, where one enormous needle was inserted into one cheek and then into the other. I promptly fainted. A year later we had the Salk vaccination and summers returned to swimming pools, and calling the telephone operator to find out the film features in Clarksdale and Cleveland. After that we cruised the towns in the Delta to meet boys and go to the picture shows. At last we were all able to eat at hamburger stands with flies. I say condescendingly that today we would have been playing computer games during the polio epidemic.

Stories

When my grandmother from Memphis died in 1949, Mother endeavored to divert Grandpapa from his depression by reading to us after the enforced polio naps. The book that she chose was *Gone With the Wind*. I was spellbound and brought Bobbie Lou into these literary afternoons.

Mother had started reading to me early in life, when a friend of my grandmother Carnes had sent me Bible stories. During an episode of the flu she read to me about Abraham, Isaac, Joseph (the most interesting to me), Lot and his wife, and then brushed it off with the Sermon on the

Mount. After that there had been *Tom Sawyer*, *Huckleberry Finn*, *Bambi*, *The Secret Garden*, *Black Beauty* and eventually we were reduced to the *Miss Minerva and William Green Hill* series. I was amazed to hear that William Green Hill had existed in Covington, Tennessee, and that he was my father's second cousin. The first book had been such a success that it inspired eighteen other books by a different author, when the original author died. All of this exciting life of children on paper inspired Bobbie Lou and me to think that we were missing out.

Until the Civil War captured our imaginations, we had been dominated by *Calamity Jane*. During that period we purchased cowboy shirts from Mr. Lamensdorf's dry goods store on the street every Saturday afternoon. The shirts cost $2.98. We played "hide-out" in my back lot and built big fires on our land next to Holmes Lake and on the empty lot near Bobbie Lou's house. In order to keep up with the characters in our books, we decided to have bad days, when we let the air out of Cousin Joe's tires and tampered with her water meter. Without telling Nan what we had been doing, mother redirected us into literature.

Mother's readings lasted into the late evenings, when she was still on the porch with a moth fluttering around her floor lamp. Bobbie Lou and I demanded that the readings continue through the winter afternoons. We would buy a box of Millionaire Turtles from Willard Rose's Sundry Store in the center of the town and rush home, place the chocolate turtles on the coffee table, stand on our heads, with our feet on the couch, swallowing turtles upside down and absorbing literature. If Mother reached a sexy part, she pretended that she had lost her place and we would shout, "You are skipping! You are skipping!"

I never read another children's book after I was eight. By the time that Bobbie Lou and I had finished junior high school, we had been introduced to the Bronte sisters, Jane Austin, Daniel Defoe, Victor Hugo, *Little Women* (which we found boring), Daphne du Mauriac, Pearl Buck, Summerset Maugham, Mark Twain, and other Books of the Month, which Mother saved for summer readings. It never occurred to us that this had anything to do with education, until we realized that we did not need to put out any effort on a book report. We were free to play.

Gone with the Wind remained my favorite. Mother read it to me five times, until I had the movie memorized up to the point where Scarlett left the hospital when the confederate soldier's leg had to be amputated. We always read it in the first edition because we liked to turn the pages. The first edition belonged to Lucie Weissenger, the intellectual of the street, having come to our part of the Delta as a governess for the Smith girls at Hillhouse, a large plantation near Clarksdale. She married their bookkeeper, Alan Weissenger. He was rotund and a cousin of mother's friend, Kathryn Henderson, and had successfully taken over her father's business. Lucie came to the door with her cigarette on a holder and her glasses on the end of her nose. When she spoke, the fact that she was also fat and intellectual-looking vanished. She impressed us as a true aristocratic intellectual in all of her mannerisms. Her walls were lined with first editions. She taught me the thrill of a first edition. It was just as it came into this world, no chance for the author to re-think, or for an editor to re-draft. Over the mantle was a portrait of her grandmother with a slash at the bottom. It had never been repaired, but was left as a reminder of what a Yankee soldier had done on their plantation in Issaquena County.

As the summers progressed Mother would telephone Lucie and say, "Lucie, Carole and I are just feeling like *Gone with the Wind* again." Shortly afterwards a little boy appeared at our front door re-delivering the first edition.

Bobbie Lou introduced me to another civil war book, *Tap Roots*. I wasn't as keen as she, for the book contained an amazing incident: the hero kissed the heroine's bosom, even kissed her nipples, which were to me such ugly brown things. Nevertheless, we hid it between the mattress and springs of my bed. Not only did the Civil War remain vividly alive, but also other stories implanted a similar personality on a large number of people in the Delta. We read for the story. A friend of mine from Germany recently visited the Delta with me and commented that we all talked alike. That is because we talk with one thing in mind, the passion for the story.

Heat, Singing, Death, Birth, 1952

The crops required three rains. Erratic seasons of drought had not occurred regularly. There was one drought in the twenties and another in the early thirties. After that the three rains promised by natural rhythms continued. No farmer had irrigation. In 1952 the first late-April rain came, producing a stand of cotton. Afterwards it struggled as weed, certainly not in the manner that cotton should blossom. The July rain did not arrive. There was one last hope, the August rain. Weeks seemed as long as months while we held our breath and prayed for that vital August rain. Cracks became an inch wide in the earth and crickets abounded, covering the front entrance to our house. We rushed inside after the picture show, but not in time to ward off the crickets. They invaded the house, bedrooms, and bathtubs, making a racket all night, jumping onto the beds.

Cotton struggled between large cracks in the earth, developed a few blooms, then squares, but the squares fell off. A farmer's business depended on a loan from the Production Credit Company in Clarksdale. This usually meant enough for his family to live on comfortably and for his hired hands to survive and to pay for fertilizer, crop dusting, mortgages on tractors and combine machines. This season left the workers with nothing to do and at the end of summer the rice farm would probably be lost. My father was fifty-seven and doubted if he would still farm at fifty-eight.

The people on our place started singing spiritual songs in order to boost their spirits and fill their time. Their singing was inspiring and soon they were on a radio program in Clarksdale every Sunday, where we listened with admiration and then pride as a song was dedicated to Daddy. The loan of the credit company covered the living expenses of the labor, although they would have no profit at the year's end, and it was highly probable that they might have to find another farm/plantation.

The singing took place on a front porch of one of the houses on our row of cabins on the other side of the street. Heat did not absorb into the earth when the sun went down. The white people who came to listen perched on the front of their cars and we still sweltered. Music provided the only cheerful part of the day. A flash of lightning would come and inevitably went away, leaving us with only the consoling echoes of the spirituals.

One wonderful night I remember Nee Nee taking the prominent place on the steps of the red cabin. She belted out her song as none other could sing. Afterwards a few men sang, then Annie, now heavily pregnant, was moved to sing her own song and she did it with almost the same voice as her mother. By this time Annie had two children, Carole Christian and W. L. Tucker.

A few days later Nee Nee told us that Carole was very ill. She had to remain in Dr. Rubensoff's clinic. Dr. Rubensoff, a good doctor who had been born in Russia, practiced medicine on the street. He quickly realized that Carole's case should be referred to a doctor in Memphis, and she was sent to the John Gaston Charity Hospital. Poor people had no health insurance, and even today there remains little assistance except for Medicare for the old and Medicaid for poor children (we await the results of new legislation called Obamacare, unless it is somehow made dysfunctional). The States has been the last sophisticated society in almost one hundred years to neglect a national health system.

Nursing this pretty six-year old little girl fell primarily upon Lizzie, for Annie was so heavily pregnant that the hospital did not think it safe for her to spend much time there. Despite the doctor's warning, Annie took many turns. Carole was never left alone. Lizzie was then fifty-seven and the only place that the hospital offered for either Lizzie or the pregnant Annie to sleep was a chair. On one or two occasions a nurse gave Lizzie her bed.

At first they thought that Carole could have polio, but this was soon ruled out. They tapped her spine. She was constantly subjected to needles while the medical students from the University of Tennessee Medical School looked on. In Lizzie's opinion, she was used as a guinea pig. Lizzie was not one to hurl accusations, for she was balanced in her judgments. But no parent can watch her child suffer.

My own parents did everything they could do. Daddy telephoned Dr. Raines, a prominent urologist in Memphis, and he looked into the case on a *pro bono* basis. He contacted other important doctors. Daddy telephoned families in Memphis and asked them to invite Lizzie to stay at their house, but she would not budge from her chair beside Carole.

We all prayed. I promised God that if she would live, I would not smoke. Then I spent the night with Bobbie Lou and smoked, as I decided that God did not care about that promise. Soon afterwards Carole died, diagnosed by the chorus of doctors as having tubercular meningitis. Lizzie's brother, Anderson, had contracted tuberculosis when Carole was very young. He spent some time at their house. Looking back over the last year of her life one could see dark circles appearing under her eyes. She was such a well- looked-after little girl that one noticed these symptoms only in hindsight. Although her life was short, she was greatly loved. Lizzie once said that she had loved her too much. In her reckoning, perhaps she had put the child before God.

The heat did not subside, usually reaching 105 degrees Fahrenheit in the shade. When the sun went down the singing began. Other churches joined the group on our farm for a final singing. A grandstand was erected on the west side of the railway track, in front of the shops. All of the chorus members were dressed in white. Everyone in town attended. This happened on the evening of Carole's funeral. I can still see the streetlight reflected on the face of Nee Nee in a white dress coming to sing.

The August rain never arrived. That year we ginned only one-fourth bale of cotton to an acre. The Production Credit Company had a squeeze on most of the farmers. Daddy was good at trading in land, and managed to sell one third of the rice farm for a good price. He took a good salaried job as the Postmaster for eighteen months, and rented out the rest of the rice farm, where they now began to grow rice. He continued to farm the D. P. Shelby land and after two years he was back onto his feet. Our standard of living was not diminished, but the transition must have been difficult, even humiliating, for he had not had a job since the Depression. He saved most of his own farm.

A month after Carole's death, Annie produced twin girls, born at the hospital on the street. It looked as though they would both live. Mother brazenly asked if she could name them and Lizzie and Annie agreed. Mother said that no one had ever been named for her and she would like for one to be called May and the other Madia, for her aunt, Mrs. Murnan. As an afterthought she said, "Name the largest one for me, because I have had enough bad health in my time and I don't want anything weak named after me." The largest twin was called May, but they decided to spell the names differently and they became Mae and Madie Bee.

The two little girls were both good looking and attracted attention when they walked down the street. People would stop Annie to say, "Just let us look at them." A heavier fence was built around Lizzie's cabin and no children came to play with the girls except by invitation. They were not allowed to swim in streams. Always dressed as little dolls, both grew to be delightful, pretty, unspoiled young women. Madie was diligent at her studies. The light over their bed would be on long after Mae had gone to sleep. Mae was good at sports and always a little taller. Lizzie said that she took Madie and Annie took Mae. Madie graduated from Texas Christian College and managed the accounts for an electrical company in Dallas before retiring a few years ago to look after her mother and then becoming a court reporter. Mae remained in Shelby and became a caregiver. They had five daughters between them. All have finished university. Two of Mae's daughters have master's degrees in computer studies. Madie's daughter Theresa is a mathematic teacher with a degree from the University of Texas and her other daughter Jenifer graduated from Baylor University. Annie had two more sons, Dan Christian (Carole's full brother who died in 2008) and Calvin Giles. Annie's children had good jobs. W. L. Tucker was a caterer in Chicago, before his health forced him into retirement and he died in 2005. Dan was a manager for several branches of Sears and Roebuck in the Dallas/ Fort Worth area before his death. Calvin, the mischievous one, ran a housing development in Coahoma County, Mississippi, preached on the weekends, and is now pursuing further studies in computer management. Much effort by the extended family was put into these children. All were given a strong Christian upbringing and were able to take some rewards from America's pool of promise.

Lessons on becoming a Southern Belle

One summer afternoon when I was about ten, my mother enticed me to listen to her advice by saying, "If you come up on my bed, I will tell you what it is going to be like to become a young lady." I was curious and she continued. "This is a time in life when you have no responsibilities to a husband or to a child or even an older parent. It is a time for you to have lots of pretty dresses and play the field. But it is nevertheless an important time. A lady who has a good 'young ladyhood' has confidence for the rest of her life. It is also important, because this is the time that she selects her husband. If she marries too young she misses her young ladyhood, and too late, they all say, 'she is on the shelf.' "

"You must make sure not to become committed to a man until you are engaged. Throughout your life you must accept that all of the balls are in the man's court, but if you know how to handle them they will protect you and put you on a pedestal. Nevertheless, they are the ones who invite you to go somewhere and they are the ones who must propose."

I didn't like this inevitable inequality, but I was intrigued.

"Remember you must treat a little boy and later a man just like a puppy. Rub his fur in the right direction. Don't ruffle him, handle him."

"You will go to many dances where you meet all sorts of young men, but the boy must ask the girl to go to the dance. You can't ask him; he must ask you. It is often the unattractive boy who will take you to the dance or dinner party where you will meet the attractive one, so be polite to all invitations. Even if a boy telephones you to go fishing, reply enthusiastically, 'I would love to go fishing; what an interesting idea! But just this weekend I am going to Memphis with my parents.' Try to at least look like you are interested in their conversations. It isn't always easy. I had a beau from Chicago who stayed so long and talked on and on about his business of selling air-conditioning to department stores that I had to tip-toe back to the bedroom and ask Mama to please come out and help me entertain him. Mama was good at that; she arrived on the porch and no one would have faintly suspected that even she was not spellbound by his conversation. She had the ability of hanging on to every dreary word."

"Remember, the most attractive and sought-after young men have doubts about themselves when approaching a girl, so don't be intimidating, simply make them feel good." That was a relief to know.

"Now I hope that you are not going to be free with your kisses. It never pays. They grow bored with what they have. Keep men guessing." I had to think about that. "Then she added, "would you prefer to be that gold necklace in Broadnax on a velvet cover behind a glass case with a high price tag or the cheap one in Sterling's that is tarnished because everyone has handled it?" Well that was a sales pitch that was hard to refuse.

"Now you will probably do all right at dances, because we have given you ballet lessons for years, but remember, if you get stuck with a boy, don't look miserable. All the boys will break the girl who is having many breaks; they follow the pack, but everyone gets stuck now and then. If you pretend that you are having a good time, someone will break in on you and you can change partners. Stay cheerful and remember that some boy's mothers have instructed them to do a duty dance with every girl from Shelby. You will be released. If you look miserable no one will come and you will dance on and on with the same partner."

"You have probably already noticed that most of the girls like the same boy, so don't go around telling your secrets. Girls will double cross you."

"Well, who can I tell my secrets to?"

"Me."

"That is not enough, who else?"

"I don't know. I always had my sister Zula to share my secrets. I suppose Jan."

"The point is," she continued, "that a woman's success is dependent on love, where a man's success is dependent on money. Don't trust a woman with love or a man with money. Later in life you will have some money and if any man tries to borrow from you, say very sympathetically, 'I can give you a little money from my income, but the principal is tied up.' Then he will be embarrassed to take a gift. Men develop many excuses to get into someone else's pockets: they need it for their children, you spend too much, and the rationalization goes on and on. Well, I am off the subject; just learn how to handle men and your own money and enjoy this period of your life."

"And furthermore, when you decide upon a husband, set your sights high. Love is important but it is not all, especially if you end up clerking in a department store every day. Don't marry for love only. Look at so many of the Murphree girls; they were pretty, but many of them only believed in love. Marry brains, not money. People lose money but brains are a better investment."

I didn't like the part about secrets, but was looking forward to all the clothes I would have.

Then she added, "You must do something about your table manners. You can't go out to dinner with a young man and spill things or put your elbows on the table, and remember not to order the most expensive thing on the menu or the cheapest, order something in between."

I replied, "I won't go out to dinner."

"Oh, you have to, when a young man is serious about a young lady or engaged, he always takes her out to dinner."

I developed a mental picture of a French restaurant with tiles on the floor and mirrors on the walls and this man in a suit with a blank face sitting opposite me, the fiancé, while I struggled with a steak. With that advice I always ordered fried shrimp. I could easily cut off most of it and dip it into the tartar sauce and make a dive for my mouth and it only cost $1.25.

Love

Throughout my school days I remained uncoupled. I suppose my dreams were too high. Becky had one steady boyfriend after the other from the time she was in the second grade, but she had dimples and a beautiful singing voice. Ann was always in love, and even after seventy was destined to attract men. Mimi was in and out of love every week. Jan found her husband, Walter Clark from Clarksdale, when she was in the tenth grade. Bobbie Lou and I remained aloof. She was clearly the most beautiful girl in the Delta, and my head was far above the clouds.

Even Bobbie Lou fell deeply in love when she reached the tenth grade and obtained a football jacket from Will Gourlay from Rosedale. I was the only one to be left with my imagination, often sitting in our car, gazing over Holmes Lake, and singing "Somewhere over the Rainbow," to myself.

Love began with the movie stars. I was besotted with Clark Gable. I would kiss his photographs in magazines and say to myself and Becky, "He is only forty years older than I am; that is not too much." Becky never discouraged me, for Becky's boyfriends did not deter her from falling in love with movie stars. We had a large poster of Marlon Brando over our beds. Then there was James Dean. Marlon Brando was only twenty years older, totally dislodging my loyalty to Clark Gable. I even wondered if Gable did have false teeth and bad breath as Vivian Leigh had alleged. When I was twenty-five I encountered Brando on an elevator in the Ritz Hotel in New York, instantly recognizing the profile from the poster. He was dressed in a silk suit and could have been mistaken for an ex-professional football player, had it not been for the nose. When I was forty-five I noted in a local newspaper in England that the then fat and pony-tailed Brando was considering buying a house in Oxfordshire. I still thought of ways of tip-toeing away from my husband and meeting my beloved fantasy. That man did more for women's imaginations than the whole film industry, which he called "Frozen monkey vomit".

Becky and I had another, slightly more approachable, crush: Richard Widmark. He epitomized all that was European to us. (Although we now know that he came from the Midwest). Perhaps for our benefit he had not changed his name to Rick Williams. It sounded thrillingly Germanic, perhaps an aristocrat. We played a naughty game and took turns being Richard Widmark. I would put on a blue pajama top and be the man. Then Becky donned the same pajama top. We kissed and squeezed each other in the missionary position, making sure to put toilet paper between our lips. We *certainly* did *not* want to touch in any significant manner! This occurred while Mother and Ruth Morrison drank coffee and passed peanut butter candy in the next room.

When I reached the ninth grade, aged fourteen, I began to go out so-cially to sub-deb dances, which were held at the Courthouse in Rosedale. The Courthouse had been designed for multiple purposes, with removable seats for dances and a Courtroom for trials. The rostrum was decorated with magnolia leaves painted silver, and there was an archway under which each very young girl was presented to Delta Society. The sub-debs had two escorts and a coterie of stags (boys) was invited, assuring us of many breaks during the dances. (Delta boys tapped a partner on the shoulder and broke into the dance; it was mortifying to be stuck and dance with the same boy for one or two pieces.)

Mary Elizabeth Wilson, an enthusiastic lady from Rosedale, sponsored these dances, because she wanted to give young people good memories, memories similar to the ones that she had been privileged to enjoy from her Delta youth. She succeeded. Each girl paid fifteen dollars to be a member of this cotillion. Mary Elizabeth also had a cornucopia of attractive male cousins who were slightly different from the other boys in the Delta. They all came from a tiny town, Sumner, Mississippi, and most of them went to Webb School in Bellbuckle, Tennessee. Not only had a large number of my family attended this school, but also Midnight Sun, the famous walking horse, still grazed in the nearby town of Wartrace, Tennessee. In Master Webb's days, whipping took place in a special building without heat. De-spite the whipping, most of the products of the Webb School, as it was called officially, were normal, sensitive, tough and well educated.

I fell deeply in love at my first sub-deb dance, when I was only four-teen. The recipient of this idolization was one of Mary Elizabeth Wilson's cousins who was already at Princeton on a scholarship for his outstanding performance at Webb School. He looked like Scott Fitzgerald and was four or five years older than I. He flirted with me twice a year, filled my dreams, danced with me, put my hand next to his chest so that I could feel the prickly hairs. There it stopped. I lived from sub-deb ball to sub-deb ball in order to see him, hoping every summer that we might somehow end up on the back seat of a Ford. I thought of cutting off my dark brown and auburn hair, my nicest feature, as a gift for him to take back to Princeton. My parent's were deeply pleased over this suspected fantasy, for it saved them from realistic worries.

I cultivated his cousin, Augusta Wilson, Mary Elizabeth's daughter, who became my best friend. I even went out with his brother and his other cousins, desperate to acquire news of him. Bobbie Lou was also lovesick for Will Gourlay. She would collect me to go to school every morning in her little maroon Ford coupe. We would listen to the soppy songs on the radio, smoke a cigarette, tease each other endlessly about our emotions and then arrive at boring old school.

The summers produced magic. There were dances all over the Delta, not only the ones where I hoped to see "The Man," but dances at the Odd Club in Clarksdale, dances in Cleveland, Ruleville, and Greenville. We became a tribe, those white Delta planters' children.

I had dances on my side porch. The most entertaining person who came was Bill Eggleston, a cousin of "The Man." He drove his grandmother's two-toned Cadillac and he was wired up, making the first Hi-Fi set I had ever seen. He erected this homemade contraption in our two cedar trees, no doubt to the misery of Madge and Charles Denton. After dancing Bill taught me about black music, tuning on to radio programs that Bobbie Lou and I had never heard on our romantic cruises listening to the Platters and Pat Boone. There was Bo Diddly, Little Richard, Jerry Lee Lewis, Muddy Waters. I was unsure of my taste in music and am no musician today, but I found the sound wonderful.

Bill and his cousin Tommy Lawrence took a drive during the intermission of one of the Rosedale dances. They rounded the curve and went off the road. The seat came up, the car turned over, but Bill still protected his forty-five of Chuck Berry singing "Roll Over Beethoven." Tommy was left to find his own way out of the automobile, but they were both back at the dance in time to hear Rufus sing Danny Boy.

Bill would telephone me and play a record from Webb School. The call was charged to his grandmother, who was his greatest supporter. Although his cousins were getting scholarships to the best universities in the States, Bill remained indifferent to his studies, and his parents despaired. His grandmother stood by him and contended that Bill was *the* genius in their family, for he had perfect pitch and played the piano beautifully without a single lesson. I protested against their pretensions and once more declared that *I* was going to be a famous actress. Bill replied, "I shall buy all of the seats in the house and be the only one applauding." In the autumn of 2002, when I was nearly sixty-two, I went to an exhibition of photographs at the Haywood Gallery in London. The banner over the doorway said, "Ansel Adams, William Eggleston." I was in the audience of many people applauding for one of the world's most famous photographers.

I lost hope over "The Man" by the time that I became a senior in high school. My only relaxation that year was to read *The Commercial Appeal* from the scroll in the school library, because I was seriously paying attention in school in order to escape. The front page depicted one Shelby Tucker. "Mother Stoutly Defends his Stormy Record." Shelby Tucker and Walter Raleigh Coppedge from Rosedale, Mississippi, both students at Oxford University, were in Moscow at the World Youth Conference. They preached in the streets against Communism. Then the Chinese offered them a free trip to China, crossing Russia on the Trans-Siberian Railway. This happened during the peak of the Cold War and only one American had ventured into Red China. The headlines for days were "Would they or wouldn't they go?" There was a prohibition by the State Department for all holding United States passports to go to either the Communist Republic of China or North Korea. Coppedge decided to forget the adventure as he had his doctorate to finish. Tucker went to China. *Life* featured him when he was finally expelled from China. (There had been a promise by the Chinese that they would not ask for passports). After ten well-feted and glorious days in The Republic of China, they went back on their promise and demanded all passports. When Shelby Tucker refused to submit his passport, he was deported and sent back across the Soviet Union on another tedious trip on the Trans-Siberian Railway. Others in the group stayed on. *The Commercial Appeal* was full of this amazing young Oxford student, who had traveled around the States and Mexico with $1.62, before receiving a scholarship to Andover Academy and after that Yale, and was set to take a degree in Law from Oxford. When he returned from this forbidden trip he would be a candidate for The House of Un-American Activities Committee. Speculation was that Tucker's passport would be withdrawn. He would lose any chance of a degree from Oxford. The President of Corpus Christi College, Oxford, fined him £5 for going away without the President's permission. Tucker returned to the States with his degree.

My legs dangled from the seat in the Shelby High School library and I declared to myself, "I can't catch "The Man," but Shelby will love me, because we are cousins and he will understand me."

Exit

My mock Scholastic Aptitude Tests had been so dismal. Sweet Briar and Randolph Macon required four years of language, which Shelby High School did not offer. These colleges had been my anticipated heritage. It was too late to go to boarding school and achieve four years of language credits, and there was another crop disaster. Our wonderful Latin teacher, the Superintendent's wife, Mary Evelyn Walker, left with her husband who became an insurance executive in Jackson, leaving us with scarcely more understanding of Latin than "*Adeste Fidelis*" and no university credit, as colleges only gave one credit for two years of a foreign language. There arrived the pregnant football coach's wife with Spanish I. Nine of us were in her class, Thelma and Mary Alice Chow, Becky, me, Sandra Godbold and Louise Ann Burris, Martina and Alfa Burgess (the Mexican family who had stayed in Shelby) and Gus Denton. Our class began at 8:05. She started every morning with "Buenos Dias, Senoritas" or "Senor Dentona" (our names pronounced in Spanish). Her imagination dropped for the Senoritas Chow. I was late every morning and she repeated the same remark, "Buenos Dias, Senorita Carnez, Senorita Carnez esta tarde." Still we sang, "Alla en el Rancho Grande," and played a few silly games and finished the textbook. The following year Senora Cotton moved to another football post, leaving us with another lost credit. Becky and I had been so happy to finally be in a class together that we had passed notes throughout the period and were the only ones who finished the year without a word of Spanish. If it had not been for the university requirement the lost credit would not have been missed.

Shelby High School was on the verge of closing its language department, when Mother and Mrs. Chow protested that their children were going to universities that required at least two years of a foreign language. (Even in my mother's day the school offered three years of Latin and two years of French.) Reluctantly they found the only person they could get, an ex-Delta debutante, who had probably studied no more than three or four years of Spanish and stayed one lesson ahead of the class. Then Thanksgiving arrived and she went off to New York for several weeks. We got our credit and took the tests required for a private university.

As my mock tests had been so dismal, even in the subject in which I was best, English, my parents hired a tutor for the summer before my senior year. Nanette Jacobs had taught school for many years until her nerves precluded the further struggle. She displayed an elaborate use of English, the ideal person to improve my vocabulary. I spent the summer mornings on her front porch. We simply made sentences and talked about the meaning of words and their derivatives. She was a wonderful and enthusiastic teacher.

My grades easily improved from a C+ average to an A average in the last two years of high school. The other side of the report card that said "pays attention in class" rocketed from a 4 to a 1. It wasn't a giant effort. However, I had to compete with baby boomers from all over the States who had received good high school educations. Good private universities were only taking one in every four applicants, and Shelby High School had probably produced no more than seven or eight students in the past thirty years who would attend an out-of-state private university that was not a ladies' society school, as Sullins had been, my mother's alma mater.

I had taken a National Merit Scholarship Test designated to find people from remote parts of the States and give them a scholarship to go to the best colleges. I was not a finalist, but to my surprise did rather well in mathematics and something called space (which I believe was simply reason).

My cousin Shelby Taylor who lived in Baton Rouge, Louisiana (the grand daughter of my Great Aunt Ellen), had recently met a lady canvassing the South for young women on behalf of Vassar. The lady had a special interest in those with talent. Shelby knew that my talent was acting, and immediately telephoned mother, but I was never allowed to apply. "Vassar is a college where you will only meet Yankee men. They are very attractive, but they are hard-boiled. They do not treat women as treasures the way that Southern men do. Many of them don't even *believe* in servants. At the end of the day, your life will be nothing but the kitchen sink. It happened to my cousin Ella Mae. Besides if you are an actress you will only have a divorce." I was not allowed to apply to any college above the Mason-Dixon Line.

Two girls from Cleveland and I were up at five in the morning on a dreadfully rainy December day. There had been another crop disaster, this time constant rain, which prohibited me from going away to boarding school for my senior year. At six that morning, I entered Juliet Kossman's bathroom in Cleveland and watched her patient mother insert her new contact lenses. They were another key to the lock for getting out. We then collected Sue Davidow, three girls from Mrs. Hart's ballet class, and drove in this blinding rain for fifty miles to Greenwood to take the tests. There we met other young people from the Delta trying to get into a private university. The rich boys swaggered. There was a second chance at the test in January.

Much to our amazement, we three girls got through. My results weren't brilliant, but there were no re-sits. Then came the tedious applications. Mine had narrowed to three colleges, Vanderbilt University, Hollins College in Virginia, and Sophie Newcomb, the women's College of Tulane University in New Orleans. (These didn't have the four-year language requirement). I also applied to the University of Louisiana in Baton Rouge in the event that I was turned down by the other three. My parents prayed that it wasn't Hollins, which costs approximately one-third more than the other two institutions, and in addition there were the fares to Virginia several times a year. Although I had a string to pull at Vanderbilt, my father's cousin Ernest Williams, from Memphis, had got busy on a law case and forgot to pull the string. Vanderbilt was only taking one woman to every four male applicants, which was the reason many women applied. Also I changed my major at the recommendation of my friend Augusta Wilson (already there), changing it from Drama to English, while walking to the interview. This left Newcomb and Hollins, which I could not afford. As for LSU, one needed only a checkbook for a state university.

Spring arrived and all of my high school classmates were busy with their senior parties. I couldn't have cared less. When they played "Peyton Place," no one dived for me. I decided to telephone Miss Dorothy Dale, the Director of Admissions of Newcomb and enquire about my application. "You are on the borderline, with those who have only had an average performance on their tests."

"I have straight As."

"So does everyone."

"Well, I really want to go to Newcomb more than anything."

Two weeks later I received my acceptance. I can still recall the exhausting relief, when I went to another tedious party that night, thinking, "I am going to Newcomb; this world is over."

The first person I telephoned was Nanette Jacobs. Her tutoring had turned the tide in my life. She was so genuinely pleased. Her sincere joy in my good fortune was poignant in this case, because in the previous year, her daughter, Kristen, a National Merit Finalist, had been offered a scholarship to Newcomb, but they could not afford Newcomb, even with the scholarship.

In late August of 1962, two girls from the same street left Shelby for the same university, Thelma Chow and me. I entered college without having written a theme, only one term paper, book reports, and a few short stories, which my mother had composed. I would proudly sit in my desk while these stories were read aloud to the class and smiled as if to acknowledge my creation. These deficits in my early education still compromise my learning of languages and also my spelling.

Thelma's father, James Chow, owned a grocery store on the other side of the railway track dividing the town. He had come from Canton, as had Kuan Jon. James immigrated to the States and to the same side of the street in the early 1930's. After establishing himself as a successful merchant in the Delta, he returned to China and brought a young wife back to the States. Her name was Mae. She was only sixteen and looked like a doll. She learned her English behind the cash register in their store. They quickly produced a family of six children, four daughters and two sons and they lived in the back of the store for many years. Their apartment was divided by thin oriental partitions, but the furniture was nice. When the girls learned to play the piano, only the best piano was acquired. James became a Christian, joining the Baptist Church. He drove a very nice Buick and his wife was well known in the children's section of Levy's Department Store in Memphis, buying her daughters only the best of clothes. I went to school with the Chow family for twelve years. I was with Thelma for another four years at Newcomb. As papers were handed out, the top grades were on the top of the pile. They always bore the name, Chow. This family also hosted refugees from the mainland of China and sent them to our school.

One refugee was in my class. His name was Jerry Jong. He was about four years older than I was, but put back in school in order to learn to speak English, although he was very smart in every other subject. I still remember his gripping story of the Japanese invasion of China and being thrown into a pit with other Chinese, their only food was fat and gristle, thrown to them by the Japanese soldiers, where I refused to eat a bit of fat that I had left on my plate.

One day we heard that James Chow had a seat on the Memphis Stock Exchange.

After that his sons were sent to Memphis University School. Margaret, his oldest child, received a scholarship to Stanford University from Shelby High School. She must have been the smartest person who ever attended our high school. Most of us had not even heard of Stanford. Thelma, his second daughter, got into Newcomb with none of the nail-biting agony to which I had been subjected. They had been the first Chinese family to attend the Shelby Schools. Before the Chows arrival, other Chinese students had gone to the Chinese school, located between Cleveland and Dockery. It was painted yellow! The segregation of Chinese took place because in the early days Chinese merchants had often mated with black women and the segregated public wanted to make sure that no integration would take place indirectly.[7]

During the summer before college, I managed to raid Memphis's better clothing stores. When an attractive boy in Shelby finally paid attention to me on the Methodist tennis court, it was too late. I arrived at Sophie Newcomb with two trunks and five suitcases, filled with smart clothes. I had also learned to wear my contact lenses. Thus began four of the happiest

7 Cobb p. 174-175

years, from which I acquired interesting and loyal friends for a lifetime. I did not think that I would ever spend any time on that street again.

Part Four

The Other Side of the Street

(May and Carole's stories, 1911-2000)

May: Description

The other side of the street scarcely altered from my childhood to my daughter's childhood. It began south of our plantation with a mill that pressed cottonseed into oil. Much later, next to the oil mill there was a compress, which compressed the bales of cotton after they had been ginned, into small packets and bound them with straps for easy export to the textile mills in the eastern States. Adjacent to the compress was Daddy's mule lot, until tractors replaced mules.

This lot was the site of a big bonfire and barbeque when I was a child. Daddy had a bad crop. The labor owed him the money which he had lent them, called "furnish," as was the custom in the system called "share cropping," whereby the farmer gave the labor enough money to live. At the end of the year, after the crops had been gathered, they repaid the farmer and were supposed to receive about one third to one half of the profits. The system was ripe with a potential for abuse and has received much criticism. It existed throughout the rural South until the mid-1950s. On a year of a bad crop, instead of simply canceling the sharecroppers' debts, Daddy treated them to a party with barbequed ribs, beer and built a big bonfire, throwing the ledgers into the fire for all to see their debts go up in smoke.

Behind the mule lot was a water tower. Next to the water tower, in full view of our house was the commissary, where the labor were paid and supplies were stored. Throughout my marriage, Hayes never needed a telephone in his office, for I could always send someone across the highway to contact him, or to tell anyone calling that he would soon be at home because he had left the commissary. It was a one-room cabin. The foundation consisted of eight concrete pillars. There was a fireplace, a safe, and a roll-top oak desk behind a partition of wooden bars, where people were paid on Saturdays. In the desk there was always a pistol in case there was trouble. There never was trouble, except once, when in Hayes's absence the safe was burgled. Very little payroll had been left in the safe, but a collection of American coins that had been in his family for over two centuries was taken and no doubt discarded, as soon as the burglar found that he could not make a purchase with antique coins. On the south side of the commissary was a counter beneath which were barrels of flour, lard, cornmeal, sugar, coal, baking powder, tea, coffee, aspirin and cured hams (in Daddy's day). The front porch of the commissary was distinguished by one simple two-by-four connected to two posts and bent by the weight of many sitters, waiting to be paid.

Diagonally across a gravel road from the commissary was the cotton gin. Then there were a number of tenant houses abutting Holmes Lake. Following these houses was a schoolhouse, (the first black school in Shelby). Mr. H. L. Wilkinson had donated it to the colored people. Between the cabins and the gin came to be the stables of Mr. Gus Blanchard. At the end of our row of cabins was a colored Baptist church. Then we reached Mr. H. L. Wilkinson's cotton gin and after that the center of the town.

Two more perpendicular concrete streets separated two concrete streets, and before that were several buildings made of tin. One of these buildings was always a dentist's office. The other was lived in by a poor lady with curvature of the spine, Mrs. Carr, a white woman who took in sewing. She fitted many women suffering from hot flushes and their children fidgeting and inhaling and exhaling as the hems of their dresses moved up and down. She slept in the next room of this tin house, and beyond that room was her kitchen and an indoor bathroom. She may have had one fan.

When one reached the perpendicular parts of the street, one of which led to the residential area on the other side of Holmes Lake, was the Bank of Bolivar County on the corner, more stores, and across the street was the

Post Office, the Bolivar Hardware Company and later a lumber company, owned by the Thomas family. Daddy and Mr. H. L. Wilkinson owned the stores on the north side of this street.

The depot, as was customary, stood behind the railway track and behind the depot a row of stores, largely patronized by colored people. There was a red brick building that served as the telephone exchange. In the early days Kuan Jon owned one of these stores. "Shorty's" bar/hamburger place was located there. (That part of the street is depicted in the photograph on the cover of this book.) I never went inside of Shorty's, but could see the layout from the street. There were two entrances: on the south was the White door; on the north was the Colored door. I am told that in the middle was Shorty's grill and bar where men gathered, facing each other over Shorty's hash brown potatoes, onions, bacon, maybe fried eggs, and perhaps beer. Then they went out through separate doors. This section of the street ended with Mike Rowe's drug store, which was later James Chow's grocery store. Behind these stores was a street always called "the Alley." I could not describe much in "the Alley" except that it consisted of a number of tin shops or joints, and the street perpendicular to "the Alley" consisted of similar structures and ended with the Caboose, a tiny red brick room with crossbars. Only the marshal and the sheriff had the key. There was no office or booking room; it was simply a lockup room.

There followed on the street the Delta Gin, which was largely owned and managed by Scott Morrison, the husband of Ruth (J. W. Thomas's sister). Hayes and I had an interest in this gin. Next to that gin were the Dentons' cotton gin, flour mill, de-linting plant, ice cream plant, a few more houses for poor white laborers who worked for the Dentons, and another quarter, called Thomas's quarter, for poor white people, and another cotton gin at the end of the street. Two factories eventually appeared. The last landmark was the Austin Grove, later called Joe Nasser's steak house.

Carole: The Rules, As We Implemented Them

The cardinal rule in the South and in most of the Anglo Saxon world is that a white woman must never sleep with a Negro man; the woman who violates this taboo will be an outcast, never to be accepted by even the lowest stratum of white society. But when a Negro girl sleeps with a white man, not only is she not ostracized by the Negroes, she becomes an object of increased allure to Negro youths.

There were laws in Mississippi against marriage between black and white people, called miscegenation. These were part of the Jim Crow laws and varied throughout the South for more than a hundred years. It was a felony for a "Negro" or "mulatto" to intermarry with any white. The penalty in 1865 was a life sentence. This statute was revoked and then renewed. It was revised in 1880 and revised again, prohibiting a person with over one quarter Negro blood to marry a white, with the penalty being a fine of up to $500 or perhaps ten years imprisonment. In 1890 this statute was revised to include a "mulatto" with one-eighth "Negro" blood. In 1906 this statute was extended once more to include Asians or a person with one-eighth Mongolian blood. In 1920 a person who promoted support for such events was punished with a fine of up to $500 or six months imprisonment or both. In 1930 such marriages were nullified. If parties went to another jurisdiction their marriages were legal. The last miscegenation statute was in 1942, no doubt made with war brides in mind, making a marriage between a white and a "Negro" or Asian void with a penalty of a fine of $500 or ten years imprisonment. The Jim Crow Laws did not end until 1967 with the decision of *Lovingly v. Virginia* of the United States Supreme Court, and thereafter the laws in Mississippi died a reluctant death until 1973.[1]

Other laws were passed, abolished, and passed again segregating transport. There were different laws for jury service and voting. I write about

---

1 Appendix C Jim Crow laws, on line

*The commissary, painted by Martha Giesler Long of
Shelby, Mississippi in the 1960s.*

what actually happened. We had close friends who had this degree of African American blood and it did not matter. Their daughters were in the best sororities at the University of Mississippi and were belles of the balls. Did their families live in the terror of a very dark child?

Lee Jackson from Rosedale brought home a very sophisticated Chinese bride after World War II. The upper middle class Jacksons didn't know what to do with her. They braced up and invited the Chinese grocer's wife to tea. Anne frankly told them that this was a very nice woman, but the kind who would have been her amah in China. She spoke French with a Russian accent, because her governess had been a white Russian. Mary Elizabeth Wilson, who lived in Rosedale, gave a tea for them. The ladies attended. This act of kindness sowed the seeds for a lifelong friendship. Lee and Anne (the most sophisticated person I ever met) were extremely nice to Mary Elizabeth's daughter, Augusta and to me, when we lived in Washington, in the mid-1960s. I feel confident that there was no attempt to enforce the statute against Lee and Anne Jackson. It was probably only used to deter mixed marriage couples from settling in Mississippi.

Every public and private facility that admitted the public had separate white and "colored" restrooms and separate water fountains, even in the courthouses. White restaurants served white patrons. "Colored" restaurants were located in the less desirable parts of the towns. Even drive-ins served only white people, although the waiters were usually black.

On buses and trains, black people went to the back, even if there were only one or two white people on the bus. I often heard the driver talk about "the situation" to an old white woman on the front row, oblivious to the majority of his passengers. It is surprising that the black people didn't riot. And yet in other ways the drivers were often extremely courteous to black people, making special stops off their route so that they didn't have to walk too far from their houses.

Black women were called women, never ladies. Neither were they addressed as Mr. and Mrs. in the post. When white people reached sixteen or seventeen, they were to be called Mister or Miss by all black people. This rule had been relaxed by the time that I grew up, but today some still call my husband 'Mister'. We were Jan, Becky, Bobbie Lou, Cahl and Mimi, and no one stopped them from calling us by our first names for by then our parents understood the close relationships which had developed and that times were becoming more lax.

All schools, churches, hospitals, and public waiting rooms were segregated. "Separate but equal" facilities did not exist. As noted in the 1896 Education statute, there were separate districts for white and black schools, which assured that the black school was in a poor district.

The neighborhoods did not mix. No one sold a house or a lot to a black person or even to an Asian. Black people lived in their part of town and it was feared that an Asian occupant may have kept the neighboring lots from being sold, so they built a nice house on the edge of town.

There was no medical assistance for poor of either races other than a charity hospital or their white employers' checkbooks. Many, perhaps most, were quite generous with doctors. It must be remembered they weren't as expensive in those days and this was part of the system of keeping labor. There was no government assistance for renting or buying houses. There were no laws to encourage equal opportunities in employment.

The implementation of law was not equal. If a white man committed a crime, he was prosecuted. Affrays by blacks among their own race were ignored by the law of "Saturday night." Black women often carried a long blade attached to their legs called a "Crabapple switch" to use in self-defense on a Saturday night. William Alexander Percy commented patronizingly on these phenomena.

> *The gentle devoted creature who is your baby's nurse can carve her boyfriend from ear to ear at midnight and by 7 a.m. will be changing the baby's diaper while she sings, 'Hear the lambs a calling,' or indulges in a brand of baby-talk obviously regarded as*

highly communicative and extremely amusing. Many white families expend a large amount of time, money, and emotion in preventing the criminals they employed from receiving their just deserts. They feel that the murderers and thieves in their service are not evil and have not been made more unfit for society by their delinquencies.[2]

The judge and jury were always white.

White people believed that a black man's libido was so high that special care must be taken not to encourage him. One placed money into the yard-man's hand by dropping it, so as not to brush against the palm and elicit excitement.

Black people came to white houses by the back door, except Lizzie, who entered the front door with her key. Then she received other black people at the back door, except her daughter, who came to the front door as well. Most white houses were equipped with a servants' toilet, either indoors or outside. Lizzie used any toilet that suited her. White people be-lieved that lavatory seats could transmit venereal diseases. I always stood over toilets at school and in the picture show, even though they were segre-gated. There remained undesirable white people.

White babies often suckled black women's breasts when their own mothers did not have enough milk. White women and children hugged and kissed black women. A handshake was the most contact they had with a black man, and this was on special occasions. They sometimes hugged an old and trusted black man, perhaps augmented with a pat on the head.

Black women ruled their society. They had the best houses on farms or plantations, if they were house servants. They had custody of their chil-dren. The men were fluid figures. Black people married often and simply 'quit' rather than obtaining a divorce. Their children were usually raised by grandmothers.

If white people loved and respected an elderly black man or woman,

2 Percy, 308-309

they called them 'Aunt' and 'Uncle', an affectionate rather than a pejorative term which many now consider it. Black people who were close to the family, sat with the family at funerals, shielded from the peering eyes of neighbors. They often sat in a pew behind the families at weddings. We also sat with their families at funerals. When Zachariah Cook died, Mother, Daddy and Cousin Fred were seated in the choir.

When I went to Sophie Newcomb (Tulane) in New Orleans, Asians were not rushed for sororities. Had Thelma Chow known this she no doubt have not applied to a women's college founded to educate upper class southern ladies, even though in our time they were anxious to recruit Asians for their academic excellence. However she seemed to like the place and went on to enjoy a junior year abroad. She later got her Master's degree from a university in California.

These rules were accepted as part of 'the system', thought to be necessary for the protection of society. The rules changed with the legislature of the 1960's and the Civil Rights movement at that time. One must not forget that Lyndon B. Johnson, not John F. Kennedy, was responsible for getting this legislature passed. Although it is amazing to me when I write or read this over forty years later that it actually was an accepted system by all I knew well and loved dearly, it also happened throughout the colonial world. The psychology is larger than my factual book. When integration arrived in the South there were more kind feelings between the races then in most parts of the country, because they had always lived in close proximity and sometimes (I do not say often) loved each other. It is said that in the South the black was an individual, in the North a generalization.

People We Remember
(Apart from Lizzie)

May: King Hollis

King lived on the other side of the street when I was a girl. He was Daddy's straw boss. Daddy called him King because of his superior manner. Daddy said that he was King of all the colored people and the name stuck. It was as much his fantasy as the one that Dr. DeMarco was a descendant of Marco Polo. King was nearly Daddy's age and he emulated many of Daddy's mannerisms. He wrote in the same precise penmanship that Daddy had learned under the monks at Christian Brothers School in Memphis. He was light skinned and even spoke like Daddy. He was not Daddy's son, for he was too old.

His children grew up and moved to the North, but King remained with us for several years after Daddy's death. Then he retired and moved to the North to live with them. We received Christmas cards from him for about ten years. They always included a precisely written letter as though written by Daddy about the events of his year. It gave me an odd sensation to see these envelopes. In return we sent him parched pecans from Mississippi.

May: The Daniels Family

I was sitting in the car outside of the commissary waiting for Hayes to finish paying people, when I saw a middle-aged colored woman and her young daughter come out and walk along the road. The daughter was about twelve years old and she walked on her ankles. She had been club footed from birth and her knee caps descended to the middle of her femurs. I met them in the mid-1930s. When Hayes appeared I said immediately, "Look at that!"

"Yes," he replied, "I was hoping you wouldn't see it. They are a good family. There are ten children, five men and five girls. They have been on our place for over eighteen months. All are all hardy workers. The first year they cleared their debts and made a thousand dollars. They were amazed." Mr. Daniels had died and the family had worked for another planter for almost twenty years and never cleared anything beyond repaying the amount furnished to them. Finally Ruby, the mother, decided to move.

"It is true that people have been treated that way."

"Well, I have seen it now. We must do something about this child."

"Now, don't pester me about everything. What on earth can we do?" he puffed.

I soon thought I knew what we could do. The Carnes family had a close friend who was an orthopedic surgeon in Memphis. He was very kind-hearted, almost as gentle as Cousin Fred. The next time that we visited Hayes's parents, I saw Dr. Lipscomb and told him about this girl, Bernice. Could anything be done?

His heart was touched, as I was sure it would be, and he volunteered his services for the operation, but he could not pay for the hospital. Hayes and his father contributed a certain amount towards the hospital bill and we even had a collection box at the commissary, so that the people on our land donated a few nickels, dimes, and quarters towards the hospital expenses. It was a joint effort.

Once the money was collected, I had reached the first hurdle. The next was Ruby. I told her that Dr. Lipscomb could operate on Bernice and he felt confident that she would no longer be crippled. Ruby sat numb. Then she shook her head. She had promised her husband that she would never do anything to the child. She would let her be. I pleaded in every way I knew possible. Finally, exhausted I said, "It is her life, not yours, or your late husband's. Let her decide. She is twelve years old."

Worn down by my argument, Ruby said that she would go home and think about it. A few days later, she returned and said that Bernice wanted the operation. "I have never gone against him before."

I would not be telling this story if the operation had not succeeded. Bernice always walked with a stiff gait, but her knee joints were put back into their sockets and her club feet were corrected. She was bright in every way, despite the limitations of the colored school in Shelby, which had now moved to a brick structure on a back street. She not only graduated with honors, she was also the first person from our farm that went to a university. She was educated in a college for colored people in Memphis and became a top-ranking teacher.

Soon after Bernice's operation, I discovered that I was expecting Carole. Ruby became our washwoman. She came to the house on Mondays and Tuesdays. Carole adored her, as Ruby had a natural way with children. Carole would not let her work for darting in and out among the clothes drying over the floor furnace. She called her Boo Boo, as she could not say Ruby. The name stuck, just as Lizzie's had become Nee Nee. The Daniels family together with Lizzie's family became our family. Rosalie, Carole's first nurse, was Ruby's daughter-in-law.

Our favorite was her son James, a good tractor driver on the farm; he performed many jobs around the house. Carole was besotted with James, and screamed and kicked from her high chair whenever he appeared. "James, James."

He quickly scampered out of the dining room, scarcely looking at the baby. Everyone teased James and asked him why he was afraid of the baby. He never acknowledged the reason, but in the back of my mind I knew that James was afraid that if anyone should tamper with the baby, he might be blamed. Colored women were Mamas, but colored men were afraid to be Papas. Throughout my life in the Deep South it had never occurred to me, until I saw James's fear of my baby.

One of Ruby's other sons, Preston, sewed. He moved north after the war, became a tailor, and had a family. He would have been much too individual for a Southern colored man. At the end of the 1940's Ruby announced that she was leaving us. She was moving to an Italian man's farm near the highway, south of town. She said that she could make more money because his land was better. He also gave her a white-painted house with electricity. We couldn't argue with that, but we were hurt.

James continued to work for us for a few years and then got a job working for a company in the town. He moved his family to the colored addition and bought a small white painted house. When he came to our house to do general cleaning, he talked of nothing but his notes and buying his house. He paid these notes to a rich man in Shelby. After about eight years of paying for his house, James was offered a job in a wholesale grocery company in Greenville. He had an opportunity to sell his house and went to this man to find out how much he still owed. He was told everything. A contract was produced. All of James' payments during those years had been interest. We were heartbroken for James. Of course he had not understood the contract, and I dare say that it had never been explained to him.

Ruby continued to come to our house if I needed special help. She liked us and she was always polite, but there was a different atmosphere. We sensed resentment. Her children had become active in the National Association for the Advancement of Colored People. Eventually she moved to Memphis and lived with Bernice[3].

Carole: Cevale, Rosalie and Jessie

I can still see an early home movie of me as a small child sitting in a wagon being filled with a bale of cotton. A very tall red-skinned man was emptying sacks of cotton into this wagon and I was throwing the cotton into the air. That man was Cevale. He had come to our farm with his father,

---

3 Ruby lived to a very old age and the Daniels had family reunions well into the 1980's. Lizzie often attended.

Jessie, from Tennessee. Jessie had been my father's nurse when he was a boy, and Jessie's father had been a slave on my great grandparents' farm near Summerville, Tennessee, about twenty miles north of Memphis.

When I was five Lizzie stopped working in the kitchen and devoted her full time to making a crop. Cevale had a new wife, Rosalie, a very light-skinned, pleasant woman who came to cook for us.

She had not been working for long when she failed to turn up one Sunday morning. The night before Cevale had been grabbed in the alley. His throat had been cut and he was left to die. Rosalie did not witness the murder, although she had been in the juke joint next to the alley. Daddy was grief-stricken. Poor old Jessie was still alive. Rosalie remained terrified that the murderer or murderers would come after her. She tried to continue working to keep her mind busy. Also, she needed what she perceived as our wing of protection.

The town marshal was of no use; he was simply a lockup man, who flashed the spotlight on the top of his car if notified that a burglar was about, making sure that the burglar vanished before he reached the scene. Daddy was devastated and contacted the Sheriff of Bolivar County in Cleveland. Men appeared and looked around the alley, but the Caboose remained empty. At dinnertime even a small child could feel her father's grief. He had brought the family down from Tennessee with the promise of offering Cevale a better job as a tractor driver and a gin hand, only to subject him to the law of "Saturday night." The Sheriff had done what was expected of him, but Cevale had not been farm labor; their relationship had gone back for three generations or maybe longer.

About six months later, Mother noticed that Rosalie's stomach was large. She was not pregnant and Mother insisted that she go to a doctor. Rosalie had a tumor. She was operated upon, but did not live very long. Their short lives made a deep impression upon me. We were left with Jessie, a thin little man, who had come down to the Delta at our invitation and seemed to shrivel away after this happened.

May: Octavia Jackson – A Free Spirit

After Rosalie died, I was once more without a cook. Carole and I were visiting the Tolers, who had moved back onto the street and into the Blanchard house after the Blanchards had moved away. Mrs. Blanchard and Mrs. Toler were sisters. We were having a nice visit, but I insisted on leaving, because a potential cook had made an appointment to be interviewed. They smiled and said, "She won't come; you may as well stay here."

"What do you mean?"

"It's part of the Disappointment Club."

This was shortly after the war and the Disappointment Club was an embryo of Civil Rights unrest. I went home, not believing them and waited for the rest of the afternoon, but no one came for the interview.

Soon after this occurred, I was riding up the highway with Hayes and Carole, when Hayes stopped to give a woman a lift. She was out of breath from the heat and very glad for the ride. Her pink tongue hung out panting. "Octavia, I didn't know you were living on our farm."

"Yes'm, I is."

"I remember you when I was a child. You were one of those women sitting in our backyard sewing up hams the first day that we all moved back from Memphis. Do you remember that?"

"I do's."

She had been on and off of our land for over thirty years and looked too old to be able to make a crop, but Hayes had given Octavia and her husband a house and provided some work on others' crops.

"Octavia, can you cook?"

"Sho."

"Well, do you want to cook for me?"

"Yes'm, I will."

Octavia Jackson

"Come to the house on Monday."

Hayes fumed. "Why did you get me into that? You know she can't cook."

"Well, we can try."

The following Monday she was there in time for breakfast. The breakfast was delicious and so was dinner. There was very little that I needed to teach her about cooking, although she could not read or write. She got up with the chickens and told the only time that she needed by two spots on the kitchen clock. At ten she put the dinner on the stove and at twelve she served it. By one-fifteen she was on her way across the street with a big sack of food for her husband and as the sun was descending in the west she returned to cook supper.

She was terrified of the telephone and held it a foot away from her mouth should she have to answer. However, she enjoyed the radio, and prefaced all of her remarks about the news with the words, "It speaks."

As for cooking, her specialty was spaghetti Bolognese. She also made hot-water cornbread, the likes of which I had not tasted. Her country steak was tender and smothered in onions, and there were okra and tomatoes fried in corn meal, turnip greens cooked on a low heat for half the morning. Her blackberry and peach cobblers floated in dumplings and were covered in whipped cream. She was adept at stealing the blackberries from Mrs. Yates's side yard and telling me that they grew on our hedge.

"How did you learn to cook such spaghetti?"

"The Sacks."

"You worked for Italians, the Saccos?"

"I did. They say to me, don't call me Miss and don't call him Mister, call me Nellie and call him Sammy. I lacked Nellie and Sammy, but there was Old Man Sack. When I worked on their farm, one day I don't have nothing, so I go to Old Man Sack and says, "I's hongry.""

"He says, 'You's hongry, Octavia, well, go over there. Eat that.""

"That was a pile of coal."

"I's hongry! I says again."

"He says, 'Eat coal.'"

"Yes'm, he says it. Dat's de troof."

The first thing that I did for Octavia was to get most of her teeth pulled. They were producing an infection and were replaced by glistening white and some lovely gold ones which were the specialty of Dr. Gazelle, the dentist who worked across the street. She felt better, but her glorious disposition was disturbed on many a morning.

"What's wrong with you again?" I asked.

"Henry, we's squabbling."

The squabbles reached saga proportions. "Why on earth did you marry Henry? From what you tell me you have never got on."

"My first husband was named Henry, he was the papa of my children, Beauty and the boy. He done proposed to me when he saw me plowing with two of Mr. Shelby's mules by the light of the moon. He sayed I plough so beautifully. I lacked him. Then he died. This one had the same name and I jes married him by the dark of the moon."

As Octavia had a good job and a little house with ten dollars a week, plus food, uniforms and medical bills for life, she soon quit Henry II. ($10 a week would be about $150 today). Although uniforms were supplied at Christmas, she always put hers back into the box and cried and said she didn't want one. Of course she had many other presents that she didn't reject. Her two-room house had an outside toilet, a fireplace, kerosene lamps, and a front porch where she was the life of her street.

She had come to the Delta from the hills of South Mississippi as a dancer in the Rabbit's Foot Minstrel Show. When the show left town, she settled on Daddy's land. Soon after she came to cook for us she was teaching Carole the minimalist movements of her dances. Their favorite was *Balling the Jack*. She swept the room to the radio and danced around the floor. It took Becky to discover, while she was playing house with Carole, that Octavia was averse to dust pans and simply picked up a rug and swept the dust beneath it. Her cooking stood to compensate for her cleaning and so did her company. She transported me. In the mornings after the groceries had been ordered, while we waited for the delivery man, I would pour each of us a glass of port and we would talk of old times, before Daddy died.

She had another gift, that of a masseur. "How did you learn to massage my back that way?"

"T's got mother wit. They says if you's never seen your pappy, you's got mother wit."

Octavia looked different from most of the other colored people, who had more than likely come from West Africa and mixed with white and Indian blood, as were Lizzie, Freddie, Mary Lee and Cevale. She was as dark as possible, six feet tall, weighing no more than one hundred and eight pounds. Elizabeth Thomas said that she looked like an African princess. I told her this and thus she became a Royal. She must have descended from Nubian stock of the Nile Valley, although she claimed that her mother had come from a Blue Gum tribe and that their bite was "pieson".

Octavia didn't lower her dresses for a long time after the war. She liked them in the middle of her knee to show off her legs. The Dentons had two close cousins, Mr. Doolittle, who was rich, and his less well off-brother who ran their dairy and delivered fresh eggs and chickens. One day Mr. Doolittle arrived with his delivery, and he teased her about her short skirt.

"Is that Carole's dress?"

"Oh, Mr. Littledoo, shame on you, you knows this ain't Carole's dress."

There were two Smith brothers, E. W. and Clifton. They were Annie Mae's older brothers. E. W. was rich and owned the store. Clifton worked in the store, where Octavia did most of her shopping. They supplied food and dry goods; it was a complete country store. Both held to what they considered to be a strong "principle" of racial prejudice. Clifton did not want his son to go to a costume party dressed as Al Jolson, because Jolson was a Jew. They were both small, but Clifton was much the smaller one.

Octavia made frequent purchases in their store, but she always called them 'Mr. Little Smith,' and the other 'Big Mr. Little Smith.'

She had also worked for Mrs. Powers, who called her "Ackie." On one occasion Mrs. Powers asked Octavia if she would clean her attic.

"Yes'm," she replied politely and cleaned the attic all day in the blazing summer heat. At the end of the day Mrs. Powers handed her a dollar. Octavia handed it back.

A few years after she came to work for us she had a minor heart attack. After that I banned her from attending church revivals as she got too excited, or pretended to do so. Lizzie watched her fall out at one church service. They carried her down the aisle with the preacher following closely behind. When she thought that no one was looking, she opened her eyes for one brief moment to rearrange her lace petticoat so that the preacher would be enticed.

She was childlike in many ways. If I left her to look after Carole, Carole, Becky and Octavia had fights with water pistols all over the house, on the beds, targeting the wallpaper. I would have to hire Ruby to look after Octavia and hire Octavia to play with the children. She always pretended to cry about this supervision.

Christmases were a big time for us and I tried to make Octavia's as nice as possible. Every Christmas she was dissatisfied. She kept asking me for a dolly. "I wants a dolly to put on my bed." She wanted a doll dressed in an evening dress, the kind that Carole was beginning to receive.

"Octavia, what on earth do you want with a doll, when we could give you so many more practical things?"

"Because I's never had one. When I was a girl in the hills a white lady give me a dolly. It was pretty and all dressed up, but when I turned it over, it was black on the other side."

I understood and the next Christmas we gave her a beautiful bride doll to place on her bed.

We had no idea about Octavia's age and neither did she. Hayes thought that she should be eligible for Social Security and went to considerable trouble to obtain some sort of post facto Birth Certificate from Edwards, Mississippi, where she had been born. This was done by getting the testimony of her older sister. It transpired that she was only sixty-five, but old enough to draw. She was even owed some back payments. Her response to this windfall was, " Now that I's drawing, there was people I had to stut, but now I'm not stuttin nobody."

Every year after the Social Security checks began to arrive, she took a vacation to the hills of Mississippi and threatened not to return once she got "up in those green hills." She never failed to catch the bus back.

She became quite extravagant after this windfall, buying a plastic raincoat from a traveling salesman for $25 that cost $2.98 in the shops. She would arrive to cook supper with blue hair, not paying any attention to what I said we wanted to eat. "Grits." She threw them into a pan and we ate a large lump. "Sausage." Our sausages were the size of hamburgers.

"You are drunk, Octavia."

"No'm I ain't." Then she sat down on the back steps and pretended once more to cry.

One day she announced to me that she was going to marry a blind man who had a lot with a mortgage on it.

"Octavia, do you know that a mortgage is not an asset, it means that he owes money on that lot? You would be miserable looking after him."

"Well, I's marrying, because the third times you marries you marries in blue." She must have picked that up from the Duchess of Windsor.

I pleaded with her and finally gave her twenty-five dollars to buy beer and have a party on her front porch and wear her blue dress. She escaped the marriage.

Octavia refused to discuss her son apart from saying that he was no good. It had been years since she had seen him and she had no idea where he was. Her daughter, Beauty, and Beauty's husband, John Scales, were given a house on our farm. They were a big strain upon Hayes, for they fought continuously. When they finally moved off our farm the doctor still telephoned us in the middle of the night saying that John had "busted" Beauty's head. He would not sew her up unless Hayes stood for the bill. They had five children. One daughter, Willie Mae, was a little older than Carole. It embarrassed Carole somewhat to see Willie Mae, who only lived across the street, because even at a young age she realized the differences in their opportunities. There was a younger granddaughter, Glory Dean. She was adorable and reminded one of Octavia. She was Octavia's heart.

One afternoon Octavia came to us in a high state of agitation. Glory Dean was missing. She thought that she knew where we could find her. We were directed to a man's house on our farm north of town. Hayes went inside while Carole, Octavia and I waited in the car. The man looked cowed and opened the door. Glory Dean came out and got into the back of our car. The man was told to leave the farm forthwith. Nothing had been found, but it was improper. Octavia began to shout, "When you gets home I's going to hang you, hang you."

Glory Dean sat mute. Finally two huge tears appeared in Glory Dean's eyes and ran down her cheeks. I assured Glory Dean that Octavia was only upset and that nothing was going to happen to her, but that we were simply relieved that she was safe, and the man was very, very bad.

A few years later I was told by others that Glory Dean was pregnant. I was not supposed to tell Octavia that I knew this. As I was worried about the birth of a baby delivered to a thirteen-year-old girl, I found a way of mentioning the matter without getting my sources into trouble. I told Octavia and Beauty that I had noticed Glory Dean hiding Easter Eggs and that she appeared to be pregnant. I explained that under no circumstances must she have this baby delivered by a midwife. We would pay for the doctor. They still clung to the midwife, for they had great faith in her abilities. Finally I prevailed, and obtained a doctor. Glory Dean and her son were fine.

About a year after the birth of this child Carole ran into Glory Dean in town and asked her how she liked being a mother. She replied with a broad smile, "I likes him."

Carole had an early puberty. Little bosoms began to appear. We were so alarmed that we took her to see a doctor in Cleveland, but he said that it was nothing. Then I took her to a ladies shop in Cleveland, The Parisian, where the buyer, Mrs. Finch, said, "We'll get her a Bobbie Bra, but first I must put tucks into it."

While she was waiting for this thrilling garment to arrive she went into the kitchen and showed her breast to Octavia. "I am getting a brassiere, look."

Octavia's cigarette, which was the fag end of one of Hayes's, dangled precariously over the spaghetti sauce when she looked at Carole. "What bee done stung you?"

Octavia retired from cooking about the time that Carole went off to college, but she continued to live in her house and came to our house for her main meals on most days. She had a serious stroke in 1962. Carole was at home with her boyfriend. We all went to see Octavia in the Shelby Clinic. Integration had not been implemented at that time and the colored ward was in the back of the hospital adjacent to the kitchen. There was my free spirit, an old lady with eyes glazed by cataracts. She was conscious and said to us, "In my father's house are many mansions, if it were not so I would have told you." A few months later she died.

May: Aunt Purdis

There were many good, God-fearing people in Shelby, but I had the privilege of knowing two perfect Christians. One was a retired Methodist minister's wife, Mrs. Eva Neblett. She was highly intelligent and today her good soul would have been spoiled with degrees in theology. She taught Sunday school in the Methodist Church. I think that she is the reason that I am not a complete agnostic. She had been the mother of four sons. Two had died and one was a disappointment; the remaining son was everything that she could have wanted. Carrying her troubles bravely and cheerfully, she and Mr. Neblett lived in a small house on the street behind Aunt Mary's house, provided by her daughter-in-law, Mary Lemoyne Wilkinson McKenzie. Possessions were not important to her, for her sights were elevated on the spiritual. I told her that she had ruined church for me, for I only went if I had a new hat because I was incapable of listening to the droning of the Methodist minister after I had heard her. She laughed in her usual broadminded way.

The other perfect Christian was Aunt Purdis, who was a colored person. I cannot imagine that she ever committed a sin. She had been married to Uncle Knox for over fifty years. They had no children and I believe that they had been utterly faithful to each other for a lifetime. They were both very dark and looked one hundred percent African. Uncle Knox took care of the yards for many people in my family. The couple lived in our old playhouse, which had been moved to the north end of the street, directly next to the oil mill and our horse barn and pasture. This remained a one-room structure. After Ruby went to work for the Italian, Aunt Purdis became our washwoman. I didn't like to see her stand up and iron, so I bought an ironing machine. She never liked it, but was embarrassed not to try to use it. Aunt Purdis did not believe in many mechanisms of the modern world because Jesus didn't need them.

When she was a girl in South Mississippi, for some reason connected with her health, she had been sent to Guatemala for several years. Hayes used to take her around the farm as she could speak Spanish to the Mexicans. She and Octavia made an incongruous pair, but Aunt Purdis "the sinless" was as accepting of the wild, bohemian Octavia as Mrs. Neblett was of a young lady who had an illegitimate baby.

Once Aunt Purdis came onto our side porch and when I asked her to sit down, she did so with reluctance. Before sitting she turned the cushion over.

"Why are you doing that?"

"Because the lady in South Mississippi who raised me told me to always do this in white peoples' houses."

"Well, don't do it here."

Gone With the Wind came to the picture show and I wanted everyone who worked for us to see it. The film seemed to me to be a part of their heritage as well as mine. Carole and I went to a movie about three nights a week and I often gave out tickets, if I thought they would brighten others' lives. Everyone accepted my tickets except Aunt Purdis. She was a member of the Sanctified Church. They did not believe in going to a movie; Jesus never went to a movie.

I argued that Jesus never used an electric iron or turned on a fan. Jesus never rode in a car or drove a tractor. She accepted this, but there was another impediment. A member of her Sanctified Church sold peanuts across the street from the picture show. He would see her. She couldn't let her congregation down. Carole intervened, "Oh, Aunt Purdis, go with me, in the night he will simply think that you are my grandmother." She refused the invitation.

Aunt Purdis and Uncle Knox had already reached ripe old ages when she came to work for us. One died and the other quickly followed.

Carole: Freddie and Mary Lee Hall

Freddie Hall had been on our farm since he was a small child. His grandfather, Wash, had worked for us all of his life. Freddie could not read or write, but he was good-looking, as were his three brothers who also worked on our land until the exodus after the war. Freddie had stayed on. He married Mary Lee when she was only fifteen. Her own mother had been ready to finish the black high school in Shaw, when she got pregnant and died a few days after Mary Lee's birth. Her grandfather had remarried a lady that Mary Lee did not particularly like (but she was always nice to the step-grandmother in her old age.) Although her birth grandparents had separated, she knew them and told me that her real grandmother came from Natchez and did not need to straighten her hair. Her grandfather had attended Alcorn Junior College for a few years and her mother's sister had married a white man in the 1940s!

Mary Lee said that she had married Freddie at such a young age in order to escape her step-grandmother. They had five children in quick succession. They also had hard work in common. Mary Lee refused to go to Chicago and live with her in-laws during the exodus after the War. So Freddie stayed on the farm to become Daddy's chief tractor driver and later they jointly became our "straw bosses". I think this job gave them a start in life. My first memory of Mary Lee was of her weighing cotton, handling the bales just like a man. She could do many things that she aspired to do and after marriage and between having five children, she finished high school and later took the Greyhound bus to Clarksdale to take a course to become a hairdresser and much later she became a practical nurse. She was indefatigable in her efforts to better herself.

My father had a great deal of respect for Mary Lee and she praised him to the last for taking her out of the field when she was expecting her last baby. Freddie and Mary Lee lived on the other side of the street from me, and like other people close to our family were of mixed heritage. Not only was Mary Lee part white, but also all of Freddie's family showed indications of a Chinese heritage.

Their son Richard was very intelligent and Daddy's favorite. They visited with each other every afternoon. When Daddy was sick, Richard went to a pay telephone and called him at his own expense. That gesture was more appreciated than any attention that Daddy received. Richard became a police officer in California and later owned a security service and several racehorses.

Mary Lee had many difficulties in her marriage, for Freddie was a ladies' man. She told her woes to Lizzie and Annie. Despite these difficulties they stayed together for nearly thirty-three years. They led a self-sufficient existence on our street, raising hogs, chickens, guineas, ducks, ponies for their children in the back yard, and vegetables, canning or freezing what was left over. They had electricity but could not afford to buy a freezer, so they rented space in the Denton's ice cream plant to keep their food. A few years after the death of my father, Freddie and Mary Lee divorced. She continued to send him chicken and dumplings. When he died of cancer in 1997, she spent his last night with him in his bed. In her words, "I loved my Fred, but I didn't want to go back."

Freddie was never without a good job throughout his life. He became a truck driver for the Ferretti Lumber Company and passed an illiterate driving test to obtain a truck drivers license. He had no use for people who could not do something and he always found time to be a superb fisherman.

In the middle 1960s, Mother helped Mary Lee to get a job teaching with Head Start, the program newly initiated by Lyndon Johnson, teaching basic skills to disadvantaged children before they attended the first grade. She remained in this and other similar practical nursing jobs all of her life. She felt that her call in life was to lift people who had parents that could not cope, who had no manners, or who even had grandmothers that had been tainted by drugs.

In the 1960s some old friends, Mary Elizabeth and Bob Wilson, had moved to Shelby from Rosedale and bought the house of Cousins George and Joe. The only Civil Rights crisis that came to town was a boycott of the Shelby merchants, because they did not provide equal opportunities for employment to both races. Mary Elizabeth tried to prevail upon Mother to make a purchase, even though Mother seldom shopped in the town.

Mary Elizabeth said, "We owe a loyalty to the merchants."

Mother replied, "That may be so. I am not sure about my political convictions, but my loyalty is with Mary Lee; she looked after me when I was sick. I will not cross a picket line if she is standing there."

Mary Lee enjoyed a comfortable existence in her last twenty years, first living in Mound Bayou, and later in a new three-bedroom brick house in Shelby overlooking the land where she had worked for so many years. Her telephone never stopped ringing and her little dog Mattie was always in her lap. She had accurate political insight and the presidential election in 2008 boosted her spirits. She was a deeply Christian person, reading the Bible in the early hours each morning before collecting disabled children to go to a school. During these visits I asked her why she never married again. She said there was another man, " He was easier with money then Freddie but he was a ladies' man as well. Then James Daniels asked me to marry him, but he was not a ladies' man."

The Middle of the Street

Carole: An Old Man

I can still envisage a clapped-out Chevrolet coupe going back and forth in front of our house. It was driven very slowly by a man well into middle age, Dr. Brookshire. He commuted to his office in Hushpuckana, (the town of about four houses, four miles north of Shelby). I was told that his practice had become, for the most part, black people. He lived south of Shelby, but I didn't know where. I often saw him in Willard's Sundry Store sipping a fountain Coca-Cola, as a break in his commute. He wore a slightly frayed gentleman's striped shirt and was very polite. People seemed to make a point of speaking to him as well, but one had the feeling that they did not know him and that this was an effort born of good manners. He made small talk with the other men about the crops and the weather and then continued his journey either north or south. Dr. Brookshire had been in the Delta since the early times.

I never saw him visit in anyone's house, but the Murphree family and Cousin Fred always used him as their doctor. That was because he and Cousin Fred had begun practicing medicine at the same time and his abilities were respected. He had delivered all of Mrs. Murphree's ten children when they lived in Hushpuckana. On rare occasions when other doctors had given up, people consulted Dr. Brookshire. He had two prescriptions, calamine and walking. My Aunt Zula, Mother's sister, went to him during a difficult period in her marriage and the prescribed walks enabled her to cope.

One day a lady named Doll Wilkinson was altering a dress for me when she began to speak to Mother about Dr. Brookshire. Mother tried to catch her eye, but Doll failed to notice and the conversation continued. Dr. Brookshire had a new wife, another black woman; the first one had died. This wife also attended the Roman Catholic Church with Dr. Brookshire. He never broke the code at church. Dr. Brookshire sat near the front with the white people, and his consecutive wives sat in the back with the very few African American people who were Roman Catholics. It was then that I discovered why he lived south of town. He lived in the small all-African American settlement called Winstonville/Chambers. He never changed houses, only wives, after the first one died. The story was put about that he came from a very good family in Arkansas. People added the usual tale, that he had been engaged to a lovely white woman who had been killed in an automobile accident and that tragedy had caused him to "cross the line."

When I was at Sophie Newcomb, I commuted with an attractive young married woman from Shelby to Delta State College one summer. Dorothy Lee Burke was finishing her degree to become a teacher, as she had married after her first year at the University of Mississippi. She graduated with honors that summer. I was taking an easier mathematic course than the one that they had offered at Newcomb to fulfill the requirements for a Louisiana Teacher's Certificate. We were very congenial and told stories all the way to Cleveland and back. One mid-day we were interrupted on the north side of Mound Bayou. There was a traffic jam and two highway patrolmen with holsters and pistols said, "Sorry, ladies, we have to stop you and search." The year was 1960 and the civil rights unrest was reaching its peak. The patrolmen replied, "Dr. Brookshire has died." Dorothy Lee and I both evinced sadness, but he continued.

"Yes, Ma'am. He was a pauper and in the charity ward of the Greenville Hospital. Then they all began pouring in. They decided to move him to the colored ward the day before he died. I am sorry, but I must inspect your car."

Behind us was a line of cars, friends of the doctor's with horns tooting, black peoples' cars decorated with plumbs and tinsel for a funeral. I assume that the patrolmen were afraid of a civil disturbance. Tempers appeared to have been outraged. Dorothy Lee and I eventually continued. We were too saddened by these events to discuss them. For one brief moment we suspended our natural congeniality, and went home to dinner with our own thoughts. Of course we would never be required to keep public order. The tragedy went deeper than rednecks. His life seemed to have been an affront to so many layers of society, and yet they had tolerated him until the day before he died.

Carole: A Young Man

In 1969 I was in the process of packing two trucks to move to England. I had torn down the old smokehouse in our garden, where I found a number of items, including photographs. Sorting the pictures was an ordeal, and I was in the midst of this when Elizabeth Thomas arrived to keep me company. I told her that I was throwing away in-laws and ugly ancestors, and continued dispatching them while she drank a cup of coffee. Then I came upon a photograph that I did not recognize at all, of a handsome young man with curly blond hair, full lips, and a Roman nose. He was wearing the uniform of a military academy in the north. His skin was a little dark for the color of his light hair and there was something that looked African in his eyes. I looked at the picture and passed it to Elizabeth, whom I called Aunt Foster.

"Aunt Foster, who is this? He is a Shelby and he is a young black man."

She smiled sweetly, "He is a Shelby and he is black. Now throw that one away."

As I was in a hurry, I did as directed. The kitchen basket went out to burn.

In the mid-1980's I was visiting in Shelby. Elizabeth was in the hospital at that time and I spent the night at their house to keep J. W. amused. He gave me some advice which I shall pass on. "If I never said anything worthy of remembering, remember that J. W. Thomas advised, don't live past eighty. It has been fun until then." After that revelation he began to have a good time, telling me stories that he would have never mentioned had he not been past eighty.

The mystery of the photograph was unlocked. When as a young man, J. W. would sit on his parents' front porch and watch the parade of people walking into town. On weekdays came the three little Shelby girls, dressed in their white linen dresses, lace petticoats, white stockings and black patent leather shoes. On Saturdays came the three little boys, equally well dressed in smart dark clothes. But their black mother, also well dressed, accompanied them. They were sent to schools in the north. All belonged to my grandfather.

The young man in that tossed away photograph was most certainly my uncle.

Carole: Landmarks

On a return visit to Shelby in the mid-1980s I noticed smoke coming out of the chimney of the commissary. "Why is someone living there?" I asked my renter, Abe Balducci.

"A man moved in. I haven't done anything about it. He pays no rent."

The other houses on my lot had either been pulled down or burned. I had given Lizzie and her family a new house when I inherited money from my parents' estate. Freddie and Mary Lee had bought their own new house after Daddy died. I began to worry about this man in case there was a fire and he should sue me. When I changed renters the following year, I gave instructions for the commissary to be torn down. This may have been the earliest structure in the town, probably there when my grandfather bought Lucknow from Mrs. Evans, one of the five first settlers. A local artist, Martha Long, painted the commissary.

*

The railway tracks were taken up in the 1960s, as trains had ceased to run. The depot became a town library. The Oil Mill and the Compress closed. The gin across the street from our house ceased to function as did many other cotton gins, leaving only the Denton's Gin and the Delta Gin. I owned 100 shares of stock in the Delta Gin. It had never paid a dividend for the twenty-four years that I had owned the stock after my parents' deaths. I was offered $2.50 a share on one occasion, and didn't think that worth considering. The certificates remained in a cardboard box under my bed. In December 1986 I received a telephone call from Mr. Victor Malatesta from Shelby asking me if I was interested in selling this stock for $5.00 a share. I replied affirmatively, and wondered if I would be able to locate the certificates. In view of their past performance, I did not investigate the value of these stocks, because I no longer knew anyone who was connected with the gin. As it was a private company, I thought that I had no means of finding the true value. The check came in and a 100 share certificates went out.

In 1993 I was notified of a proceeding for the winding-up of the Delta Gin. There had been a recent decision by the Supreme Court of Mississippi that had said that a director of a private company owed a fiduciary duty to the shareholders to tell them the actual value of the shares when offering to buy stock, otherwise the sale was void.

I employed Pascal Townsend, a good Mississippi lawyer, who walked into court in his Panama hat, read one case to the judge, and subpoenaed the lady who kept the books for the Delta Gin at the time that this transaction took place. The evidence accepted by the Court was that the value of the shares was about $20,000 when my transaction for $500 took place. Judgment was granted in my favor. Then Mr. Malatesta exploded into a tirade of abuse directed at most people in the court, accusing the judge of wrongful discrimination and threatening all who participated in this trial. The huge black sheriff rolled his eyes upward when he heard this remark. I was anxious to leave the premises with my judgment, but Pascal paid no attention, shuffling out of the courtroom, speaking to everyone, crossed the street to use his son-in-law's photocopier. Then he eased into his Cadillac directly in front of Mr. Malatesta and we drove off to the Clarksdale Country Club for lunch.

In the meantime the judge issued an injunction against Mr. Malatesta prohibiting him from contacting any of the people whom he had threatened in open court. After that the Delta Gin was also pulled down.

In 1995 I returned to visit the Delta and to Shelby. I found that the other side of the street, which I still owned, had been trespassed by a site for used equipment. I sold it to the squatter for the purpose for which it had been occupied.

*

In the late 1990's James Chow died and his good grocery store was sold. The telephone exchange had not existed for a long time. By that time The Bolivar Hardware and Lumber Company were defunct. The whiskey store remained open; the Caboose and the water tower remain intact.

It was inevitable that the people from the other side of the street now live on our side, or what is left of it. Half of the houses on our side of the street have been torn down and the shops stand empty. The schools were finally integrated in 1973. There were different views and shades of similarity or points of view on the subject, but the Delta had never been dominated by rednecks. Civic-minded people stepped forward and tried to lend a calm hand. Apart from that minor picket, there were no serious disturbances in Shelby. Lizzie's church caught on fire in 1962. Was it intentional? No one was injured and they built a new one in the town. That doesn't mean that there weren't hot heads. In the 1960s people took godchildren back from their godparents if they seemed too liberal. Churches were split into the First and the Second congregations. Most whites objected to the mingling of the races, and some blacks did as well.

I once saw a photograph of Lizzie's family taken a long time ago and said, "Nee Nee, your mother was half white." She shook her head in disapproval and replied, "Those were near to slavery times, things happened." She was clearly not pleased, as Mary Lee seemed to have been, and did not want to discuss the event.

When integration became a fact in the late 1960s, a friend from an old Delta family said to me, "Maybe things will go back to being *them* and *us* and the others will pick up their tool boxes and go." That was not to be. We (the planters) moved to the larger towns that provided private schools, or realized that we could rent our land and live more interesting lives elsewhere (London, Paris, California or even Jackson, Cleveland, Clarksdale or Memphis). The small towns throughout the Delta became rural ghettos in the 1980s. We, not the poor whites, left the black people to fend for themselves, not altogether happy or successful. Although a black middle class has developed in the South, there is a large underclass, wielding considerable power through crime and drugs. The complexities of the problems are beyond the scope of this book. I have tried to write about these people in the hope that someone will understand their lives from the inside and that my stories will enhance understanding of both black and white people who lived in these times. Lizzie constantly said, "There is good white peoples and bad ones and good colored peoples and bad ones. It's not all one way." No one ever called Lizzie "Auntie," for she ruled our house as a kind despot.

Had there been a Marshall Plan for the South after the Civil War instead of political slogans like "Forty Acres and a Mule" for people who did not know how to read a seed packet, the Jim Crow Laws might have been changed or abolished; civil rights need not have waited until the 1960's and its cultural wars. One must remember that the rural South was faced with black people numbering 9 to 1 by that time who suddenly became the masters, as Senator Roberts so aptly described (Appendix A). At the same time the white community were pulling themselves out of five years of civil war, a depleted economy with many young men killed, leaving spinsters and orphans behind. Most colonial societies throughout the world in Victorian times and before that believed in the supremacy of the descendants of Northern Europeans. Such attitudes were not unique to the southern part of the United States. I often heard my mother moan that had they not assassinated Abraham Lincoln, followed by that incompetent Andrew Johnson, things might have been better. Maybe a more intelligent man, and less vindictive one, may have seen the need to give the black people more advantages than a vote. Education does change attitudes. I remember the somewhat hesitant respect that my father showed toward Judge Green of Mound Bayou, as if by calling upon him he were putting a toe into an unknown stream. Even Senator Roberts acknowledged that in the early courthouses at these times the judge, jury and advocates were all black and ill trained, but they were not prejudiced against a white defendant. The South could not put up with the overnight transition of power and troubles became fanned by ideology. Later came further ideology such as The White Citizens Council of the 1950s. Today things are different? We simply have different ideology.

Part Five

Rolling up the Mat

Carole's stories

(Mainly from 1962-2010)

A graduate who thought she would
never see much of that street again.

Funerals

When I was a child we had Oriental place mats on the dining-room table. I entertained myself while waiting for dinner by pulling out the straws. Eventually my mat became quite ragged, with only a few straws connected by some thread. The street came to look like that, dilapidated yet still intact.

On an early March afternoon in 1957, I returned from a visit to Clarksdale. Cars lined the driveway. Grandmother had died. We had visited her the previous summer in a nursing home in Dallas. Zula had brought her from Colorado to a Texas nursing home called The Recovery Center, from which no one recovered. She had to share a room with another old lady. The three sisters arrived, fussing. Mother was mad at Zula and stayed at a hotel. Eleanor was also mad at Zula, but didn't want to spend the money on a hotel. They met wearing hats and gloves at the Recovery Center for two days and spoke to each other.

Having lost the weight that she had gained in middle age, Grandmother was once more quite beautiful, except that she could scarcely see. She had become a Christian Scientist and notified no one that her sight was dimming from cataracts until it was too late to operate. Despite this omission and the fact that she had developed breast cancer and failing kidneys that she also neglected to mention, she remained cheerful, not compromising her animation. She laughed about her lack of sight and guessed that Daddy was wearing a blue shirt, because it was his favorite color.

Mother said, "Mama, they say that Carole looks just like you." She replied, "I can only see the shape of her face."

Then she said, "Is Carole affectionate?"

Daddy replied, "No, not at all."

"Oh good. I never was either—can't bear sentimental affection."

She looked sad only in the last few minutes of our visit, when she commented, "I do wish that you girls could get along."

I hadn't realized that I loved my Grandmother until that visit. I wanted her to come and live with us so that I could visit her every afternoon after school. It was too late.

The funeral was a small affair in a chamber of the Memphis Funeral Home on Union Avenue. Elizabeth and J. W. Thomas sat in the family section with us. Zula and Eleanor and Aunt Zula and Uncle Sam did not come. This was only a Shelby funeral. Isabel was there with Cousins Joe and George, Cousin Fred, Nan and Gwin Shelby, Annie Mae, Ruth Morrison, Madge, Charles and Flemma Denton and some of the Murphrees. Then there were the multiple Memphis relations from Daddy's family.

I went into the chapel to take a last look at Grandmother's remains and remembered Lucille Patterson's story about Grandmother's view of the hereafter. "Lucille, I don't think I shall get much out of heaven, no good food, no parties, no pretty clothes, just floating around listening to music, and I never understood music."

Lucille replied, "Anna, I don't think you will get much out of heaven either."

Now, she was going to have to make do.

When I returned from viewing her, Elizabeth Thomas commented to me, "There were two profiles, exactly alike, looking at each other", my grandmother and mine's from the casket.

I replied, "How do you think I felt?"

She was buried beside her husband and her first child, Frances, the last grave in the Shelby lot at Elmwood Cemetery.

Ruth Edwards Shelby had died four years before Grandmother, after Cousin Fred finally placed her in the Gotten Turner Sanatorium in Memphis. Her excesses had led to dementia. Like Grandmother, she too regained her youthful looks when weight fell away. Her hair was plaited on the top of her head and she wore a stylish blue robe with embroidered beads that covered her bosom. Her eyes were once more vibrant.

She had two gentlemen callers. There was one with whom she was constantly furious. That was her husband, Fred. He had put her there. The other was Dr. Shelby, who sent her flowers and chocolates every week and took her out to dinners on Sundays. Cousin Fred outlived Ruth by about six years, but he never threw away her clothes or her shoes. I occasionally peered at the shoes in the shoebox footstool, always kept in his bedroom.

A year after Grandmother's death it was Cousin Fred's turn. He had been operated on ten years before at Mayo Brothers Clinic for prostate cancer. It returned when he was nearly eighty. He suffered very much in his final illness and was grieved for by all his relations. Shelby Edwards, his stepson, Gwin Shelby, his nephew, my mother and Janula, all felt that he had been something of a substitute father. There was also his younger brother George. He was a substitute grandfather for the younger generation.

Uncle Gerald (Fitzgerald) died in the early 1950's after he had slashed his wrists, then screamed for his cook, "Adah, Adah, come quickly, get me a doctor, I am committing suicide." He was diagnosed with hardening of the arteries to the brain, and was sent to Whitfield, the State Mental Institution, where he was interred for a few months before dying.

I borrowed a book from Cousin George during the Christmas holidays of my first year at Newcomb and returned it to him in the mid-term break. He came down the stairway to my doorbell summons with his face covered in bruises.

"Cousin George, what has happened to you?"

"Girlie (the name he used for Cousin Joe, who was not in the least a girlie) went to El Paso to see Sarah Gwin, so I just got drunk as hell."

It was his last toot. The following summer he was out on his plantation with Cousin Joe in the late afternoon, where he suffered a heart attack and died. The sun was setting. The cotton was full of blooms.

We gathered at Gwin's house that evening. Cousin Joe had never been defeated, but she lay on a couch in her son's den and simply said, "I now have more on one side than the other."

Ladies tried to rally her for bridge parties and she bravely attempted the occasions, but she had had an attractive, manly husband for more than fifty years. Despite his wild streak, he had been totally loyal to their family. She could not find consolation in ladies. A year later she died of a stroke in her garden where Jo Gwin, her granddaughter, found her when she visited after school. There remained Jane, who remained and remained and remained, into the 1990s, staring into eternal blankness.

Aunt Mary died in 1961. She had been bedridden with around-the-clock sitters for almost ten years.

Mr. Will Denton died in his mid eighties in the late 1950s.

Mrs. Thomas died in the spring of 1958, smelling a lilac in her garden.

Mr. and Mrs. Murphree continued to walk down the street holding hands for several more years, to the sound of the Baptist Chimes until Mrs. Murphree died of a brain tumor in the late 1960s. Mr. Murphree lived into the early 1980s, bravely taking his medicine. Madge and Charles Denton and her sister Flemma lived into the 1970s and 80s as did Mrs. Mike Rowe and Mrs. Tom Yates. Alan and Lucy Weissenger built a new house and moved off the street, as did Madge and Charles Denton, but Madge and Charles moved no further then a lot behind Madge's sister's house. This concluded the third generation of our close friends on the street.

The Rush to Memphis

Ladies from the Delta were almost colliding with each other in the 1960s to reach the Gartley Ramsey Hospital in Memphis where they received electrical shock treatments. Why is not difficult to answer. Why it didn't happen to the previous generations makes one ponder. That generation had no treatments, only summer resorts, children, the business of caring for plantations, short lives, and looking after other relations. The next generation faced the realities of life with husbands absorbed in farming, hunting, and other women and the ladies collapsed, leaning upon each other. Very few worked unless they were widowed, divorced, or of limited means. Bridge, shopping, beauty parlor, visiting, carrying for family, reading, and consoling each other, occupied long stretches of time. No one can say that Delta women are not well read. They did not need to cook or clean house and it was certainly either too hot or too cold to garden. They were birds of paradise, perfectly turned out, always in stockings, dyed to match skirts and sweaters, and silk or pure cotton shirtwaist dresses. They lived for literature, preferably novels. My mother, Dot Murphree, and several of my own close friends were to receive the fashionable electric shock treatments, about fifteen women from one small community. Their prime function was to be imaginative good mothers, especially for girls. They let the land take care of the boys.

Ann Morrison Coopwood was a beautiful young married woman. Her husband had later gone to dental school and became a prosperous dentist. She had three children, who were individual and very attractive; the last children on the street were Betsy, Scottie, and Candy, my substitute nieces and a nephew. Betsy came roaring down the sidewalk in a little motorized jeep that J. W. had built for Ann shortly after the War. Scottie had the railway track and train that had been built for Ann, which covered their back yard. Ruth and Scott Morrison built a new house on a lot at the back of the Street, and their grandchildren had the run of their comfortable house. Scottie kept a raccoon on the front porch and claimed that it was his best friend. Although the house was full of pets and servants, the parents' lives were falling apart. Ann went to bed for eight years. On occasions the raccoon was let into her bedroom. Her husband drank. Intelligent ladies tried to help, but there was no one who could pull her out of this quagmire, until she picked up her bed and walked away. The beauty fled to find another life.

Air conditioning had eliminated many of the smells. Fewer people were sitting on front porches, which had been an integral part of Southern life. People had sat on the porch in the afternoons after four and after supper. These hours meant that one was free to call. The porch also served an inhospitable purpose. If some one called whom one was not used to receiving, they were seated on the porch to state their business. By the sixties, most porches had been covered in glass. People began to live in the back bedrooms of their houses in comfortable chairs before the television. It took a long time for the doorbells to be answered. Then one was met with, "Carole, how nice to see you. You know, I don't go out anymore." Coffee would be served with a thawed-out Sarah Lee cake and the conversation proceeded politely, but the seldom-answered doorbell told all.

I was in college during much of the period when my society seemed to collapse. Although I came to Shelby in the summers to entertain my parents who paid for my expensive education, I spent most of my time at the swimming pool or on the golf course with Mimi.

Revisited 1962-63

Graduating from college is quite a shock for those who can no longer rely on parents to provide further stimulating experiences. One longs for non-directed communal life that offered easy intimacies and youth on every side. I quickly came to be an alien in my own hometown amidst people who did not care about my last four years. I went to New York in the summer of 1962 after I graduated to bid my best friend Sue Anne Kenney goodbye, when she sailed for a year in Europe. My other close friend Virginia Bass went to Paris to live with the writer Larry Snelling, with whom she had begun an affair during our senior year at Newcomb. My trip to New York was the first time I had ever been in an integrated lavatory. I still remember seeing my face in one gold leaf mirror and a black lady's face in the other and I thought that the reflections reminded me of portraits around the walls of Southern houses. I never noticed integration again. Mother and Daddy were of the firm view that I had had enough of New Orleans. They hoped that I would marry the rich cotton planter from Louisiana to whom I became very loosely engaged during the summer following my graduation or settle in Memphis.

I had graduated with a major in Modern European History and minors in American History and the History of Art. At my parents' insistence I acquired a Louisiana Teacher's Certificate, although I had no inclination to become a teacher. I applied for no jobs. August arrived. Daddy pressured me to move to Memphis. I was reluctant, but confident that it was too late for me to find a job in the schools. He thought differently, for he had a string to pull. His friend, Julian Bondurant owned the Wells-Fargo Company in Memphis and was also president of the Memphis School Board. Daddy took me to see Julian and told him of my predicament, as if it were *my* predicament. In order to please Daddy, I put on a nice suit and visited Julian's office. Daddy was semi-proud of me, if only I would get a job, marry or move to Memphis, and hopefully do all three. Julian sat me on his stool, an elephant's foot, the trophy of a shooting safari in Africa. He had no hesitation in pulling the string and telephoned the lady who was head of hiring teachers in Memphis and arranged an interview for me that afternoon.

Daddy couldn't go into the interview room as he had done at Julian's office. He had, however, typed my resume on his old Underwood and that was the end of his participation. He waited in the vestibule. Yes, there were a few spaces left for teaching positions. Then the competent lady asked one last question, "Why do you want to teach school?"

I replied, "Because my mother said it is the only reasonably decent job a young lady can do for a year or so before she gets married."

Labor Day arrived with me still unemployed.

Then I received a telephone call from my favorite cousin, Shelby Taylor (Aunt Ellen's granddaughter), from Baton Rouge, Louisiana. She had given me a second home throughout my college years. We were on the same wavelength and she was concerned about my options (marriage or Memphis) towards which I was being pressured.

She had the package: "Why not take a business course? You can string out old Soule Business College for a long time." I had my own money, having inherited a bit of Aunt Eleanor's thrift. I had saved from gifts of U.S. government bonds, Christmas and graduation presents. The sum amounted to about six hundred dollars that I volunteered for my tuition at business school, where I was to learn typing and shorthand.

Albert Murphree quibbled, "Why didn't you just go to Drone's Business School?"

I smirked.

Shelby Taylor set up a place for me to live with her madcap friend, Sheila Rafferty McGuiness, a divorcee, who had a house in the New Orleans Garden District on Seventh Street. Shelby's own daughter, Ellen, had received a late acceptance to Sophie Newcomb, but was not able to get into the dormitory. She and I could share a room at Sheila's house. The rent was $125 a month for a shared room, the use of the house and two meals to be cooked by Millie, who had worked for Sheila's mother. The same two trunks and five suitcases of clothes that I took to Newcomb were repacked, and once more I boarded the City of New Orleans in Grenada, Mississippi for New Orleans.

When I arrived at Sheila's house, I liked everything that I found. We sat around a large table in the evenings with one of Sheila's ex-husbands, her teenage daughter, Sharon, and her brothers and sister-in-law and my cousin Ellen, and all raved, as Southerners are brought up to do, about Millie's cooking. Sharon was soon into my suitcases and looked much prettier than I in my clothes. Soule was just around the block from her house and I went there and applied. This was the moment I realized that I had not returned to Sophie Newcomb.

Old Habits, New Friends

The first weekend in New Orleans I was back with my old friends and went to Slidell, Louisiana, to Leon Irwin's country house with my college boyfriend. Late that Sunday night, Sheila greeted me. She had spent the weekend on the Mississippi Gulf Coast in Pass Christian, which had been the former home of her family.

"You are going to take my job. It doesn't amount to anything. Old Soule can wait. All you have to do is to be nice on the telephone. I work for the law firm of Drury, Lozes, and Dodge. You will adore Jim Drury. You can look after the house and please look after Sharon."

"I can't type," I replied.

"That doesn't matter. You only have to type a legal docket once a week, and you can do that on two fingers. The job pays $375.00 a month. I will only be gone for six weeks. I am going to Europe with Catherine Tucker. Her stepson, Peppy, has been visiting. He has been hitchhiking all over the world. You must meet him. He is at home now, writing a book about India and Thailand and Australia and Japan."

Soule waited and the next morning I went into Drury, Lozes, and Dodge, where Sheila showed me the ropes. The job was marginally more complicated than she had described. It took me a whole day to type the one-page legal docket. The partners would pop into the reception room and ask if the typewriter needed oiling. An important duty was to make the morning Luzianne Coffee from the French Market. On my very last day, they all congratulated me for making the first good cup of coffee they had drunk in Sheila's absence.

Sheila and Catherine departed on the evening of the 29th of September 1962, my twenty-second birthday. Before leaving, I heard more of the young man who was writing a book and realized that this was the Shelby Tucker about whom I had read during my last year of high school. Sheila couldn't wait for me to meet him. Shelby Taylor, my cousin, was visiting and she tried to catch my eye, shaking her head. She encouraged me to meet that nice young man who worked for the Monroe-Lehmann law firm to whom Sheila's brother, Nigel, wanted to introduce to me. She also said that Jim Drury was a wolf. It all had the effect of making me more excited, but I didn't want Sheila's family to detect my interest.

On the night that Shelby Tucker arrived I was wearing a pair of Bermuda shorts and a white blouse. I was very conscious of a spot on my white blouse, but I didn't want them to notice me changing clothes, so I met him with the spot on my blouse and the standard gold circle pin on my collar.

He was a little different from what I had expected. Probably at his father's behest, he wore a dark brown suit and looked sensitive and slightly insecure. We could not take our eyes off each other. Everyone sat around

Sheila's dining table with loud voices and lots of drinks. I looked straight across the table at Shelby, who had dark brown hair, blue eyes, and very regular features. His eyes gave nothing away, but his mouth was sensitive and full. If he were teasing or not telling the truth, it could always be detected by his mouth. Despite his thinness, his physique was perfect.

We went to the airport and the ladies climbed the steps onto the plane. After they departed, we stopped at a bar in the airport and I talked to Shelby's father. He was still a handsome man at fifty-two and very agreeable. In a matter of ten minutes we seemed to have much in common. He spoke in a Mark Twain voice derived from West Tennessee, Ripley, and was my distant cousin. He confided to me that although his sons never wanted to return from Europe, he always longed to get back to his roots, to the business that he had created. I understood this, for I had never left my roots. I had not been north of Nashville until I visited Sue in New York that previous summer. In the group was an adorable younger brother, Bruen, only twelve years old. He was the child of Shelby's father's second marriage.

We returned to Sheila's house and somehow the older and younger groups disappeared and left Shelby, Ellen and me on the front porch. Shelby began to tell us his ideas, values, and comments on local issues. Ellen argued, for she was only eighteen. I listened, realizing that I was upstaging Ellen, who was better looking than I, having inherited her mother's light eyes, regular nose and light brown hair. Nothing conquers a man like listening.

He Called

Before the week was over I received a telephone call from Shelby Tucker inviting me to the Mississippi Gulf Coast for the weekend. Ellen responded, "I can see it now. He will make an interesting first husband. You will probably have four."

Shelby did an unusual thing and told me to reverse the charges on my call to him (or rather to his father). This had never happened with New Orleans boys. That weekend, after the first week's work of my life, I took the bus to Gulfport, Mississippi, where Elizabeth and J. W. Thomas met me, for they had a summer house in Pass Christian and I was supposed to spend the weekend with them.

Shelby's father paid for the initial evening. He was keen that his son, who appeared to be marooned in an attic writing his travelogue, have a normal girlfriend. Well, I was normal. Otherwise our experiences were at opposite ends of the pole.

The menu at the Friendship House was twenty pages long. We both ordered a flounder and Shelby selected a Graves wine. After dinner he drove me down the Mississippi Gulf Coast to Ocean Springs and took me to a playground, where he put me on a swing and stood on either side behind me pumping the swing. I felt the intensity of his muscular legs. Later he kissed me goodnight. My parents telephoned the following morning, for they kept an ear to everything that I was doing. What did Elizabeth and J. W. think of this man? J. W. replied that he thought that the planter from Louisiana had his feet on the ground more than this one.

Shelby collected me for lunch the following day and took me to the Bay St. Louis Yacht Club. I relayed J. W.'s comment. Shelby said for me to tell J. W. that he had had his feet on the ground in Pakistan, Afghanistan, India, Thailand, Australia, Malaya, Japan, Alaska, Central America, Mexico, Russia, China and Europe, more ground than the planter had ever thought about.

Shelby's father had tiptoed into his attic in the early hours after our first evening and awakened him with, "Well, what do you think of her?"

Shelby looked at his watch and replied, "Just nine more hours and she will be gone." His attic had been invaded.

*

I could never have believed that he had told his father that morning that he wanted me to leave, for our conversation the following day at lunch over fried chicken and iced tea was an hour of instant congeniality. We spent the afternoon visiting his childhood haunts in Bay St. Louis and hearing his stories about growing up there with his friend Penny Cole. We drove in the open pinewoods behind the bay and both gasped at the beauty of an old wooden bridge. I commented that it was the type of structure that would cause my father to shake his head and say, "Look, when are they going to tear that thing down?" We saw the world through the same eyes and when he took me to the Gulfport Greyhound Bus Station, he invited me back the following weekend.

The next weekend was on his terms. He didn't take me to a restaurant again, but took me into his sleeping bag on the end of one of the many wooden piers that lined the man-made sand beach of the Gulf Coast in Pass Christian. There we gazed into the water and I discovered that it was neither brown nor gray, but yellow, blue, green, black and brown, the colors of the three wooden boats painted by Monet. He lay with his head in my lap and looked up at me and said that I reminded him of a combination of Kit, his best friend from Oxford, and his mother, from whom he had been estranged for almost ten years. Shelby was a searcher, a wanderer, and a highly educated man. In his trip to India and the Far East he had explored the three major Eastern religions and to his surprise had been converted to Christianity by missionaries whom he had met in India. It would not be an easy path for him to follow. His life had been that of a libertine. He hoped that he could best serve his ideals by becoming a writer. A writer cannot live in solitude; he must experience the fullness of life. When he was a boy, living in Bay St. Louis, Mississippi, he had three things that he wanted to do: go to Oxford, write a great book, and have a great love. One could not write a great book without the support of the latter, would I marry him? The differences in our ages, experiences and perceptions of life did not matter.

I said, "Yes."

**

Thus began my reconstruction. It did not come automatically and not without protest from my parents, many old friends, and me. Shelby opened the windows. On the weekends, which were all spent at his father's house, in the attic, with the sound of the waves coming through the front window, I lay on a bed and read, while he typed on a ping-pong table and cast his pages in my direction. I read as I had only read in the hot afternoons in Mississippi, when Mother forced me to take naps in order to resist polio. I had been far too behind with my work at college to read for pure enjoyment. During a short time I read most of Evelyn Waugh, Pasternak, C. S. Lewis, the Phillips version of the New Testament, and some of the Koran.

Downstairs there was another student. Shelby had ripped the television plug out of the wall. By the time that his father found someone to repair it, Bruen was also a passionate reader, a habit that has lasted for both of us. Shelby darted between his typewriter and overseeing his protégées, Bruen and me.

The engagement, though real, was not absolutely binding on either of us. When the weekends were over, I was quite relieved to be going back to New Orleans with Sheila's brother Michael, stopping at a roadside joint for a beer and oysters and working on Monday in a world that had become my home. Shelby was claustrophobic. There was still an old boyfriend in New Orleans from college days. That was my real pull, not the planter. I had gone full circle when I was in college from "The Man" to one who was hairy, muscular and rich. Now I was turning back in the direction of "The Man", although one who was much more forthcoming.

Sheila had two couches in her living room. During the first few weeks of my engagement I necked with my old boyfriend on the soft comfortable couch and saved the more elegant couch that had belonged to Jefferson Davis for Shelby. After one of these sessions on Jefferson Davis's couch, Shelby was dreadfully sick, for he had punished his system in India, once living on an egg a day for eight days crossing Iran, when his travelers' checks had been stolen. He had amoebic dysentery, and weighed no more than one hundred and thirty pounds. No wonder he looked vulnerable on the evening of our first meeting. His body convulsed over Sheila's kitchen sink and I put my arms around him to protect him and somehow knew that I would always do so. When he recovered from the agony of the moment, he turned to me and said quite simply, "Carole, your life stands for absolutely nothing now. Please let me make you into what you could become."

Later he said, "Come with me, take a chance on life."

It was a challenge that I could not refuse. After that the double sessions on the two couches ceased.

***

During this time there occurred the Cuban Missile Crisis. Sharon's school, Country Day, planned to evacuate to a gymnasium in Homer, Louisiana. New Orleans was within the range of fire, or so they said. On one of these early afternoons dominated by fear, I took the St. Charles trolley home. From the trolley I gazed at once grand houses on the Avenue with old people in rocking chairs on the front porches, people without any teeth, long white plaits behind their ears. I had a vision of death. The effect was to make me grab for life. Would my parents try to drag me back to smother in Mississippi? Would I die a virgin?

When Sheila and Catherine returned and my job had finished, I moved with my two trunks and five suitcases, a hair dryer and curlers, to Shelby's father's house. Shelby, who had hitchhiked around India living on a shilling a day to emulate the life of an average Indian, was simply baffled by my Delta assemblage of clothes. By that stage we had begun to make love in the attic and claimed to all that we were 'engaged.'

The Mississippi Gulf Coast was one of the three most beautiful places in which I have ever lived. It was at its prime in 1962, before Hurricane Camille of 1969 washed away so many of the nineteenth-century and turn-of-the-century cypress houses surrounded by large screen porches, designed for the gulf breezes. There had been private piers belonging to many of the beachfront houses. The area abounded in live oaks covered by Spanish moss. There was a kindred spirit between the Delta and the Mississippi Gulf Coast. The Delta never acknowledged Jackson (the state capital). Memphis was the capital of the Delta and after that they skipped on to the coast. Similar people populated the two sections of the state and they ignored the hill parts of Mississippi, except Natchez and Vicksburg.

Shelby's father's house faced the Gulf. The houses facing the Gulf didn't need air-conditioning. An attic fan and porches created cross ventilation and screens kept out the mosquitoes. There was scarcely a cloudy day in the winter or the need for a coat. We were enveloped by nature. When it became too cool to sit on a pier, we made love in the car at Henderson's point, or in the pinewoods, or during the afternoons in the autumn woods at Ocean Springs on the estate that had belonged to the artist Walter Anderson.

The coastal area comprised a string of adjoining communities. Across the bay from Pass Christian were Bay St. Louis, Waveland, Poplarville, Pearl River. Behind these settlements was Delisle, where many inhabitants still spoke a patois version of French. On the east side of Pass Christian were Long Beach, Gulf Port, Biloxi, Ocean Springs, Pascagoula, Moss Point and the Alabama border. Pass Christian, one of the first Spanish settlements on the North American continent, had been governed under the Spanish, French, United States and Confederate flags. Hurricane Camille flattened most of the beachfront, including Shelby's father's house in 1969, when wind reached 190 mph. About three hundred lives were lost, but the residents braced up, returned and rebuilt the coast, including the Episcopal Church and the graveyard. In September 2005, Hurricane Katrina arrived, with less ominous winds, only 135 mph. But the winds were 500 miles in diameter and drew a surface water of half the Gulf of Mexico. The whole area has been destroyed including the house and many of the works of the artist Walter Anderson in beautiful old Ocean Springs. Our love affair encapsulated much more than ourselves.

In a place of such beauty one also found charming, easy-going people. "Just don't rock the boat," is all they seemed to ask. Shelby's father was often out of town and Catherine went to New Orleans leaving us to look after Bruen. We walked with the child at night on a moonlit beach and I mastered re-heating the midday meal that had been prepared either by Catherine or the cook, Purmelia.

Return to Shelby

This idyll had to come to an end. Shelby had had a stormy relationship with his stepmother, Catherine. The moment was quiet and his father wanted to keep it that way. In late November his father's older brother died and he had to go to the funeral in Kentucky. Shelby's grandmother was eighty-four and blind. It seemed like a good idea for Shelby to finish his book in Ripley, Tennessee, which was on the way to his uncle's funeral, where he could ease his grandmother's pain at the same time for Shelby had always been her favorite grandchild. I was deposited at my parents' house in Shelby on their way to Ripley, and my two trunks and five suitcases followed on a Greyhound bus. That is how I happened to return to this street.

What followed was a winter of enlightenment. I continued reading prodigiously, but my friends were disappearing. In November we went to Bobbie Lou's wedding. Becky had married two years earlier. They both lived in Cleveland. Mimi had broken up with her love, Jack Cheatham, but was becoming attached to a handsome and wealthy young man from Cleveland, Mike Sanders. Jan became engaged to her childhood sweetheart, Walter

Clark from Clarksdale, and her mother, Janula, married again and moved to Dallas. I thought that I was engaged.

During this long engagement I learned to type by writing a misspelled love letter every day. I had tutorials in cooking from Lizzie (who had returned to our kitchen after Octavia retired). The lessons lasted from ten to twelve each morning and I tried to write it all down saying, "Nee, Nee, how long do I cook the rice, chicken, snap beans, beets and cornbread?"

She always replied, "Til they get un." Then she would say, "Is you ever gonna clean up as you goes?"

No novice could have had better advice. I continued to persist with my typing, and after a few months, compiled a cookbook of personal recipes from this street. I have used them throughout my life.

Shelby came to see me every weekend, and the weekends lasted for days. To my parents' consternation he would hitchhike from Ripley to Shelby, a distance of about one hundred and thirty miles. People doubted that he had been to Oxford or Yale and certainly didn't believe that he was a lawyer. People who had not even finished college, or certainly not gone to prestigious one, declared in unison that I was mesmerized by a pseudo-intellectual. He wore tennis shoes. Would a lawyer do that? Why would this man hitchhike? The only person who seemed to think that he was genuine was Johnny Sacco, who owned a service station on the northern end of the extended street. When we stopped to fill the car on the farm account, Shelby would speak a few words of Italian to Johnny. "That's it. He's speaking it. That sho is it," responded an excited Johnny.

Finally my father tried to pay Shelby to travel on the Greyhound Bus, humiliating enough to Daddy. Shelby did not accept the money, but promised to take the bus, although he always hitchhiked to Clarksdale and took the bus from there to Shelby, a distance of twenty miles.

We viewed another place with new eyes: the Mississippi Delta. With Shelby the winter was no longer dreary, for together we looked at the stark brown horizons of muddy earth that ranks among the richest land in the

States. In front of these fields was the water tower and beyond that lone cabins sitting on tiny slopes with a few puffs of smoke coming from the chimneys.

Spring comes early to the Mississippi Delta. Daffodils bloom in February and buttercups come up along the railway banks in March. Wild onions appear in February. April is glorious and in May the heat usually reaches eighty degrees Fahrenheit; day lilies, violets, nandina, rosebud, verbena, crepe myrtle and flag irises cover the yards. The pecan trees put out their tassels, oak trees their leaves, and there is the smell of the privet hedge in bloom.

Shelby reconciled with his mother, who lived in Memphis, and we spent other weekends there, making new friends, going to the touring Metropolitan Opera Company to hear James McCracken sing in *Otello* and Joan Southerland in *Traviata*. We unearthed more childhood memories from Memphis. I commuted to Memphis on the bus, and we clung to each other in the station as if some disaster were impending. Following one visit Shelby wrote me a love letter and enclosed a tin coin that he had printed on a machine in the Greyhound bus station. It said, "I love you, Peppy." (Peppy was his family's nickname for him)

People in love think that they are invisible. Shelby and I made love in an abandoned cabin on the plantation of my ancestors, Monochonut. It was highly romantic to know that two cousins, who shared two generations of Shelby ancestors, had afterwards found each other and returned to these roots. We spent afternoons with a picnic in the woods behind the levee of the Mississippi River and a night on the top of the levee. All the stars in the hemisphere seemed to appear, which we took as a sign of eternal blessing. Other afternoons were spent behind a black Baptist church on the Brooks plantation. We were absorbed in our future plans. At night we parked the car on our plantation road, and afterwards we drove about the town, me sitting next to Shelby without any clothes. We never thought that there were other people, not as easygoing as the crowd on the Mississippi Coast, people who in their diminished futures had nothing better to do than to follow us.

One spring afternoon Shelby and I went for a walk in the new addition behind our house. Daddy must have heard something, for he warned us, "Be careful, people in little towns do not have much to do but to absorb themselves in the lives of others. You don't even see them, but they see you." I thought this was an odd warning, for we only intended to walk along a sidewalk. We proceeded on this course and then cut across our cotton field to a pecan grove that was near to a new housing development. We had a blue Indian blanket and spread it on the ground. The inevitable happened. Shelby took off my clothes. Suddenly I was staring into the face of Stony Stone, Margaret Murphree's son, followed by the school biology class taking a field trip! Shelby quickly covered me in the Indian blanket, but the field trip had discovered an unintentional lesson in the biology of Homo sapiens.

Shelby finished his book at the end of May and our plan was to proceed to New York, where he would get a job in a law firm, using his spare time to take his travelogue to publishers. I still had money that had not been spent, thanks to the infusions from Sheila's job. When Daddy put me on the plane for New York, he let me spend my own money, hoping it would soon be depleted and that I might return and meet that mythical young lawyer from the Monroe-Lehmann law firm. Daddy saw Shelby once more before he departed for New York and said, "Take care of her."

New York
(Summer 1963)

Shelby soon followed me and found a job in a law firm on Fifth Avenue. My Xeroxing skills did not count for much in New York. Like most graduates with a Liberal Arts degree I was sent to interviews for jobs in publishing. (Of course I had never even thought of publishing when I was in college). The lady from the employment agency would say, "I have a charming young lady, perfectly suited to become a copywriter." I inevitably had to take a typing test and despite my practice on love letters, I only typed ten words per minute. One publisher politely called the agent and said, "She is charming, but she can't type." (I couldn't spell either, but the interview never got that far.)

I found a slot on a waiting list at Time-Life as a "research assistant," a fancy description for a university graduate who files. But I had no trouble getting a job selling clothes at Best & Co., across the street from Shelby's law office in the 666 Building on Fifth Avenue.

Every morning I had to wear the same little black dress. My job was in the sports department and the title was 'Buyer Trainee', but in reality I was merely an extra summer sales clerk. I did, however, have delightful company in Andrea, due to complete her last year at Vassar. She too was clerking in the sports department and "engaged," but the memory of her fiancé was quickly dimming while he spent the summer in Hawaii. He was an Englishman, a graduate of Cambridge and a friend of Jonathan Winters, during the period that *Beyond the Fringe* was all the rage in New York. As Shelby wanted to return to live in England, Andrea and I spent our spare moments contemplating the rigors of a life in England: cold water flats, not many telephones, penny-pinching wages, and socialized medicine. To rally some enthusiasm for this untested destination we took our tea and coffee breaks (twenty-minutes twice a day as stipulated by the union) and went to the British Sportswear Department on a lower floor, where we tried on Weatherall raincoats and hats, collapsing at the image of ourselves in these sensible ensembles. Would we also have to wear heavy stockings and lace up oxfords?

I was anathema to the permanent staff of sales ladies, Mrs. Orenstein, from Queens; Mrs. Clages, who stood in front of the counter by the elevator eating potato chips all day while being strategically placed to catch the first customer; and Mrs. Domingo, an unassuming Italian lady from the Bronx. Mrs. Orenstein had her eye on the big fish and paced up and down the rack of clothes by the dress/coat department in order to snatch one of their customers and get a commission on a larger sale from that department as well as her own. Her sales pitch was "Hit's snot a match hit's a blend, you catch, you like, you know what I mean?" The second pitch was, "Hit's the layered look." Which meant that one could not buy a pair of Bermuda shorts and a shirt, but in order to be stylish one also needed a turtleneck jersey to wear under the shirt and a vest to wear over the shirt, plus a cardigan.

Shelby would collect me for lunch, and one day my stock rose when I mentioned that he worked across the street in a law firm.

Mrs. Orenstein commented, "A lawyer! He will make lots of money."

Mrs. Domingo slapped her forehead with her hand and said, "Oh my Gawd, I thought he was the elevator boy!"

A few weeks later my stock crashed the day that I acquired a customer from South America, who bought everything that I suggested. If one had a customer in the sports department, one was allowed to take that customer to the dress/coat department, so as not to break the spell of the sell. My tally (bill) cascaded down the counter. This was treading on Mrs. Orenstein's ambitions. She and the other salesladies stood at the counter saying, "Look at the kid, look at the kid, selling all over the store." Then I took my goods into the wrapping room where two ladies stood at a table all day staring at a treasured magazine photograph adorned by a pink satin bow, of Jacqueline Kennedy, Caroline and John-John.

Shelby and I lived in Greenwich Village and were introduced to the New York of stand-up counters at Choc Full O' Nuts and Horn & Hardart. Shelby even insisted that we have dinner at Woolworth's one evening, an offence that I nurtured for a considerable length of time. That summer was a far cry from my previous summer of dallying about proposals and throwing away prospects for good jobs. I didn't dare recall the *noblesse oblige* of Jim Drury's law office where he had raised the salary of a secretary because she had threaten to quit and he could not let her go out into the world to get the sack, or Sue Anne Kenney's home on Long Island and lunches with her father in the Rainbow Room at Rockefeller Center.

Then I had a telephone call that ended my life of docking in and clocking out.

Just a Short Spell
September/October 1963
(Written 1964)

My father is dying. It may be tonight; it may be a week from now. He had an operation. They found a spot on his lung. It spread to his back. He received radiation, but shortly after that he suffered from heart failure. If he lives much longer, he could be bedridden. The specialist in Memphis said that at the most optimistic prediction he had two years. But he won't live. They sent him back to Cleveland in an ambulance so that he could die near home. The ambulance stopped in our driveway on the way to Cleveland. Mother and I were there and so were a line of people from our farm. The black people came and stood in a respectful silence. Suddenly my father's eyes filled with tears.

The operation and shock were too much for his heart. Today he had an attack. He survived it, but it is a question of hours. For several days now he has not been himself. The illusions or revelations that come before death have begun. Black people know that when you start seeing and talking about people who are already gone, this is the time you won't pull out. I expect they are right. They are usually right about such things; they live closer to it than we do. They are the ones who stay by your bedside when you are old and stripped of your life's remaining faculties, toting your bedpan, sharing your fears, secrets, and anguishes. The knowledge is not something I want to delve into, but if Bertha, Daddy's nurse, says that after three hard rains in a row, somebody is going to die, I'm not going to smile knowingly and say she doesn't know what she is talking about. She is the only one who has sat and listened for those three hard rains when the rest of us were busy with our golf, worries, or bridge games.

I love my father. But I am so busy hating all of those people who hang around with their air of troubled concern helping Mother that I can't grieve for him. Mother doesn't know that he is going to die. They keep giving her hints to PREPARE her, just enough of a hint that when they leave, after talking about roses and grandchildren, she can lie awake all night and wonder: Is he going to die?

"May, I don't think you realize how awfully sick Hayes is."

"He has always protected you so, May, someday you are going to have to face things as we have faced them."

"You know, May, you don't think about God as I do. After Bob died I used to just slip away from my family and go and sit in the church and get down on my knees and stay there for about thirty minutes. Have you ever done anything like that?"

"No, it hurts my knees," Mother responded.

Uncle John came down from Memphis today. He got emotional because Daddy said that Cevale had been in to see him. Cevale was murdered over fifteen years ago. At first Uncle John tried not to notice and said,

'Haven't you had any company?' Daddy smiled and said, 'Oh, yes. Papa was here too.' Daddy's delusions didn't upset me. Dr. Ringgold had told me that he was going to die and dying men can experience worse things than seeing Grandpapa. Such a serene look came onto Daddy's face.

I was in New York with Shelby when I got the news. We had spent a few days at the end of summer driving through Vermont and on into Quebec. I had never been out of the States before and was enchanted by the narrow cobblestone streets of Quebec, men wearing berets, speaking French. That was six weeks ago. Charlotte and Judy had left messages for me everywhere. In case I should miss the note on the hall table, there were notes on the refrigerator, on my bed, and over the washbasin at the women's residence house on 12th Street, which was my official residence. "CALL YOUR AUNT MILDRED." My hands were glued to the telephone. Aunt Mildred gave me the facts immediately. Daddy had been convalescing from his operation when they had found something else. There were a lot of terms that I didn't understand, but the message was clear that his days were numbered.

Later I sat on some stone steps somewhere on K Street, near Washington Square. Prissy men passed with their dogs. Shelby held me in his arms but there was no warmth that could stop the crying. I thought, "Daddy may never see me again." He had been worried about my affair with Shelby. I had told him another lie so that he would let me come to New York. It is expected to tell a consoling lie to one's mother, but a father knows what is happening and the lie will register and mean more than the fact to a father.

Uncle John left early so that night would not catch him on the highway. But the ladies remain all over our living room. They sit with you when you are sick, or when you are busy, or when you are worried, or when you wish they'd all drop dead and sizzle. They consider themselves to be thinking about others.

Miss Mary Dodd Poston said, "May, why don't you rent out that apartment?"

"I don't want it rented," I snapped.

That was where Shelby had stayed. Shelby had spent each morning and each afternoon typing there. I would hear the typing noises through the wall in my room. Sometimes he let me sit in the apartment with him while he worked. After everyone had gone to bed I would put a coat over my gown and creep into the apartment and talk in whispers to Shelby and watch the blue and yellow flames in the gas heater until it was time to put on my coat and creep back into the house.

It was during this period that the ladies had begun to follow us everywhere, without us having the slightest idea.

I know that this night Daddy will be dead. He is already dead in everything but name. All that remains is for the doctors to make their little pronouncement and for the morticians to take him away for their expensive preparations. But only in that first awful night in New York did I acknowledge the void. Then I came home immediately. I had to be brave. Now it has become a hospital ordeal.

I went to his commissary today to get some papers from the safe, and sat in his swivel chair that once fascinated me as a child. There I had played in the commissary office, the part that was partitioned from the rest of the room by wooden bars. The bars reminded me of a jailhouse. Every Saturday Daddy paid the labor. I would watch his bags of money coming from the safe and thought that we must be very rich.

I was very partial to Daddy then. I knew nothing of boys and parties and fashions. Later I became Mama's baby. Sometimes he took me with him when he went to talk to the people on the farm and sometimes he let me ride Duke, Zechariah's horse. Some days I got to go to the Denton's cotton gin and was put into a corner of a bale of cotton with Sherman and his powerful suction machine that pulled the fluff into the gin, after the seeds had been taken away. It frightened and excited me to imagine myself being pulled into the gin with the cotton, but I kept far away, even then knowing that gins are dangerous.

There was a picture of me on Daddy's desk, taken when I was three years old. In the desk drawers were receipts, letters to the Production Credit Company and the Staple Cotton Association, bank statements and a ledger with entries: Blue and Gold Super-market. James Chow's Meat Market. Octavia and Lizzie's social security accounts. Cash—Carole Carnes. Cash—Carole Carnes. Newcomb College $2,500. Chi Omega Sorority $150. Town and Country. Levy's. Goldsmith's. Halle's. McCauley's Welding Shop.

The night wore on. It was ten o'clock. They sat. We all sat. Talking, waiting and waiting for a telephone call from the hospital. Miss Mary Dodd sat in the brown chair. Gussie Phillips was stretched out on the couch. Gussie wore bedroom slippers. Her days were spent doing so much good that she never had time to completely dress or wash her hair. How much longer were they going to stay? There was no telling how long Miss Mary Dodd would feel like "May needed her."

Miss Mary Dodd's first husband, a doctor, had committed suicide. She didn't care much for him. Her second husband was a silly alcoholic. She loved him dearly and worked like a dog for him. Then, after he died, she went about saying that you are never too old to marry again. Now, her lips clamped together, her hands folded tightly, she stated out of the silent night, which had fallen upon us: "I never could understand why a man would marry a woman that he had slept with."

"Neither could I," replied Gussie, closing her eyes and stretching her big feet. She had led the group following Shelby and me the previous winter.

My stomach twisted into three knots. My throat contracted and I had to concentrate in order to manage an interested expression. If only Shelby would come back from New York and, in a perfect rage, smash their false teeth down their throats. If only he were here to tell me that he still loves me. If only Shelby would come back.

I took a deep breath, so that my voice would be completely controlled.

"Gussie," I said, reverting to an earlier conversation, "I don't agree with you about nursing homes. I think they are one of the few sane ideas this generation has produced. Why should old Uncle Blot or Aunt Blaa ruin perfectly useful lives?" I knew that her life had been dominated by attending to her mother and her old aunt.

Where was Shelby? I needed, needed desperately to talk to George, who shared his apartment, someone who might know where he was. The telephone did not answer.

"Carole, what ARE you doing back there? Miss Mary Dodd is ready to go home."

Oh, Miss Mary Dodd, you are so much fun! "Just a minute," I said apologetically. "I have put in a long distance call."

I had brought the telephone into the bathroom, which is large and square, not like those economy bathrooms in modern houses. It has the kind of bathtub that you can really lie in, one that stands on legs and isn't glued to the floor. The gas heater installed in the fireplace is the only concession to progress. The mantel over it, with its clutter of hair brushes, cold cream, foundation creams, astringents, mascara, powder puffs, pins, rollers, a hair dryer perched rather precariously, eye shadow, polish remover, cuticle remover, deodorant, nail scissors, had been put to the same use by three generations of vain women, because the light here is flattering. Mother primped in front of that mirror when she went to dances. I dressed there, and that evoked memories of Peter, who came from Missouri and took me out for several years when I was at Newcomb. I remembered when I first met him. He saw me coming from the library and asked where I was going, and took me somewhere for coffee. He walked me back to the dormitory and caught my hand. Every evening was full of promise then. Now I am with these bats. I looked into the mirror only to see Miss Mary Dodd half way in, her girdle already pulled down.

"Excuse me!" I said and flew out.

When the operator finally called me back it was to report that Shelby's number had not answered.

"Carole, are you through talking? Miss Mary Dodd is ready to go home. Were you calling long distance again? I don't know what I am going to do about that telephone bill."

I came out. They all looked. They were thinking about the telephone bill. Miss Mary Dodd kissed Mother goodnight and marched down the steps. She wasn't the kind of lady one needed to assist. I started the car; then there came that awful silence, the one that comes before a talk.

"Carole, I know it isn't any of my business."

You're damned right. If only I could say that. But the best I could do was a stony stare.

"You know I love Hayes. And I love May." I suspected that she didn't love Mother, as she would have been jealous of Mother's easy life. I hoped she could feel my coldness. "I don't know whether I love you or not. I expect you are awfully spoiled but you're a pretty thing."

"Oh, Miss Mary Dodd, what can I do to make you love me more?" I didn't say it.

I ran a red light, nearly colliding with another car. Its driver shouted at me. I wished he had hit me. Not killed me, but just hurt me enough so that I could be unconscious for the whole terrible rest of this.

Mother was sitting alone in the front room when I returned from running Miss Mary Dodd home.

"Has anyone called?" I asked.

"No. From whom are you expecting a call? Why do you suppose he hasn't called?"

Why hasn't George called to tell me where Shelby is, I thought? George was always in the apartment.

I began to gasp for breath. I couldn't say a word. I dare not let Mother see me and suspect that we had problems. She would use any weakness in our relationship to stick in the thin edge of her wedge. I tore through the house to the kitchen and out onto the long back porch, bumping into a stepladder on the way. It has been six weeks since we have seen each other.

And that last letter sounded so remote, as if he were only writing to me out of an obligation. And last week there was only one short letter, and Mother said, "You don't suppose Shelby is letting you down?" They all think it. They are all waiting for it. Can this be happening? Just six weeks ago we were the most important things in the world to each other. My life swirled about me. What did it amount to? What was real? Fifteen months ago Missy Green and I were eating cheeseburgers and sipping cokes by a swimming pool at the Buena Vista Hotel on a Chi Omega house party. It was certainty, a trivial world. Nancy Snellings and Courtney Ann Parker were coming out that year and there would be lots of parties. Would it be Peter or the New Orleans man or the planter or would I meet someone new? My thoughts were on finishing college and hopefully not having to use my teacher's certificate and having a big diamond ring placed on my finger and having my picture all over the paper and five beautiful children. My house would not have false beams or be painted in rose or aqua. My house would be painted a pale yellow and bask in the sun amidst mosses and wisteria. There would be a pond with lily pads. If only a lily pad would come along now, and I could board it and float away.

Someone was watching me through the screen!

"Freddie, is that you?"

"Yes'm, Miss."

"You want anything, Freddie?"

"No'm. I don't want nothing. I just felt like coming. There waddn't nothing else I could do."

I opened the screen door and sat down on the steps beside him. But I couldn't say anything.

"Why you cry so, Cahl, Miss, child?"

"Freddie, it's so awful, I feel like it's always going to be awful. Nothing better can ever happen anymore. Everything's changing, going wrong. And, and... it's these people, these awful old people."

I felt like I had to say this to someone, even if it did sound so trite.

"Miss Cahl, you ain't paying no mind to them folks, is you? Folks always gonna talk, specially if you's fine looking and you's got rich blood."

It sounded so simple the way he said it. But thoughts didn't occur to him about how barbaric and destructive people are. And there was Shelby, so remote in New York? I felt like I was drowning.

"Things goes. Just like my back goes. For a while in de winter time it gits so bad I think I can't stand no more, and sho as I do, de Laud," he rolled his eyes up to the heavens, when he mentioned 'de Laud,' "he come and send a fine dry day and gives my pains a rest for a short spell."

The night smelled sweet and dusty. I could hear the cotton gin across the railroad tracks chugging away. It would stay open almost all night. We sat and listened.

"Freddie, you remember when Daddy used to take me up in the field and put me on the horse with Zacharah and I'd ride Duke?"

A grin broke all over his face and the moon was reflected on his teeth. "Sho! Duke, he's still alive. He got so fat, ain't no¬body been on him in three years or mo, but in his day he was a fine Tennessee Walking horse"

"How old is Duke?"

"You remembers. He was born on your birthday."

"Of course. When Mother was having me, Daddy told you to call him when Melody foaled. No one was quite sure which one was born first."

He laughed and said, "You go off to school all dis time so you could forget all you knowed. What done happened to yo mother wit?"

Freddie got up a little stiffly, because of his back, but he was still a relatively young and good-looking man. "It's night time for sho. I guess I better go on."

"Thank you for coming, Freddie, we really needed you tonight. And you know if you need us…" the conversation stopped.

"Yes'm. I knows dat."

There was the sound of the telephone ringing. "That's the telephone, Freddie. I'd better get it."

"Go ahead, child."

My father died that night on October 5th, 1963. His nurse said that he looked up and said, "God help me." He had not been a desperately religious man for he loathed the hypocrisy and the piety of churches. His religion was in his deeds. He was educated at private schools, loved sports, and became the pitcher for the Memphis Chickasaw Baseball Team. Several people with whom he played baseball had made the big league and we would hear about them when we tuned the radio onto the World Series. He had come from a good family in West Tennessee, but hated cities and learned to love the Mississippi Delta, its freedom, and its expanse. He had eventually married into the family that had been his surrogate family for many years before he even noticed my mother. He looked after her as if he had been her father. That was his life.

A Power House of a Woman

I gathered the crop while Daddy was ill. This was done with the assistance of a good man, Mr. Billy Greer, and Freddie. Freddie didn't like anyone else on the scene and managed to pronounce Mr. Greer's name to be Mr. Grahr. I would ask him about something and his reply was, "Mr. Grahr says to do it this way, but us don't do it this way." Stuck in the middle, I would always say, do it our way. We all made a big profit, Freddie included. Mr. Greer was glad to see the end of this job, which he no doubt took out of friendship.

Six weeks after Daddy died I tied up enough of the business to go back to New York for a visit with Shelby. Annie Mae stayed with Mother, which I thought was an excellent solution. Mother pouted: "I had a husband; now

I just have Annie Mae."

Shelby and I had a beautiful time in our little flat at 16 Gay Street in Greenwich Village, the location of the Janet Leigh film *My Sister Eileen*. That was the only thing to distinguish the flat other than a bird's nest with an egg, left by the previous occupant. We had one single bedroom and George Allen, a Harvard graduate and an editor for Oxford University Press, had the other single bedroom. The kitchen was stuffed into a former broom closet and consisted of four ranges beneath a gas oven and a refrigerator beneath the ranges. One washed the dishes in the bathroom sink. This was supposed to be a find of a place in the Village. I learned about garbage and carried it out regularly in Safeway sacks. In Mississippi someone else had carried out garbage and also lined the can with *The Commercial Appeal*. Housekeeping was part of my initiation. I prepared dinner for Shelby and George in the evenings; my luxury was the twenty-five cents that I spent on mushrooms from the corner green grocer. The words of one of the ladies at Best & Co. resounded in my mind, "Tony Curtis came in here to buy a suit. Where else can you see that but New York?" New York seemed a high price to watch Tony Curtis shopping.

During this period I interviewed for jobs. In upper Manhattan, Bellevue Hospital wanted a new image, beyond craziness. They planned to produce a paper called *Better Bellevue*. I was to promote this image. Now the telephone greeting became "Better Bellevue." The office was illuminated by a fluorescent light and the rest of the hospital was darker, with depressed people shuffling down the corridors in pajamas. I smiled as politely as I could manage and escaped onto the street and the subway in the midst of an early snowstorm. That night we went to see the film, *Tom Jones*, and afterwards the city was covered in a blanket of white. For twenty-four hours New York City relaxed and took on the demeanor of a normal life. People paused and contemplated the snowflakes until the slush resumed.

Shelby's friend, Ray LaMontagne, married in the Chapel of Yale. We drove to New Haven with his friend Norty Wright and his fiancée, Susan

Watson. Norty was the director of the television program for children, *Captain Kangaroo*, and Susan was staring in a Broadway hit musical, *The Fantastics*. I was introduced to a world of new and sparkling people. But in our cramped apartment one could hear one's neighbors brush their teeth and I heard one man say to another, "Aldous Huxley has died."

The reply was, "Elvis Presley has died?"

"Naw, just some wyter."

Then Greg Taylor telephoned me from Rego Park City in Queens, where she and her husband, Norris, were living. Greg was from Memphis and I had told my mother that I was living with Greg and Norris. "They have shot President Kennedy. He is now in a casket, leaving Dallas." Two hours earlier my Aunt Zula, who lived in Dallas, had stood beside the road and watched the cavalcade, waved in her usual perky manner and said, "Hello Jack, Hello Jackie." Then she heard the bang. At the same time my friend from Shelby, Rives Neblett, was sitting in his very good fraternity house at Ole Miss when the news was announced and he watched the boys snicker. He walked out.

I continued to job hunt and even added "Managed a Plantation in Mississippi" to my resume, which inspired one employment agent to describe me as "a power house of a woman." Finally a light appeared for my future employment. The slot as a "Research Assistant" with *Time-Life* was mine to begin in January. I went home to a brave Christmas on Mother's behalf and watched her put on boots and walk in the snow to a coffee party hosted by a lady with whom I knew she was not in the least congenial. She was trying to become a widow.

It was still exotic for me, coming from New Orleans and Memphis, to take the elevator to the 46th floor of the *Time-Life* building, but that was the only interesting part of my job in the biography department of their library. They had files on everyone whose name had appeared in *Time*, *Life*, or the *New York Times* on at least three occasions. These were contained in manila folders which cut one's fingers. My supervisor was a lady from

Lithuania who spoke seven languages. She tried her best to interest me in some complicated procedure for indexing. All that I was able to manage was to stare and wonder how anyone who spoke seven languages would do this job. The head of the department was a New England lady named Miss Content Peckham who wore woolly red stockings. As she marched through the library, she came upon me crawling on my mobile stool reading the manila envelopes. They even had a file on Shelby, because he had been to Red China and had developed in his sophomore year at Yale an import/export business. She snapped, "Reading doesn't get filing."

I spent half my work time at *Time* in the infirmary of the corporation, because the new birth control pill obtained from the Margaret Sanger Institute made me sick. I also broke out with hives from the tedium of the job.

Then Ann telephoned. Mother was going off the rails. Annie Mae had left and Lizzie was staying there, but no one could cope. I had to come home.

Shelby and I had three days. He had already decided to go back to live in Europe in late April. He knew that he did not want to spend his life in the States. His father was planning to accompany him on part of this trip. We had considered a marriage on a ship. This news wrecked those plans. We parted on 24th of March 1964.

The Lady of Whitfield

Mother was indeed in a bad shape. She could not walk or talk. She had been taking medications prescribed by a psychiatrist at the Gartley Ramsey Hospital, which she complemented with port ordered from the grocery store and delivered to her house. At the suggestion of Gussie Phillips, she had added bromide to this cocktail for nerves. For six weeks she remained in the Gartley Ramsey on a drip. One day the nurse said to me, "She is such a pretty lady; we can see it now." By that time she had recovered her faculty to talk, somewhat incoherently, but could not walk. The doctors said they could do no more and I would have to take her to a more permanent place. Blue Cross was reaching its limit. I couldn't find anything on the spur of the moment and the few places mentioned cost a fortune. Although she was well off, her income would vanish at the suggested private institution in Alabama. It charged $6,000 a month in 1964. I hired an ambulance to carry her to what was officially called the Mississippi State Lunatic Asylum in Whitfield, south of Jackson.

I have never experienced a sadder drive than that lonely country road to Whitfield. The words of Jason Compson from *The Sound and the Fury* rang through my head: "Blood, I says, governors and generals. It's a damn good thing we never had any kings and presidents; we'd all be down there at Jackson chasing butterflies."

The grounds were large and the buildings of red brick secured with bars. I remembered Mother's friend Kathryn Henderson and the fifteen years that she had spent there. Elizabeth Thomas's elegant mother, Mrs. Kirk, had tolled up twenty-five years. There were Uncle Gerald and several other people from Shelby who had died at Whitfield in the remaining months of their lives. I assumed that this might be my mother's fate. And what was *I* to do if it were?

Her very intelligent doctors learned as much history as I knew, including her father's suicide and Aunt Ellen's. Then I told them of the drugs that she had been taking. When I mentioned the word "bromide" they looked at each other and nodded. The drip had certainly improved her condition, but she was still unable to walk. They placed her in a room with a skinny little rough woman with long facial hairs called Mag, and they were contained within a locked corridor. I was instructed not to return for two weeks.

I went home to sit before the television with Lizzie. We watched Susan

Watson singing in *The Fantastics*. I had known an interesting world. The plunge from romance and stimulation had taken only two months. Was it now going to be taken away?

On my first visit, I found Mother walking down the corridor between two good country women, who were practical nurses. She immediately complained of the food, had forgotten that Daddy had died, and was riveted by the tales of her roommate, who "got into fights" and was now able to leave Whitfield, but didn't want to go! I investigated having a restaurant send her food, but Whitfield was ten miles away from a restaurant. She had to make do with Coca Colas and candy bars to supplement the hospital fare of watery vegetables, creamed corn, a tiny nibble of fatty meat, and light bread, which she refused to eat.

On the second visit, two weeks later, she had a new roommate, Mary. Having borne thirteen children, Mary was in this institution because she wanted another baby! Mother was thinner and walking better with the assistance of the nurses. She looked at me with a perplexed expression when I said, "Now, Mother, don't you remember, Daddy is dead."

"Daddy is dead?"

She understood, but it didn't go deeper.

During the following two weeks, she had a gentleman caller at Whitfield, an old beau from the Coast, who had heard that Daddy had died and of her predicament. When I told my neighbor, Lucille Flautt, she responded, "They should have locked up both of them."

On the next visit, the doctors said that Mother was ready to come home. She had been given a number of electrical shock treatments, probably more than in the Memphis hospital, but they also gave a good followup drug. The poisons had been expunged from her system; healing would take place at home. Whitfield serviced an outpatient system, and if she had a panic attack, she could telephone them at any time and talk to a doctor. I wasn't sure if I could cope, but no one gave me a choice. Mother packed her bags and got into the car and declared that she would have never been carried on a major highway with me driving unless it had been to leave Whitfield. I looked out at the early summer fields covered in a golden afternoon sunlight and mused that whatever Mississippi lacked in cultural and educational facilities, it certainly had a good loony bin. This form of socialized medicine has existed for a long time in the state of Mississippi. Mother entertained me all the way home. I was grateful to have her.

The house had been newly decorated, thanks to a burst pipe. Mother climbed upon her four-poster bed and her room was immediately filled with well wishers. After Whitfield she was thankful for what was left of her life and able to cope; she never had to return to another institution. That summer she looked especially pretty at Mimi's wedding to Mike Saunders, dressed in a smart new suit to show off her new Whitfield figure.

Europe

My trip to Europe went through Memphis and Washington. I tried to get out of Shelby the summer that Mother was sick by attending summer school at Memphis State and returning to Shelby on the weekends. Bob and Mary Elizabeth Wilson had moved to Shelby from Rosedale and bought the house on the street that had belonged to Cousins George and Joe Shelby. Bob was a descendant of the early settler who had died of yellow fever caught from nursing his friends. Their three children, Augusta, Bob, and Mary Elizabeth were in Shelby part of the time. Augusta had been my close friend in high school, when I was in love with "the Man," for she was his cousin. She had finished Vanderbilt University, obtained a Master's Degree from the University of Mississippi, and now she, too, had to face the job market and found a job in a bank. I joined her, sharing a cheap apartment behind the Baptist Hospital in Memphis and took French and typing at summer school, and after the summer school closed I worked for temporary agencies, making enough to support me each week. I had one foot in one world with Shelby and the other dangling. Shelby and I broke up in November 1964 because he reached the conclusion that he could not support me in Europe and have the life of his design.

As Mother was much better, Augusta and I decided to move to D. C. despite the protest from everyone I knew. In unison the older generation declared that I was escaping my duty; Memphis was my place. One important cousin had the ambition for me to stay there and re-establish the Carnes name. Someone whom I liked very much proposed to me. I wondered for the next two years why I had not accepted it. I was twenty-four and longing for security, a congenial mate, a house on Walnut Grove Road, and once more to put on a pleated skirt and cashmere sweater and push a trolley at Cecil's Delicatessen. But there was another world and I had to be a part of it. There remained my $600 dollars to finance the move, replenished this time from my salary at Time, Inc.

*

I had no idea what I had got myself into when I took a clerical government job in the Civil Rights Division of the Department of Justice. One had to have a security clearance and the FBI had a big time with me. The investigator went to the cheap apartment building where Augusta and I had lived for a few summer/autumn months in Memphis and flashed his badge at the receptionist saying, "What do you know about this girl?"

"Well, she was never very friendly," replied the terrified woman. No, because I was darting into the lobby to search my post box and found very few letters. Then the FBI went to Shelby, Mississippi. The field trip with a man who had been to Red China was on everyone's lips. At the same time a young man from Shelby had stolen a tractor that had belonged to the federal government. The citizens of Shelby were anxious to give him as good a report as possible for his investigation.

The FBI even wasted their resources by going to New York City to interview George Allen. "Did she live in this apartment with Shelby Tucker, unmarried?" George was somewhat more intelligent than the investigators and replied, "Yes, she lived here just after her father died; she shared the apartment with us. Shelby slept on the couch in the living room."

Despite much travel and interrogation they couldn't find anything to prohibit me from getting a grade 3 job (the lowest in the Civil Service), which amounted to reading reports on Ku Klux Klan activities in the South and summarizing them for their lawyers in the Civil Rights Division of the Department of Justice.

I changed jobs frequently during my two years in Washington, eventually moving on to a job on the Senate Judiciary Committee, editing a calendar. When applying for this job, I intimated to Senator Eastland that I had many relations in the Delta, and his assistant wasn't astute enough to realize that they were dead and would not help to save the Senator from the new conservatives of a Republican variety. It was embarrassing to continue using the same references, and on my last job I gave Augusta's name as a reference, for she had a good job with "The War on Poverty" in the Johnson Administration. They re-investigated my file on a morning that Augusta had told her boss that she was not coming into work, but was spending the weekend in New York. He begged her to finish something, and she consented, on the condition that she could dry her hair in the office and not receive anyone. That was agreed. The FBI agent appeared, flapping his card, and was ushered into my referee with rollers in her hair under a ballooning hairdryer. The questions became gritty, "We hear that she is quite attractive? Is that true? What does she look like? Would you call her impetuous, making love in the broad daylight with a man who has been to Red China?"

Augusta had more regard for my record than I did and insisted that I write a letter, a lie of a letter, and place it into my file, to counteract this mendacity. It occurred at the peak of the civil rights unrest. Augusta wrote the letter, dressed me in a pale blue skirt and sweater with a green and blue striped blouse and sent me to see a very sympathetic inspector of the FBI. I told my side of the story, blaming it on Mississippi, small-mindedness and exaggeration, definitely not naked-in-the-open, making love. He seemed happy to accept this misrepresentation.

The FBI didn't know that I continued to receive letters from Shelby. We were small fry. On a summer morning in 1965, Shelby telephoned me from Italy. He had returned from a trip to Saudi Arabia selling mutual funds, and substantial commissions were pouring into his bank account. He felt confident that he could afford to marry me and write books as well. He had bought a camper and was going to India, via Afghanistan. "Come with me."

I declined. I couldn't do that and leave Mother in Mississippi; she would go downhill immediately. We had a mutual blackmailing system. If she had a panic attack, which she continued to do, I would yell and scream and tell her that she was ruining my life and that I must be free. She would calm down, but I also knew the limits of the panic attack technique. She would not have coped in Afghanistan. One imagined her dressed each night in silk pajamas and a silk quilted robe, sitting around the camp fire with Afghans eating beans and camel kabobs and drinking water with a drop of iodine to purify it, measuring her medications, and spreading her sleeping bag over a ground sheet with a fading memory of sunsets which ended in salted nuts and cocktails. My great friend Sue Anne Kenney, said, "Don't marry, and don't miss Afghanistan." This was not possible for a person with a dependent parent.

**

The following year I was able to save a hundred dollars a month from my salary on the Senate Judiciary Committee. In early February 1967, I crept down the corridor of the Senate Office Building and placed a telephone call to Billy Burke at the Bank of Bolivar County in Shelby, dimes and quarters clinked into the phone. I wanted to borrow about three hundred and fifty dollars and as I opened my mouth to explain my facilities for repayment on a tax rebate, he replied, "All right. It will be in the post," and hung up. This was the first time that I had the occasion to borrow money, and was amazed to see how easy it was to do.

I sold my car and, with the money that I was saving, financed six months traveling throughout Europe without stopping at a youth hostel. Mother could cope with my going to Europe—something she understood—but not Afghanistan.

Mother came to visit in Washington for a pleasant month before I left. I told Senator Eastland that I was going to be married and that my mother was giving me this trip, a grand tour *before* the wedding. That kind of lie was still credible for the Deep South and I thought it advisable if I ever needed a reference, as most of the employees on the Senate Judiciary Committee were there until they collected their rather generous pensions.

In April 1967 I boarded the Italian ocean liner, Michelangelo, part of a cruise stopping at five ports before landing in Naples, from whence I went on to Positano to visit Larry and Virginia Bass Snelling (friends from Newcomb days). Afterwards I traveled to Greece at the very end of the '67 revolution, then Italy once more, Austria, France, Switzerland, Germany, Holland and Denmark. In Denmark a tall, handsome Dane, Jorgen Cold-ing, a mature medical student who was Sue Anne Kenney's boyfriend, met me at the railway station in Copenhagen. He asked me how long would I be staying. That put one on guard for the way that Europeans thought. Visits were and still are for a short break only, not as in America or Australia. We spent a happy week sailing around the fiords on Jorgen's boat, accompanied by Sue's friend, a young scientist from England, Dr. Ian Kerr. The first night, after a drink of hospital alcohol mixed with orange juice and a bag of raw English peas and no dinner, Ian and I were sent ashore to share a tent, as there was very little room on the boat. The timid Ian and I turned onto our opposite sides and went to sleep with the simple thought, "This is Scandinavia." Then I went to England to spend a month with Philippa Henderson, an Australian friend whom I had met when traveling in Greece and Italy.

Today my fellow camp mate has just retired from the forefront of investigating viruses in cancer at Lincoln's Inn Fields in London. Sue and Jorgen sailed to Antarctica and South Georgia when they were in their fifties. Virginia founded a charity in Tennessee called Poplar Creek Camp, teaching underprivileged children; Larry is a southern writer of considerable publications; and Philippa is an artist and biographer of repute in Perth, designing new towns. They have remained a close part of my life. I developed a determination that this was to be my future, but I had no idea how to implement the plan. I knew from the beginning of my story that I would get away. Life is seldom an accident.

***

Throughout the trip I had letters from Shelby. He was returning to the States from India. One letter came from the still undeveloped Seychelles Islands and a collector of stamps at American Express in Paris gave me a bottle of perfume in exchange for this stamp. We decided to meet in Oxford. Then I received another letter at American Express in London, quoting a song by the Andrews Sisters: "Bingle, bangle bungle, I'm so happy in the jungle." He was headed for East Africa to visit a friend who had coffee plantations in the country then called Tanganyika and after that he went on to South Africa. I felt a delightful sense of relief and Philippa and I bought a ticket to see *Fiddler on the Roof*, which was playing across the street from American Express. Later I went to Oxford on my own.

In 1967 tour buses and language schools had not discovered Oxford. The only people there that summer were a few students on the verge of taking a third and the rowing teams. My room was exactly like the one that Shelby had described to me where he had lived with one window, a metered heater, and a single bed. I walked as I had not walked since my first day in Paris, took a picnic to Christ Church meadows, and gazed at the buildings from the river. "This," I thought, "would be the perfect place to live." I had very little idea that these daydreams would come to fruition.

After one more month in Paris at a small hotel on the corner of the Boulevard St. Michael, I boarded the Queen Elizabeth I. This ship and the Queen Mary met in mid-Atlantic for the last crossing of the Queen Mary. Mother and Lizzie watched the Atlantic encounter on television in Shelby, but Lizzie was not impressed. She reminded Mother that on Noah's Ark people had scant regard for the powers of nature and were dancing on the upper deck. Mother disputed this passage in the Bible. Lizzie never supplied the Biblical reference, an invention of some fanciful sermon.

I waited at the apartment of my cousin Ellen in New York with five dollars to spare. Then I received a cashier's check from Mother, which was enough for me to take the Greyhound bus to Memphis, meet her, and help select a new winter coat. I returned with a resolve in October 1967: I would never live in a big city again or take another meaningless job or be pressured into marriage. I suggested to Mother that we go to Mexico for six months. She could rent an apartment for us and enjoy the change of scenery. I would study art. She pouted. She wanted me to get married. I had turned twenty-seven, the age that she was when she had married. This was late enough. Hence I sat in Shelby for six weeks, raking and picking and selling pecans, for I was broke.

Breaking Out

I received a letter to make a telephone call. It had to be conducted from the call box next to the city hall on our street, so that Mother would not be upset. I spoke to Shelby. He was very nervous, but I was calm. We agreed to meet in Memphis.

On an early December morning Mimi and Carolyn Laudig Gaines gave me a ride to Memphis. Mother thought that it was a routine shopping trip, notwithstanding that I had very little money for shopping.

Since Shelby had departed for the jungle he had hitch-hiked through Tanganyika, Kenya, Uganda, climbed Kilimanjaro, continued hitch-hiking through Zambia and Rhodesia and on to South Africa. He had flown across the Atlantic Ocean to South America and hitchhiked from Chile to Argentina, Bolivia, and Peru, visited La Paz, Cuzco, Machu Picchu, Lima, Bogotá, Barranquilla, crossed the Straights of Turbo, walked through the jungle of Panama, had been attacked by a man with a machete in a bordello, was bumped off a plane which then crashed, killing all passengers, and arrived at his home on the Mississippi Gulf Coast after crossing Costa Rica, Nicaragua, Honduras, Salvador, Guatemala and Mexico.

I had grave doubts about going back to him. Despite these doubts I dressed in one of my smart Washington ensembles, a royal blue mini-dress with a double-breasted jacket, and a green, blue and black silk scarf, and met him in a shopping center in Memphis. It was about ten in the morning and I told Mimi and Carolyn that I would most probably meet them at half past one at the Women's Exchange for lunch. I missed the lunch and stayed in Memphis for three days, telling Mother that I was visiting my old university friend, Martha Shoaf Espy. Then I returned to Shelby and announced to Mother and Lizzie that Shelby Tucker and I were getting married. I invited them to the wedding. Mother said that she would go, notwithstanding her misgivings, for she never missed an event that promised to be entertaining, but Lizzie replied, "I'll go to your next one."

As things turned out, we did not marry for seven years, but that summer I returned to England with Shelby and as in Evelyn Waugh's autobiography *A Little Learning*, ".... I climbed the sharp hill that led to all the years ahead."

Bad News
(1968-69)

J ust because one has endured meaningless occupations does not require one to become a round peg in a square hole. I tried to do this in England in the autumn of 1968, where I was accepted at the John Radcliffe Hospital as a nursing student; the education was to be paid for by the National Health System. All I had to do was to work for a meager wage for three years and take a few examinations. Room and board was provided.

The other students, much younger than I, bored me. I had to live in a dormitory at age twenty-seven and eat an institutional breakfast. How I longed for my own cup of Nescafe and a piece of toast individually grilled. This was my route to live in Europe. I began to write stories on my little portable typewriter in some vague hope that they would direct me to a more congenial path. When classes and work finished, I threw down my nurse's bonnet as quickly as possible and went to a pub, *The Bear*, on Blue Boar Lane. There I met delightful young men over steak and kidney pies. No amount of *après* hospital could compensate for the time spent cleaning the sluice. One night I was put on duty in a geriatric ward and had to calm an old man who had decorated his bed with little round balls of ordure. I greatly admired the qualified nurses and still do, but I soon came to realize that I did not fit. I began to ride again and decided that I would become a nurse in the Himalayas and track from village to village on a horseback giving out needles, syringes and tablets. This image kept me going from September to December. Also, I did not prefer old people, so I considered becoming a theatre nurse (where I would not see any patients at all) or a pediatric nurse (children being more appealing). Some mornings I looked at the old ladies and thought, *What am I doing with them when my own mother is missing me and needs me?*

Mother planned to sail to England and spend the winter for a reduced rate of £7.50 a day ($20.00 in US terms) for a room and breakfast at the Randolph Hotel (the best in Oxford). I told myself that this was far more interesting than Shelby, Mississippi, and that she could have dinners with Shelby and me at pubs in the evenings and go to the theatre.

This plan never materialized. Augusta Wilson telephoned me at the Arthur Sanctuary House, my residential establishment, and told me that Mother had been in the Shelby Hospital under the care of a Dr. Warrington, running a low-grade fever for three weeks. She didn't want me to be notified, as she did not want to wreck my plans. After several weeks of mother running a fever, Dr. Warrington had made an investigation and found a mass (all without notifying me). Mother had been moved to the care of a surgeon at the Coahoma County Hospital in Clarksdale. It was most probably ovarian cancer. I flew out that next morning.

I am not the best of fliers, partly due to a near-fatal accident while returning to Washington in 1966, when my plane dropped five hundred feet in a storm. This trip home entailed a snowstorm from New York to Memphis. When one is traveling in the direction of something bad, one seems to survive to meet that destination. Gwin Shelby met me at the Memphis airport.

Mother was charming and delighted to see me. She now had everything that she wanted. When the surgeon arrived, she mused, "Isn't life amazing, I get up in the mornings and have coffee, orange juice and coffee cake and you get up in the mornings and perform an operation. But I have been a mother and that is the greatest opportunity of all. It is the opportunity to mold a personality." When the Orderly arrived with his stretcher, she said, "Wait, I haven't put on my lipstick."

"Mother, you don't need lipstick where you are going."

"Do you think that just powder will do?" She powdered her nose.

It was ovarian cancer and it was large and hard to extract, but Mother believed that they would simply "pick it out." Isabel sat there assisting her fantasy as she had done since Mother was a child. Eleanor telephoned and whined from California, "Oh dear, I am so far away and I can't do a thing, and this is costing, costing, costing."

Mother replied, "Eleanor, it is me who has the cancer," and slammed the telephone.

Zula had died nearly three years earlier, after she and Mother had made up.

We waited for the biopsy without much hope. Then it came back showing no spread. Everyone was in disbelief except Mother. She came home and enjoyed dinner parties and long distance telephone conversations with anyone whom she cared to contact. Her hairdresser came to the house, but her thick, curly, perfect hair was thinning. She became tired. One evening she asked me to come and sit beside her bed, as she felt somewhat frightened.

I tried to be optimistic saying, "Don't count your chickens before they hatch."

"I don't think I have many more," she replied.

"More what?"

"Chickens."

A few weeks later, it was determined that her white blood count had gone up and she was readmitted to the hospital in Clarksdale. Within two days she fell into a light coma. Just before the twilight arrived she took off her big diamond rings and said, "Take these, I have always enjoyed them and I hope that you will do the same." The coma deepened during the next two weeks and the doctors ceased to visit. One night, I was advised to have a private nurse all night, for I had been staying at the hospital on a fly bed. I went to the home of my distant cousins Lucie Lee and George Maynard (Fitzgerald relations) in Clarksdale. An angel of mercy arrived from Memphis on the Greyhound bus. She was a very light-skinned African American nurse who knew what she was doing. Mother was given a large injection. Early in the dark of the following morning the hospital telephoned me at the Maynard's house and said that Mother had died. It was a merciful death and the "mistake" made by the pathologist, who failed to detect any spread, meant that she had not been subjected to mental anguish. I turned a blind eye to what happened that night, but always believed that that injection was kindly intentional.

The first person I saw at six that morning was Mr. Murphree, dressed as usual in his bow tie and three-piece suit, walking down the corridor. He simply said, "I had to see about the girl." His daughters had not caught him when he slipped away from home at age eighty-seven, pressed his toe to the accelerator, and did as he pleased. After Mr. Murphree, Elizabeth Kirk Thomas arrived at about seven.

At her funeral in the Methodist Church on the street in Shelby, I had two thoughts. The first was that I would never know another person so well. The second was that perhaps she was with her father.

She bequeathed to me a treasure of stories, the love of land, and the value of truth.

Confronting 1970s

Although it had taken years to effect changes in Delta society, integration was officially completed in 1968. This event not only coincided with the sixties, but with a boom or bubble in the price of land in the Mississippi Delta, a fluctuation that resulted in mass unemployment. Small town lawyers and property dealers acquired partners from as far away as Switzerland and Nigeria. Ordinary farmland was selling from a thousand to twelve hundred dollars an acre, better land for fifteen hundred dollars an acre, and some prime land owned by a distant cousin went to a big fat Nigerian and a man called Red for two thousand five hundred dollars an acre. New government farm programs gave the farmer almost as much per acre as the rent he was paying. The words for selecting a renter had been, "Good safe men, in good safe hands." This expression was no longer relevant. One always got paid the farm rent, even if the crop had been a disaster. Rents rose from twenty-five to fifty and sixty dollars an acre.

The cord had been cut with my sepia-tinted images and I moved to England into a harsher light of contemporary life. I took advantage of every rise in the price of cotton, every drought in the Sudan, to increase my income, so that I could study law in London (1971-1973), and afterwards became a pupil to a barrister. When I returned home a big black man in a big blue Cadillac met me at the Greyhound Bus station in Clarksdale, whisking everyone away, saying, "Miss Cahl is ours" and took me to George and Lucie Lee Maynard's house. I would raise the rent, visit Lizzie for a month, talk of old times, embark on another bus for Memphis and a plane to New York and London for another year in Europe.

Lizzie and I had a wonderful time reminiscing during these visits. I reminded her how she had erased my guilt by comforting me whenever I was naughty. As a child, I would lie on the swing with my head perspiring on her lap, while she kicked the swing back and forth in front of a window fan and stroked my hair, saying, "You's been so bad today, so bad. How come you scratch that little girl's face when she ain't done nothing to you, jest cause her name was Carole? Hey, hey, hey, so bad."

I had been rocked to sleep secure in love no matter what I had done. Lizzie made me adore being sick, for after she had fed me beef broth and finished washing the dinner dishes and had taken her afternoon nap, she would return to sit beside my bed. After our naps there would an iced Coca Cola, a salty premium cracker, and her hand. I never wanted to get up. In the winter mornings she would warm my underclothes over a gas heater to mitigate the rigors. During one of our visits at this time a strange lady came into Lizzie's house and Lizzie said, "This my daughter." The lady's jaw dropped in astonishment.

I lived economically, as a student would live in Oxford, commuting to London to law school for one pound a day. I took with me my two New-comb trunks, packing only the essentials, renting out the house in Shelby as well as the land and storing furniture in a warehouse. While I was packing Lizzie looked at me as if I had lost all couth and said,

"What is you going to put your cream and sugar in?" She stuffed a sterling silver cream pitcher and sugar bowl into my trunk and to this day I polish them in memory of Lizzie. I suspect they were the only sterling silver cream and sugar set in a bed-sit in Oxford.

My Delta income made me "a woman of independent means" in Eng-land, enabling me to support myself in law school and Lizzie as well. The first time that I returned to Mississippi after Mother's death, I found Lizzie blooming. She was seventy-six, her color was good, and she was splitting logs in her front yard. She had a boyfriend called Bull.

The following year, 1972, I brought a scholarly Englishman, Rory Wil-liams, to visit Mississippi and New Orleans. He had received a Double First degree from Oxford in classics, taught at Eton, and was now obtaining his doctorate in sociology at Nuffield College of Oxford University, because he simply wanted to do good in the world. His father had been a governor in the Colonial Services and he had grown up in Northern Rhodesia (now Zambia). He should have been suited to this part of the world. Also, his thesis was directed around the disintegration of working-class societies and the result of government programs that took the wrong direction.

Rory was subjected to Lizzie, Annie, and me, juggling the various gov-ernment programs. I had found a new house for them. It had three bed-rooms, a living room, a large dining room, kitchen and garage. This was financed by one of Lyndon B. Johnson's programs. The ex-Eton professor was put into the back of a pick-up truck and taken to Cleveland, where Annie and Lizzie were dressed in their bests to impress the powers that dispensed these houses. I helped convince them that despite Lizzie's age and retirement and Annie's lack of resources, they would be suitable purchasers. I agreed to act as a guarantor. Behind the scenes I paid the notes for thirty-three years, until the house was fully theirs. Then Rory was asked to hold their good bags, while they took shabby bags into another government office and collected their food stamps. Then we went to Kroger's with the stamps and filled the back of the truck with sacks. Idel, Lizzie's niece, had a husband who owned the truck. He shouted to Rory, who sat between mounds of groceries while I held the deeds to a house in the front seat, "This here is the gravy." Annie's five children and Lizzie took possession of the new house that week.

*

Young farmers so rich that they could not leave Shelby moved from the smaller communities to Clarksdale and Cleveland, where their children could be privately educated. The two schools in the smaller towns—Shelby, Shaw, Rosedale, Leland, Ruleville, Drew, became filled with the black students.

During this period I took every opportunity to travel as much as my breaks in law school allowed, hitch-hiking around East Africa, spending a summer in the Seychelles, traveling through Egypt and the Sudan, making many trips to France, Germany, Sweden and Denmark. In 1974, I was called to the Bar in England and Wales and entered into a pupilage in the Inner Temple. I believe that I was one of two Americans practicing as a barrister at the English Bar and the only one who did that and farmed as well. I practiced at the Bar for five years.

My land was rented to Alex Balducci, who had grown up on a farm almost in the center of our land. I returned to Shelby every August to see Lizzie, look at the crops and make reasonably certain that I received my one-fourth share. Alex warned me to never do this again as no one else would be honest with me, but he was honest. I knew enough about farming to ride over a field of cotton or soybeans and see more or less what the yield should be.

Farming was becoming such big business that people cut down every acre of wetlands before a law was passed prohibiting this. I owned twenty acres of woodlands and wetlands with Rives Neblett, who owned a similar amount adjacent to mine. On one trip I investigated clearing this. Twenty acres cleared was twenty more thousand dollars. Rives looked at these woods and said, "Carole, you don't need it, I don't need it. The woods are beautiful. Some must be left." Billy Barksdale, Cousin Isabel's husband, also pointed out to me a small whirlwind in the distance. "See that, Cah'l (the name some called me), this is what I am afraid of. They have taken every tree away in order to farm with airplanes. We could end up with a dust bowl." My woods triumphed over my greed.

Five families offered me second homes in Mississippi during this period. George and Lucie Lee Maynard in Clarksdale and their daughters Lucie Lee and Elsie were my close friends. They kept me supplied with Southern stories. Ann was always family, so I was never without her home on the street and watched her children grow up. Emma and Stuart Lytle lived on a plantation in the country near Perthshire, four miles west of Shelby. Emma was a good artist who painted and filmed the Delta as only one born to love this land could do. We had many civilized days walking the fields with their dogs, blending into the beauty of the brown, brown mud and afterwards sitting with Stu and Emma in the library before the fire with a glass of whiskey, enjoying her cook Zell's rice cakes for supper and discussing books and philosophy. Gertrude Conner, who, with another chance in life, would have been an interior decorator of repute, gave me many evenings in both of her charming houses, looking at the Delta from the inside. Isabel and Billy Barksdale treated me as a niece at their plantation called Rosebud, about fifteen miles north of Clarksdale. Thus I retained a home in the Delta.

I rode Rives Neblett's horses on his family's plantation, Allendale. He invited me to ride with him to see the New South. "Carole, I can't stand to look at another cute painting of cabins. Poverty is not beautiful! These are the houses that we are building for our tractor drivers."

The cabin replacements were made of red brick with three bedrooms, a living room, dining room, den and carport, but only five houses were needed for a fifteen hundred acre plantation. This would have once supported ninety families. I wondered how investors could pay fifteen hundred to two thousand dollars an acre for the land, hire expensive managers, buy tractors worth over a hundred thousand dollars, cotton-picking and combine machines worth over two hundred thousand dollars, chemicals, costing many thousands of dollars per month, hire a few competent men to drive this equipment and also build these houses. What was happening to the rest of the community in Shelby? Only two factories employed a total of about a hundred people, the hospital employed a few practical nurses. As a result, welfare became rooted into the community. Drugs and serious crime followed. A planter or farmer who once lived comfortably farming between six hundred to a thousand acres would soon retire on his rent check.

Rives Neblett was practicing law in Shelby as well as farming and running multiple businesses. He hired an artist to paint the town as it could become. The depot was sold to become the library. That is as far as the dream went because the shops were closing. No one could put Humpty Dumpty together again. But the landowners continued to prosper.

On one of these visits I was distressed to here that Freddie was in jail, accused of shooting someone at a joint that he had come to own. My first thought was, 'What is this going to cost me to try to bribe a Judge?' My second concern was that I had just qualified as a barrister. Mercifully his family pooled their resources and found just the right lawyer. The complainant/witness never appeared in Court and Freddie was released before I had to attempt to open my purse or compromise my career.

**

In 1976 Shelby Tucker and I were married in the Anglican Cathedral in Zanzibar, East Africa. We were married by the first African Canon of this Cathedral, Canon Sudi, who was the son of Stanley's cook. His father had been with Stanley when he found Dr. Livingstone. His mother had been a slave. It could not have been a more appropriate setting.

We hitchhiked through Idi Amin's Uganda and took a steamer from a horror of a place called Juba to Gondar in the Southern Sudan. There we took a train across the Nubian Desert to Khartoum and then another train across the desert to Wadi Hafi and on to Egypt. We flew to Jordan and hitchhiked around Saudi Arabia, Jordan, Syria, Turkey, and back through Europe before returning to England. I brought interesting photographs to Shelby, Mississippi, had a slide showing and gave an extra set of wedding photographs to Lizzie. She was relieved that I was married and had come to like Shelby very much, but the photograph of us with Canon Sudi jarred her expectations. She never framed it.

***

During the 1970's, Lizzie had three operations for cancer of the colon. Dr. Hollingsworth, who ran the clinic and small hospital on the street, telephoned me in England each time that she was operated upon. He was convinced that these incidents were separate forms of cancer and sent her case to a medical journal. Despite this she continued managing a little job when she was into her early eighties, looking after a child who had a working mother and giving her parties on my old tea table.

Mae (one of Annie's twins) married in 1972 and had three daughters: Schutrina, Sherona, and Shalah. Madie (the other twin) finished a university in Texas and became a bank examiner and later managed the accounts of an electrical company in Dallas. She is now married and has two daughters, Theresa and Kimberly, and became a court reporter.

In 1979 Shelby and I had to return to the States because of his father's failing health and his difficult marriage. Shelby's father had telephoned him in England and said, "I need you."

I sulked. Why did I have to interrupt my career as a barrister and my stimulating life in England to return to a world in which I had lost all interest, New Orleans? Places that had once been a beautiful part of my life now seemed claustrophobic. I would walk down the beach in Pass Christian, crying, "He has four children; why am I here?"

Shelby also despaired, for his writing was just reaching a satisfactory point when he had to stop and find a good job with a top law firm in New Orleans in order to make his father's last years happy. I left my chambers at the Bar and we rented out our house in England, taking an apartment in New Orleans. The Mississippi mud remained on my heels.

That Lonesome Road
(1979-1980)

Ahead of me, Shelby started to work in the law firm of Phelps, Dunbar, Marks, Claverie, and Simms. Our horrible little apartment in the French Quarter had a mouse that lived in a hole in the bathroom wall to keep me company. I began a crash course to prepare for the Louisiana State Bar Examination, which planted seeds that led to litigation and ultimately to suing nine Justices of the Supreme Court of Louisiana to obtain a Temporary Restraining Order that allowed me to sit for the dubious privilege of being examined for the Louisiana Bar without attending law school in the States. The morning that I took the examinations at a motel in New Orleans, I was on television and felt like the little girl who inspired Noel Coward to write, "Don't Put Your Daughter on the Stage, Mrs. Worthington." The last thing that I returned to the States for was to become a Civil Rights issue. I dallied in England until December, only visiting Shelby in August 1979.

In July 1979, Dr. Bob Hollingsworth had telephoned me from Shelby about Lizzie's colon cancer. He said that this time she would not pull through. She was nearly eighty-six. I did not think that I could give her up and told Lizzie of a new treatment, when I visited her house that August.

"It is called chemotherapy, Nee Nee. It could slow down the cancer for some time, but it has side effects, nausea, and one loses one's hair. You would have to be treated at a hospital in Jackson."

"I don't want no mo knife or no mo treatment," she answered.

I returned with Shelby to visit her that December. Lizzie was in the hospital on our street and many of her family were there. Dr. Hollingsworth called me into his office, "I was waiting for you to arrive as I did not want to place the entire burden upon Annie. There is no hope. I think we should cut off the supports."

I am a quick one to pull the plug and agreed immediately. In Lizzie's private room, I watched her sleeping in a pretty nightgown that Madie had bought, a tube in her nose and a drip in her hand. I remembered Octavia eighteen years earlier in an annex ward to the hospital kitchen. Withholding Federal grants from hospitals that did not integrate brought about a major change for the better in medical treatment. Shelby looked down at Lizzie and commented, "Have you ever noticed what beautiful hands Lizzie has?"

"Of course, I learned to walk holding that finger."

I waited to take Annie and Willie Bell (Lizzie's good-looking younger sister) into the corridor to relay Dr. Hollingsworth's advice.

Shelby had teased Willie Bell and she slapped him on the behind and said, "I knows how men's bees."

When Lizzie heard their laughter she opened her eyes and said, "You hush, people will think I got no folks."

That evening she propped herself up in bed, ordered supper and removed some of the support tubes herself. A few days later she walked out of the front door of the hospital that passed through the reception room to a car and returned home. Lizzie had contempt for people who ducked out of the hospital by a side door. "They's jes bees pitiful," she would say. In January 1980 Lizzie was well enough to enjoy a big family reunion, demanding second helpings of turkey and dressing. She was low once more in late February, while I was in the midst of three days of Bar Examinations.

Annie had gone into town to shop, leaving Lizzie with a cousin for an hour. Lizzie sat up in bed, held out her arms, and said, "Oh Lord."

She stared the Almighty in the face and fell back onto her pillows, looking directly at death and it took her.

*

In New Orleans, one forgets how cold the Mississippi Delta can be. I took Southern Airlines wearing a black suit and sling back shoes and no coat to arrive in freezing conditions. The ground was covered with ice. Dan, one of Annie's sons, and Willie Bell met me at the Greenville airport. I felt awful for I had a hangover. After finishing my Bar Examinations, I had let off steam and we went out to dinner with two close friends from England: Kit and Beckie Molloy. Southern Airlines stopped in Baton Rouge, Monroe and Greenville. My eyes were intent upon the paper bag in front of my seat as we bumped up and down, constantly thinking how Lizzie so disapproved of alcohol.

People had come from Arkansas, Chicago and Louisiana for the funeral at Zion Grove Baptist Church. The original church had been burned in the Sixties and the new one was only a block from Lizzie's house, but the burial was in the old Zion Grove Cemetery, near my farm, where the first church had once stood.

Annie sent Dan to Helen Aaron's store, still operating on the street, to get more white handkerchiefs. When I tried to decline accepting one, she pushed it into my hand and said, "You's gonna need it."

As friends and relations arrived, they slapped Annie's hand and filled it with dollar bills. The table groaned with food. Julia Mae (Lizzie's great niece) came from Chicago. I had not seen her since she was a girl riding Mr. Blanchard's horses. She remained the same robust spirit. When the preacher went on and on, she exclaimed in a stage whisper, "Why don't he just say a few nice words and sat down."

Annie was right. I did cry. Not from what the preacher had to say, but when I saw Madie's real grief. Lizzie had only one child, but at her funeral there were seven children (some surrogate) and several great grandchildren. The church was packed and even the hospital sent a large arrangement of flowers on an easel.

We crossed the abandoned railway track to reach the cemetery where Lizzie's parents and Carole had been buried. Some people in my car who had returned from far away began to spot familiar sights. It might have been only a bump in a field, a cedar tree. "That's where Willie Washington lived." "That's where Harrison Jenkins lived." Their old community revived for a brief thirty minutes.

None of the graves were marked, but Annie walked around confidently pointing out where each member of her family was buried. My thoughts were of a pauper's grave, unmarked. Mozart was unmarked and so was Edgar Allen Poe. Then it became too cold to think such thoughts. Although I wore a coat borrowed from Annie, my sling back shoes sunk into the ice. Crying could not compete with the freeze.

We returned to Annie's house to eat and visit. I asked suddenly, "Where is Calvin?" Calvin was Annie's youngest and most mischievous child. Some rolled their eyes. Annie said, "I didn't let Mama know. He's in jail. When he finished school he went out to Texas to stay with Madie Bee. He got to running around with a bad crowd. They was mugging. There wadd'n nothing Madie Bee could do. I went out there when he went to court. Oh it hurted me, it hurted me so bad. When the Judge say he's gonna go to prison for two years I stood up in the court and say to him, 'Yo Honor, Yo Honor, you let me have him. I'll whoop him, I'll whoop him good.'" Annie's punishment would not have been nurtured by Constitutional Rights.

"Now he seems to be doing better. He's got two specifics in religion."

Everyone tried to assure her that he had had a good upbringing and would learn his lesson and come home.

The following evening in New Orleans, I walked through Jackson Square. There I heard a lone saxophone playing, "Look down, look down that lonesome road, before you carry on."

Look Away
(1980s)

In June of 1981 I returned to England. When I looked at Shelby's stepmother for the last time, I thought, *Your troubles are not mine. I did not come into this world to devote my life to in-laws.* A person, unlike a rose, can be replanted in the same position, but I did not return to the same world that I had left. My close friend, the writer J. G. Farrell, had drowned while fishing from a rock in Ireland in 1979. Although today his family and some friends have not let him die, publishing a biography and a book of his correspondences helped him to win his second Booker Prize for *Troubles* (1971) posthumously in 2010. (*The Siege of Krishnapur* received The Booker in 1973). My career at the Bar was all but finished, due to losing touch with the solicitors who had sent me briefs. I had to change sides of the legal profession to become a solicitor, which involved more examinations when I was in my forties. I have had a good life, but I never replaced those golden years when I was in my thirties. They are probably the golden years for most people.

Shelby went back and forth to the States for a few years to finish business. I had no intention of looking back after I entered the blue interior of the British Airways plane in June 1981, happy to leave the purple carpet of the New Orleans airport. By that stage I also realized that I would probably not have children and must put my full energies into another existence. In October 1981, I made a brief visit to New Orleans to see Shelby Tucker and also to be sworn in as a member of the Louisiana State Bar and the United States Supreme Court, a credential that I have never used, but Shelby and I certainly benefited from the money that we had invested during those three years.

When I was in New Orleans, visiting Shelby, I telephoned Madie to ask about Calvin. He was due to be released.

"Madie, please get him out of Texas," I said. "When I took the Bar Examinations in Louisiana there was a case where a young man who had no previous convictions, was sentenced to twenty years for mugging in Texas. This case went to the United States Supreme Court and was not overturned."

She agreed. Calvin came home and neither did he ever look back.

Shelby's father died in 1982. He had been a delightful father-in-law, not intruding until the last two years when he could not help himself. His role had not only been parental, but that of a very amusing friend. My roots in the South were being pulled up, especially when my favorite cousin Shelby Taylor died at age fifty-nine while I was in New Orleans.

During the early eighties, I went to a party at the Ritz in London. The guests were prominent in the financial world, and I heard someone say, "The Mississippi Delta is over."

Alex Balducci stopped farming. On one of my visits to see Shelby in New Orleans, I telephoned Rives Neblett for advice on my farming. He said, "Look away until the 1990s when there will be new farm programs." On some of the years in the 1980s I had difficulties in even renting my land.

Aunt Eleanor died. Shelby Brown, Zula's son, and I inherited a small amount of land from Eleanor's portion of our Grandfather's estate. This bordered US highway 61. At that time it was rented to Abe Balducci, Alex's brother, for $60 an acre. That was the last of the gravy. My other land was on the verge of lying fallow when Abe took it over for about $25 an acre to put it back into shape, for I had had several unsatisfactory renters after Alex. Luckily Abe continued to rent the land, eventually paying $40 an acre. Rents fell throughout the Delta. And yet the land remained good to me.

Shelby Tucker is one of the most economical men I have ever known. In about 1985 he was given a speeding ticket on a U. S. Highway driving from New Orleans to Memphis. Instead of paying the ticket, he let his Mississippi driving license expire and acquired a Tennessee license, for his mother lived in Memphis. A few months later the doorbell rang at our house in Oxford. I was away and Shelby answered.

"Are you Shelby Tucker?" asked the postman.

"Yes."

"Will you please sign for this?"

Shelby looked down to see the bold lettering: Mississippi State Highway Department.

"No," he exclaimed. The honest English postman replied, "You have already identified yourself."

Shelby glanced once more and noticed that the bundle was addressed to Mrs. Shelby Tucker. *Oh Lord*, he thought, *what's she done?* He knew that I was a bad driver. There was no alternative but to sign for the package.

The contents were not as adverse as anticipated. This was a letter from the Mississippi State Highway Department saying that there had been a clause in a contract written almost a hundred years before, stating that if the railway's right-of-way, which passed through the town of Shelby, had ceased to be used for twenty years, it reverted to the original owners of the land. Over five acres of the land going through the city limits of Shelby, along the street, and north of the town, reverted to the heirs of my grandfather, Darwin Shelby. Other land went to families of other early settlers, some to the family of Mr. Godfrey Frank, my grandfather's great friend. Mr. Frank's heirs had been represented in a trial at the Rosedale Courthouse, to settle the price of this land, for the Mississippi State Highway Department wanted to buy it and make a four-lane highway through Shelby and north of the town. The jury in Rosedale had decided that $10,000 an acre was a fair price. Our share for something that we did not know that we owned was $54,000. I had to tell them about Shelby Brown (Aunt Zula's son) or the entire check was waiting for me to deposit.

*

Although the street continued to be good to me, most of my roots continued to be pulled up as friends and relatives died. By 1986 Elizabeth Thomas put up a brave fight against multiple small strokes for a few years.

Ann and I visited before her disintegration. We sat on each side of her bed and told stories. She looked so happy for at last she had the two daughters that she had never produced. She had spent her adult life trying to find a soul in others, no matter how obnoxious they may have appeared to most of us. She was no Pollyanna, but simply tried to see something good in humanity. Her cousin in New Orleans once told me that Elizabeth and her mother saw the world through rose-colored glasses. When I relayed this remark, Elizabeth smiled sweetly and replied, "Yes, I do wish they had some."

J. W. lived on for a few years and even planned to have his nephew, Scott, Ann's son, take him to Vienna, before he finally had the heart attack at eighty-six that he had been dreading since he was fifty-six.

Isabel and Billy Barksdale died in the early 1980s after spending their last few years in nursing homes. Janula Poitevent Davis Anderson, Dot Murphree, and Lizzie's sister Willie Bell Luster also died. I had grown up not only in the love of my parents and Lizzie, but that of many substitute aunts who never failed to attend a school play in which I had a part. They even attended my piano recitals! Ruth and Scott Morrison, who also died, were among this group.

Ann had divorced and remarried Paul Bode, a private school headmaster, and moved to North Carolina and afterwards to the Mississippi Gulf Coast in Pass Christian.

In 1985 Gwin Shelby was diagnosed as suffering from Anatrophic Lateral Sclerosis, a motor neuron disease that attacks the lateral nervous system. There remains no cure. He fought his fate bravely, walking into town until a few weeks before he died in 1986. I went to see him in December 1985. He called me aside and told me that he thought that I had managed a most interesting life. That was his way of saying "well done," to a life that was certainly not conventional in his world. Gwin was the last of our family to live in Shelby and in many ways the best, always responsible and charitable, a good husband, father, and stepfather—and very good-looking. He had spent his adult life under the cloud of the tragedies that took his two brothers and maimed his sister while fortune smiled upon him. He dutifully took care of all who came across his path and needed assistance, supporting seven families on his plantations who were no longer able to work. Gwin was a keen hunter, for he loved the woods and loved nothing more than to be in a boat in the middle of the Mississippi River with Sporting Life or Playboy and a bottle of whiskey. He remained handsome and manly to the last.

At the end of the 1980s I found a new tenant for my land, Jane Pirani, the daughter of my cousin Shelby Edward's son (and the granddaughter of Ruth Edwards). Life goes in tiny circles. She had inherited Cousin Fred Shelby's land from her father. This land adjoined my land. Farming was becoming a bigger and bigger business. Abe Balducci quit farming in the 1990s. I had to scrap for renters for the land that Shelby Brown and I had inherited from Aunt Eleanor, until Rives Neblett rented it after buying Shelby Brown's share in the land.

My visits to the area became brief. In 1989 I visited Shelby, Mississippi for one day, and spent the night at the house of Lucie Lee Maynard in Clarksdale. She was living in a hospital bed at her home, with around-the-clock caregivers. Lucie remained just as gracious and interested in everyone else as she had been when she was in good health, never showing the slightest irritation about her condition. She never failed to thank the nurses for each glass of water handed to her. George (her husband) had died in the early 1970s. Lucie Lee died in 1990.

By the 1990s my roots in this society had almost vanished, with exception of Annie and her family. I only returned for a day in 1990, after my mother-in-law's funeral in Memphis, and for a week in 1993 on a law case, but I did not return for a proper visit until 1995.

A Magic Carpet
(1995)

Alfred Levingston, my lawyer for many years from Cleveland, wrote to me that I might receive two bites at the cherry. The environmentalists had succeeded in preventing a four-lane highway from passing through the town of Shelby and now they were going to build a road behind the city. This road would also transgress upon our land, but the price they were offering was much lower than the one that we had received in the 1980s. I instructed Alfred to negotiate the matter, but after I paid his bill, Shelby Brown and I received very little more than the $1000 dollars an acre that we had been offered. Notwithstanding, I was glad that I had been firm.

I also needed to return to negotiate a lease on the land that Shelby Brown and I had inherited from Aunt Eleanor. My airline ticket was to expire after three weeks, which made me nervous about my negotiations. There was the further problem of my town lot, which was now half of the block on the other side of the street. Bo Ming had encroached upon this for his used equipment business. I had to find him and bring him to a lawyer's table. When the lease of the land, the sale to the highway department and the sale to Bo Ming were concluded I had three days at the end of the trip to visit Ann and her husband Paul Bode on the Mississippi Coast, so exhausted that I did not dress and ate on trays before the television set.

While waiting for three weeks and pretending that I had infinite time, I spent a few days with Rives and Jenny Neblett in Clarksdale. Rives announced that we were going to the other side of the levee for the weekend. The big levee of the Mississippi River was built after the floods of 1927. It is about a mile away from the banks of the Mississippi River. Behind this levee is a wilderness, a wild world in its third growth of cane that resembled Mississippi when my great-great-grandparents arrived. Rives belonged to a hunting club of twelve people who also loved the woods. The club owned 36,000 acres of what resembled virgin land. Flooding restricts the growth of crops to every four or five years, hence the formation of hunting clubs.

The highway from Clarksdale passed Hillhouse, scenes of big Delta dances at the Smith House, where W. C. Handy's band played in my father's youth and Memphis boys came to the Delta to meet pretty girls and dance in a pavilion to the music that had originated on their Beale Street. We were soon near to Perthshire. Rives swerved and deposited an old mattress into Emma Lytle's garbage bin which was sitting by the side of the road, waiting for collection. He said, "She would kill me if she found out."

Within five minutes we were into the woods, driving down a dusty road, passing a pasture of horses. I thought of Emma, the golden child of the Delta, who had turned down Vassar because she could not take her horse, a privilege that Sweetbrier had allowed. After two years at Sweetbriar (which she liked because she claimed that the food was marvelous), she sent the horse home and graduated cum laude from Radcliffe. There students had debated the merits of the League of Nations in her last year. She had two happy marriages, three intelligent and attractive children, and was an excellent sportswoman. In middle age she discovered that her medium was art. In her late fifties, Emma and her husband Stuart Lytle returned from Illinois to her roots in the Delta, where she accomplished her best works, baptismal scenes of black people and sculptures of people that she knew. We had met throughout my life, first at the horse shows, where she was a top rider. I felt an instinctive liking for her when I was only thirteen. Emma was a friend of my father's from the horse world and the world of her father. Friendships in the Delta are handed down from generation to generation. I met her again shortly before Mother died. The next time that I saw her was after Mother's funeral when she walked into Dr. Hollingsworth's office and announced, "I've had a blow out." That was her mother's oxygen tank. We were both instinctive and knew from this meeting that we were to become good friends.

Emma Knowleton Lytle at 75.

The lack of spare time over ten years had limited my visits with Emma. Suddenly I thrilled to the realization that my friend was there. We had corresponded over Christmases, but had seen each other much too briefly. The real and natural friendship needed nourishment. She had written to me in her inimitable scroll, "94 was an active year in spite of my 1910 birthday. A movie, *Raising Cotton*, which I made in 1941, has through the Center for Southern Studies (Tom Rankin) created quite a publicity stir. Besides my painting was productive. I'm pretty well recovered from a crisis at Thanksgiving" (this had been cancer, which she described as an "interesting experience"). "So I can confirm that I'll be here in August/September and would be delighted to see you. My current motto is, giggle and go on".

Our camping party consisted of Rives, Jenny, their children, their children's friends, and me. We arrived in the afternoon and Jenny put out the deck chairs on a sandbar of the Mississippi River. It was their secret spot on the other side of the levee. Rives and I drove into Shelby to fill up the air mattresses. The service station was now inhabited by threatening looking people.

James's Chow's grocery was closed as well as Guy Phillips's. James had worked though much of the 1980's, and his children always took a part. Although most of them were members of the professional worlds, when they came to Shelby each did a turn behind the cash register in his supermarket. It was a Chinese way of showing respect for their parents. We scratched about and found a few supplies from Johnny Mangialardi's Grocery and returned to the river.

Jenny was preparing a gourmet meal on the two burners of the camp cooker. We opened the Absolut Vodka and the conversation loosened to subjects which we would have never mentioned if we not been on "the other side of the levee." Two boys in the party had shot a deer and it was already hanging. They were allowed to cull one hundred deer a year to keep the stock healthy. After dinner we drove through the woods in Rives's truck and watched the tiny illuminated eyes watching us. There was no one to stop or accuse us of being over the limit; there were no roads, only animals and woodlands. I was overcome by the beauty of my roots and called Annie from the telephone in the truck (an invention novel to me at that time).

"Annie, this is me, Carole. Guess where I am? On the other side of the levee in a pick-up truck."

"You ain't been in no wreck is you?"

"No, I will see you day after tomorrow afternoon."

I awoke before the others the next morning to the sound of the birds, and then immediately behind my tent there was something that went "gee-gee." I looked out and there was a hissing doe. Mallards and snow geese flew over the river on their trek south accompanied by the purring of the barges going south as well. I walked about the sand bar taking photographs. Then Jenny enticed the two burners to produce breakfast and we washed dishes with sand instead of soap. Afterwards we saddled some horses and rode over that unspoiled land.

Rives told me that he had heard that Mimi was in Shelby, visiting her father. I telephoned Albert and told him to keep her, but not to tell her who was coming. Within five minutes of our reunion, two women now into their fifties rushed into the bathroom to exchange confidences. It was the same bathroom where we had first shaved our legs and told all before and after the dances.

Mimi had a man with her who wanted her to marry him. He was extremely rich. What should she do? I had no idea. Rives and I thought that he looked fine.

When we returned to the levee, Venus had arisen from the Mississippi River. Jenny, having bathed in the river and washed her hair, looked more beautiful than any woman I can remember seeing. We spent another night to the same nostalgic sounds of the Delta and the following day I left them to visit Annie.

The distance of the road from the riverside highway to Shelby is only four miles. I passed Emma's house at Perthshire. This dark-red brick colonial house had been built by Dr. Maddox, Aunt Mary's father. It was the site of her wedding and her proposal from Uncle Tom Poitevent. The next landmark was the former site of Miss Laura Mae Keeler's house. It had been larger than anything I have ever seen in the Delta, High (Texas) Victorian. The Keelers kept to themselves and there were rumors of gypsy blood and of a padded room where old Mr. Keeler had to be locked when he got drunk. Some said that Miss Laura Mae had been a belle in her day and that gentlemen's carriages had lined the road on Sundays when she was a young lady. There were other rumors of a serious suitor who was a widower. Her mother had denounced him, "I don't want any warmed-over love for my babe."

Soon the carriages became fewer and then there were none. Laura Mae donned the khaki clothes of a male farmer. Her face became leathered by the sun. She wore a man's hat and lived in this amazing house near her brother and nieces and a nephew until they all flew away. Few people were ever given the privilege of entry. Now it had fallen to a demolition company.

In the late 1920s a black trustee at Parchman Prison, the vast state farm penitentiary located five miles on the east side of Shelby, was said to have raped a white woman, the daughter of one of the prison managers. He had been serving time for a previous conviction for rape and working as a trustee in their house. He escaped. People claimed that the girl had been engaged to marry and that her fiancé had broken the engagement because she was now 'ruined.' The Bolivar County sheriff's posse offered a high reward for anyone who brought him in alive. I heard the award was $50,000 (at least one million by today's calculations). Miss Laura Mae Keeler captured the man single handed, hid him in her kitchen and was on her way to hand him over to the sheriff and make her fortune, when the mob surrounded her car and demanded that he be given to them. She had no choice. The mob took him from county to county; eventually he was burned alive in Tallahatchie County. I questioned this tale and was told by an old man in the 1950s that it was true.

"How do you know?"

"Because, as a young man, I followed the mob and watched it."

I passed the spot that had been Monochonut Plantation. The house had burned, but all of the trees and shrubs remained, as if the garden was waiting for someone to live there once more.

The next spot on my right was the Shelby Country Club, golf club, swimming pool, the site of the horse shows and the football and baseball games. Then I passed the cemetery with the cement-vaulted graves of my mother's childhood friends, the Humphrey children. The vaults were a bit cracked and the whole graveyard was parched. Bulbs would not have grown there. I quickly noticed my parents' graves and the tiny scrub bush on their lot that did not appear to have grown one inch in twenty-five years. On the other side of these landmarks was the long stream called Holmes Lake, still lined with some cypress trees, where the lily, named by the Native Americans, once bloomed. Before I reached Shelby, I passed a mound on my right with a cistern in the center. Here remain the graves of my great-great-great uncle, Dr. Thomas Neil Shelby, and his young wife, Bella, first settlers, who were buried on their plantation during the Civil War. Then I reached Shelby and drove to Mae's house, where Annie now spent most of her time.

As I pulled up near the door of the red-brick duplex, built with federal funds, Annie shouted, "You lock your dooh. My niece didn't lock hers and her car was stold."

I arrived at a propitious moment that the preacher's dinner was waiting on the kitchen table to be delivered that evening. We got the first bite which consisted of fried chicken, Freddie Hall's home grown turnip greens, okra fried in corn meal with onion and tomatoes, corn bread, black eyed peas, a blackberry cobbler and several sweet potato pies, to be washed down with mint iced tea. Both Freddie and Mary Lee were waiting to see me. Divorced for fifteen years, they remained friends. Freddie lived in a similar brick house behind Mae's house.

Mae was working in Ruleville, twenty-five miles away, as a caregiver for an old person. Now 43, she had just begun to put on a little weight. Still in her white uniform, she reached for the telephone. The call was from Sunflower College in Indianola, where her youngest daughter, Shalah, was a student. Mae's other daughters, Schutrina and Sherona, had diplomas. Shalah was in the infirmary. They inferred that she was pregnant. Mae left immediately in a second-hand car to drive eighty miles to see her baby daughter. It was difficult for me to envision Mae as a middle-aged mother. I still saw the two little girls across the street from my house, substitute baby sisters after Carole died. Then I remembered Mae as a young girl, a stunner. Mae was so beautiful, without the smallest element of self-consciousness. *Why can't she become a model*, I thought? But it was not to be.

The talk at lunch was about the Delta as it stood today. Freddie said, "When you sees something you just looks away."

Mary Lee agreed and paused. "I am going to make a phone call."

She telephoned her daughter. I could hear her daughter complain about her hair.

"Forget your hair, I want you to see somebody."

Reluctantly the daughter, Nini, arrived within minutes, wearing a very smart dress which she said she had bought from Miss Helen Aaron's store, still operating on the street. Nini worked as a supervisor at Parchman, the State Penitentiary, and she now lived in Margaret Murphree Stone's old house. I quickly learned that many houses in the town were now identified by their former white owners' names. She was furious with the kind of people that she viewed at work on a daily basis. "They don't wanna work, they simply don't want to."

Mary Lee reminded her that when she was a child she had refused to pick cotton. Mary Lee had walloped her and said, "You's gonna do any kind of work you can do, and at the moment, this is your work."

I assumed that these complaints about the present condition of the society were being said for me. I ventured that, "Despite everything you are saying, your lives must be better now. Many of you are in the white people's houses; all of you have indoor plumbing, and a reasonable standard of living. I can't comment on the schools because they are so complicated and riddled with drugs."

They agreed. Then Annie said, "But it was better then. Us would get up in those fields and have a good time." They all roared with laughter.

"This was because you were young."

"Yes," replied Mary Lee, Annie, and Freddie almost in unison.

After significant thought, Mary Lee added, "But then there was someone behind us. Your parents were behind us, but now there is no one. I live in Mound Bayou. I like to exercise and walk with a friend very early in the mornings before any of *them* is up. After that I take my car and take disabled children to school. I am afraid of *them* even in the early mornings."

To my amazement they all appeared to agree, although the young daughter could not have remembered the past, she was only disgusted with the present. There was her father who could neither read nor write, but he had always held a foreman or a truck driver's job, despite a bad back.

I later digested this conversation with Emma. She was not surprised. Was Emma ever surprised?

Emma came to the front door looking none of her eighty-five years. I handed her a present in memory of Stu, and our many quiet evenings with a drink, a fire, and philosophy. I had heard about the success of her movie, "*Raisin' Cotton*," and asked to see the video. Before pushing that into the machine, she built a fire. One could not contemplate her birthday, as this slim beautiful lady crawled on the floor, poking the fireplace. Nathan, once upon a time, built a fire to which one only had to strike a match, but he had long since gone. Then Emma arranged the screen that her daughter Suzie had painted on her last visit to hide the library from public view, Emma's curtains were now beyond repair, and she was neither a decorator, seamstress, nor a cook. She was an artist and a seeker of truth.

The home movie was an effort to see ordinary life through the eyes of a Mississippian. Emma had simply tried to show how cotton was grown. She had filmed the transition from mules to tractors. The event included the Mule Races in Rosedale, which became a social event. The film ended with cotton in the mills of North Carolina. She commented, "I filmed it because it was there."

Other objects in the house were the wonderful busts of Zell, Nathan, and Johnny (John Henry), then the young boy working in the house. He had now become the probation officer and Emma's caretaker. Her baptismal scenes were reintroduced to me before going to bed with a book about William Alexander Percy (a Delta poet and writer).

I recalled our many visits in the 1970s, when even then I could not believe that she was sixty, old to me at that time. After divulging her eighty-fifth birthday, she added, "Life is now." At eighty-five, Emma was still living for now.

We had stayed up until the early hours of the morning, but Emma claimed that she was glad because her daughter, Eleanor, had left the previous day and she needed another boost. John Henry prepared a breakfast of grits, toast and bacon, and although exhausted, we both ate our breakfast in another room that had been painted by Emma and beneath a beautiful charcoal drawing that Emma had done of Elizabeth Kirk Thomas, capturing all of her compassion. It was one of Emma's best pictures and a fitting place for our departing breakfast. She felt a little weak, planned to go back to bed, but afterwards would go on to Greenwood to a luncheon.

Before leaving I spoke to John Henry about my conversation with Freddie, Mary Lee and Annie. As a probation officer he was closer to the social problems than any of us. He confirmed that there was too little work, drugs, and a disintegration of family and community support. I turned to the road back to Memphis.

Driving out of Shelby there was a junkyard in place of the flattened Texaco Station with dead dogs by the side of the road. Then there was another empty and seared spot where Johnny Sacco's station once stood.

Johnny had the habit of keeping cash available for making small loans. He was robbed and murdered. Soon his service station too ceased to exist, exploding into a burst of flames because of the chemicals poured on to the soil for so many years.

The first town on my route was Clarksdale, a thriving community of about forty thousand well-heeled people. In the old days it had been known for its inhabitants, who were "As rich as Croesus and wild as bucks," for the land in Coahoma County was better than the land in Bolivar County. The school had been better than most in Mississippi. Clarksdale had been the first town in our part of the Delta to have a swimming pool that had faced a small zoo with monkeys and peacocks bordering a stream. Now there was only a place called Sugar Ditch. The zoo had long since vanished. Clarksdale looked like a ghost town with the two picture shows closed; the Elks Club (site of many dances) now empty, its ballroom draped in cobwebs; Garmon's ice cream parlor, where we once met boys, boarded over; the Alcazar Hotel closed. The only thriving businesses were the travel agency, where Elsie Maynard Milligan worked, and the Gift and Art Shop with its infinite supply of Francis I for Delta brides. The town was still rich, but it was moving further and further into a suburb that had once been a cotton field, with the fine old houses turned into law offices or torn down. Chain stores such as Wal-Mart had taken the businesses away from the smaller stores. Television here as elsewhere had ruined the picture show. The entrance into Clarksdale looked like a slum, and the old houses had suffered from proximity. Like Shelby, much of the town's center was boarded-up.

The next sight was Tunica, a town no larger than Shelby. It had been a landmark to all in the Delta because it had boasted two service stations, east and west of highway 61, where the ladies from the Delta stopped, dressed in their hats and gloves on their way to and from Memphis. The dilemma at this point had been pie: on the east side (toward Memphis) was the coconut pie and on the west side, the chocolate pie. I stopped on the west side for the service station on the east no longer existed. To my dismay I found only packaged Moon Pie and a faded memory of ladies in hats and gloves. (This landmark has now resumed its former glory as the Blue and White Café revived.) Towering above Tunica and calling attention to the site for miles in each direction were vast billboards advertising the new casinos. Ringo Starr's face shone over this Delta town.

After Tunica, I reached an overpass that had always signaled me when traveling south from Memphis, telling me that I had left the claustrophobia of city life and was entering into the flat, free-spirited Delta. One quickly reached the outskirts of Memphis and I was soon into its south side. This was no longer the city that had thrilled my heart when first entering as a child, the city of Levy's and Phil A. Halle and Halle on Main, stores of elegant ladies clothes, where I could smell the new in my dresses after taking them home. There had been the department stores of Goldsmiths and Lowensteins with exuberant Christmas decorations, Santa Clauses, and a delicatessen in a tunnel. These institutions had either closed or moved to shopping malls in East Memphis. The southern part of Memphis looked almost flat until one reached the Peabody Hotel and the First National Bank Building on Main and Second. In south Memphis, I locked my car doors when I stopped for a red light, but a bleary-eyed drugged man seemed to be approaching me. I made up my mind that if he put out his hand I would have to step on the accelerator, even if I ran over him. The light changed and I shot off. My magic carpet had turned into a mist and then evaporated by the time I reached my sister-in-law's house on South Goodlett Street and a security system that made a dreadful noise if one forgot and ventured into the kitchen at night to get a glass of water. The locks on the doors of suburbia had turned over.

A Call in the Night
(1997)

At three in the morning in November of 1997, the telephone beside my bed rang.

"This the Rev. Giles."

"Calvin!" Calvin's life had definitely taken an about-face since his youthful misadventure. He now managed a housing estate. He was also an itinerant preacher and held services in country churches each weekend.

"Mae and the baby done burnt up."

Seconds turned into minutes to take in what he was saying.

Shalah had indeed been pregnant when I last saw Mae. A pretty little girl had been born and Annie had sent me pictures. There had been a big family reunion in Texas and Mae and Madie were together with Lizzie's first great, great grandchild in the center of the photograph.

Mae had moved from her brick house in Shelby because the rent was too high, and had rented a mobile home in Mound Bayou. She looked after the baby part-time to enable Shalah to continue her education at Delta State College in Cleveland. Mae had worked that day and Shalah went out in the evening. The young grandmother and baby went to bed at about nine o'clock in the same room. The old lady whom she looked after expected her the following morning, but she did not appear. Another caregiver telephoned Annie. "Was she there?" "No." As Annie told me later, "It was a day that I wished had not existed."

The same night her twin, Madie, who lived in a suburb of Dallas, felt as if she were burning with a heat from no discernable source. She twisted and turned and pulled her nightgown around her neck, but was unable to rest. The following morning she also received the same call from Calvin.

Both bodies were found intact, overcome by the smoke. Neighbors saw the mobile home on fire quite suddenly.

Annie, Dan, Mae, Madie, and Calvin.

The coroner's report revealed nothing except the cause of death, as-phyxiation, a waste of twenty-three sheets of paper. We did not believe that it was an accident, but Annie did not want to take matters further. Madie said, "There is more to this story; she had smoke detectors in every room. She had no enemies. She was a clean living person." No drugs or alcohol were found in her body. Mae's life was simple, she went to work, to church, went out with her boyfriend, who was in no way suspected, and she did not even smoke. The one cigarette hole on a couch was not hers.

The owner of the mobile home came to see Annie immediately with a check for the remainder of the month's rent and no insurance money. The following morning I called Annie and was told by one of Mae's daughters that she was at church. All the family pulled together in a valiant effort, in-cluding Shalah who had suffered both the loss of her mother and her child. Her courage was amazing. When I talked to Annie, two days later, she said, "I had her for forty-four years."

There was one of the biggest funerals in Mississippi. Annie remained frightened and refused to live in her house alone.

Annie Rises Above the Ashes
(1999 - 2009)

I did not return to Mississippi until the summer of the year 2000, when Shelby had several book-signing parties and it was time for me to negotiate a new farm lease. However, I kept in touch frequently by telephoning Annie. She had been robbed on one occasion when she was away from home. She told me that the man knew her and he knew that she would not be at home. This man had been released recently from the

State Penitentiary. "He took all my jewelry, some money I had hid, my microwave, television set and my 'riffle.' If I had been there he would have killed me."

Knowing that Annie was an excellent cook, I asked out of curiosity what she used the "riffle" for, thinking that it was some interesting kitchen gadget.

"To shoots people," she replied.

A seventy-nine-year old great-grandmother had no business housing a rifle to shoot in self-defense. She had now acquired a room in her Cousin Mattie's mobile home and only returned to her house during the daytime. Mattie's mother, Sister Baby Wesby, owned the land, and three other mobile homes had been placed around Sister Baby's house, forming a compound for safety. Annie had been very sick the previous year with infections in her colon and had lost vast quantities of blood, but she declared, "I don't wanna take no knife." She had only been in a hospital once before this happened, when she had Mae and Madie. Now she was on the mend. Her time was spent between her children in Dallas (Madie and Dan) and Calvin in Jonestown and her cousin Mattie in Shelby, with visits to Mae's daughters in Memphis and Nashville. I asked her why she did not visit her son and relations in Chicago. "Chicago, that's the Devil's first cousin; I ain't never liked it."

Shalah had produced two more babies and so had Sherona (Mae's daughters) and Theresa (Madie's daughter) also had a baby. Time did not lie on her hands. She was cooking for everyone. When Shelby had a book launch party in Memphis in July 2000, Annie and Calvin arrived in a car loaded with sweet potato pies.

*

During the time that I was away other important people from my life in Shelby had vanished. Freddie died of cancer and Emma Lytle of burns. She had got up in the middle of the night and fell against an ancient shower and was scalded before she had been found some hours later. Typical of

Most of the Street has been torn down, boarded up, and the front porches of the few remaining houses painted black.

Emma, she put up a brave fight in the burns unit of the Greenville hospital for six weeks. Albert Murphree also died when cancer returned after over twenty years of remission. By 2005 all of the Denton boys and their wives, Billy and Laurie Alice, Joe and Marion, Jack and Lola, David and Carolyn had died.

One of the few houses that stand on the street in a proud condition is that of my Uncle Will and Aunt Lula Poitevent Connell. It had become a bed and breakfast with a restaurant for all of the commuting farmers. I was taken there to a delicious lunch of southern cooking as guests of Jutta Feretti, Carolyn Denton (before she died) and Kate Hollingsworth.

Nan Shelby, Gwin's widow, moved to Cleveland. In the year 2000, she looked sixty-five despite her eighty-five years. She skipped around her library, pulling down book after book and talking until two each morning, always alert at eight the following day and perfectly turned out. Gertrude Conner tried a spell at a sheltered accommodation when she passed eighty-five, but returned to her charming house in Shelby to face the music (I hope without a rifle). Nan and Gertrude both died at age 92 in 2007. They had been close friends since they were young girls. All of these ladies were the last steel magnolias. They had been tolerant, compassionate, amusing, well dressed, and globally thinking.

After my visit with Nan Shelby and Scott Coopwood in 2000, I had intended to stop by Shelby on my way from Cleveland to Memphis to speak to Annie and Mattie before departing for England. Then I recognized a landmark near Alligator, a roadhouse that had once been Brown's liquor store. I had driven past Shelby on the new motorway without noticing that the street had vanished as well.

*

Annie celebrated her eightieth birthday with a surprise party at the Shelby school, given by her children and grandchildren, but in 2004 Annie did "take the knife." Madie moved her to Texas and I visited her there in February 2004. When Madie met me at the airport, she warned me that

Annie was talking about and to people who were dead. The hospital was filled with patients on Medicare and could not have been more pleasant, with large rooms on the ground floor and facilities for patients to have meals at a table in the hall. Madie slept in her mother's large room every night, because Annie in her eighty-five years had never spent a night alone. We visited for two days, but Annie never ventured out of the bed. Madie's three-year-old granddaughter, Bria, programmed a radio alarm. We admonished her and she replied, "I wants Miss Annie to wake up and say, Bria, shut that thing off."

This was not to be. All of the fat had vanished from Annie's face, taking with it the traces of her African heritage. I looked down and saw the face of a Native American. Could it have been the tribe who lived around Natchez? Perhaps one of the first slaves who had the sinews of his feet cut by the Indians, or a slave that had been sold into the West Indies and came back to Mississippi through other trade routes?

When I left, I squeezed Annie's hand and said that I was going to Atlanta to visit Mimi. She knew that after Atlanta there would be the Atlantic Ocean. She said, "Oh, no."

Annie had a big and very dignified funeral in Shelby. Many people celebrated her life as a cook at the hospital, a mother, a good Christian who had remained strong and cheerful until the end, as did her forbearers.

Our house was torn down at the end of the 20th century, having lasted over a hundred years. Freddie and Mary Lee's grandson bought the former house of Madge and Charles Denton and the Henry's before them, as well as our lot, which for a while became a flower garden, now just an empty lot with a few dead trees and one valiant Nandina sprouted in the middle of the lawn, a descendant of a planned garden. There were too many faded memories almost screaming at me, so loud that I did not want to stay very long and like everything else in the summer it was parched dry.

Mary Lee Hall was in her a new three-bedroom brick house in 2004, on the extended end of the street overlooking our farm where she had worked for thirty-three years. It was named Cindy Cole Street for a lady active in the civil rights movement. Her children and her little terrier, Mattie, attended to her, and she continued to be employed until 2007, taking disabled children to school. I stayed with Mary Lee on both of my last visits in 2004 and 2005. We were no longer black and white people, but two old friends who had shared much of the same life. She drove the car, while I selected healthy food for our dinners, enjoyed white wine with dinner and shared the same views on national events, watching her vast television set. We were both excited by the prospect of Barack Obama's bid for the White house. After the last two visits we spoke on the telephone about two times a month. Mary Lee, in her later years, was prone to complaining that no one paid enough attention to her. A friend from Missouri called almost daily, her children were always dropping in, and even Freddie's outside children came by to see her frequently, because she had always been good to them and if they needed shoes, she made sure there were some. My last conversation with Mary Lee in the summer of 2009 was the most peaceful. She said, "I feel fine. I am going to go back to work in the autumn taking children to school." Then she visited a friend on a Sunday in July in Mound Bayou after church. She felt very hot quite suddenly and died before she reached the hospital. It was an ending that most people would wish for, but I still miss my friend who is no longer on the other end of the line. I can't bring myself to delete the name Hall from my telephone. Others can't let go either. Her church celebrates her birthday every spring and print t-shirts with her photograph on them..

I have often heard banal suggestions about relationships between the races. First, Northerners said that we, the white people, never knew a black person. In the South some people said, "They did not love us. We thought that they did, but they didn't."

These accusations came back to me when I read Barack Obama's book, The *Audacity of Hope*, whose words were significant:

Most blacks know the black story...they know what drove that homeless man to drink, because he is their uncle. That hardened criminal they remember when he was a little boy, so full of life and capable of love, for he is their cousin.[1]

Black people are not the only ones who realize that culture is shaped by circumstances. White people have received an infinite amount of love from blacks and they have as well. We have watched their microscopic progression from slavery to a century and a-half of toil, poor wages, poor education, segregation, and the Jim Crow laws. We have watched black people creeping into middle class jobs, at first being turned down for application after application, and accepted the transitions of race. There is a First Lady who probably descended from slaves, for whom many whites in the Delta applaud. An African American doctor is married to a white lady in Cleveland and people no longer seem to notice. But there are vast inequities in wealth. Shacks exist on the edges of towns, which look worse than ever existed on the old plantations, for rural poverty has been replaced by ghetto poverty. Many black people have a life behind bars. A number of white people have now walked across the road and try to understand. And Delta wealth goes on with extravagant entertainment, iced swans filled with orchids and Christmas lights as if there were no global warming.

It remains to be seen whether the settlement of the Delta was a misadventure. The rich land continues to produce soybeans, corn, wheat, sunflowers, rice and two bales of cotton to an acre for the world (often to a stock pile of subsidized products). The price of this land has rocketed, as people are once more coming down the river from the Midwest and paying three thousand dollars an acre for farm land and four thousand an acre for shooting land located on the other side of the levee. They will have little idea of the world that I remember. Has it vanished never to be returned, or

1 Obama, Barack, The Audacity of Hope, Crown Publisher, New York, (a division of Random House Inc.) First ed. P.255

is it just beneath the surface?

The Delta gave us many good writers: Walker Percy, William Alexander Percy, Willie Morris, Shelby Foote, Tennessee Williams, journalists Hodding Carter and Curtis Wilkie, only to name those with five stars. Charlotte Hays and Gayden Metcalf have recently written delightful mannerist books. It gave us the artist Marshall Bouldin and many others not as well-known, potter Lee McCarty, photographers Bill Eggleston and his first cousin Maude Schuyler Clay, Byrnne and Frankie Keating. It gave us spirituals and too many blues musicians to name, such as B.B. King, and rock musicians such as Ike Turner. The great actor Morgan Freeman has put a great deal of money and effort into reviving the Delta. Art came from the unique qualities of the Delta and suffering. The same land continues to roll over its many broken lives. I hope that the people I have described may be remembered.

Appendix A

"After the War Between the States," by senator W. B. Roberts

Any Southerner whose ancestor was a soldier of the American Revolution has a proud heritage, but even prouder is his whose forbear followed R. E. Lee, rode with Forrest, was wounded at Shiloh, or fought at Gettysburg. Beyond that, one whose parent was a trusted member of the Ku Klux Klan during the early days of Reconstruction in the central South may be proud of his ancestry.

Only those who lived through those dark days can know of the horror of having one's slaves become his rulers. A proud people were governed by their servants and remnants of the Union Army, reinforced by a horde of office-seekers who came to prey upon a fallen foe like jackals and buzzards.

The end of the war in 1865 left the South prostrate financially and almost hopeless of the future. It is hardly possible to vision conditions as they existed at that time or even to trace the heroic efforts of our people to care for their families and restore their civil government. Our lands had grown up in bushes, our houses were burned or dilapidated beyond repair, we were without money, and we had no friends in Washington. Federal soldiers were at the election places, our women were being forced off the sidewalks by the insolent blacks, and despair was everywhere. It was in these conditions that under the secret leadership of General Bedford Forrest the Ku Klux Klan was organized for the protection of the defenseless, the preservation of law and order, and the traditions of the South. Their meeting places were secret and none but brave men, willing to risk their lives, were admitted to secret membership. I remember, as a small boy, my mother arousing me from my sleep to come to the window to see the parade of the Ku Klux Klan on some errand of mercy or, perchance, of vengeance upon some miscreant who had violated the traditions of our people. Few in number, their work was of necessity done in secret. I remember knowing, even as a boy, that if work was to be done in a town or near a town, clansmen from a neighboring town would quickly, after night, enter the town, do their work during church hours, and then quickly disappear; while all clansmen in the neighborhood were conspicious in the church, loudly singing hymns and listening to a long sermon, with a perfect alibi.

There can be little doubt that there would have been many more outrages upon our people in those dark days had it not been for the restraining influence of the clansmen upon the newly enfranchised blacks, inspired to devilment by vicious white interlopers bent on keeping the defeated Southerners under the existing rule, in order that their system of plunder might be perpetuated as long as possible.

With these conditions confronting them, our people determined to free themselves of the existing government of Negroes and Carpetbaggers. In 1875, the white people of the state, under the leadership of George, Walthall, Clark, Lowry, Barksdale, and others, rid the state of Negro and carpetbag officials; but it was fifteen years later before the last of them retired from office in Bolivar County. As late as 1882, the negro population of Bolivar County was so dense that the 250 white voters in the county were confronted with over four thousand negro voters; and all kinds of trades and so-called frauds were resorted to, to rid the country of this irksome condition. The state had a negro United States Senator in Washington, elected from Rosedale in Bolivar County, B. K. Bruce, by name; a negro Congressman, John R. Lynch, who, by the way, was living in Chicago a year ago when the writer enjoyed an hour's conversation with him about people of fifty years ago. Both Bruce and Lynch were able men, fairly represented the people electing them, and exerted a good influence among their race; and their influence, together with that of Isaiah Montgomery, J. H. Bufford, George Gayles, and others of the colored race, went far in creating amity among the people of the county.

In 1882 and 1883 the older men called me into conference with them and in deep earnestness explained to me that to retain even a show of white supremacy, which they regarded as necessary, it was my duty as a young lawyer and citizen to use my brains and skill to devise ways of preventing negro control by any means in my power. And so all of us worked toward that end. I regret that space and time permit me to mention only a few of the ludicrous occurrences in our efforts to control the elections.

On one occasion Congress had passed a law providing that the Federal judge should appoint two inspectors at each box to guarantee a fair election of Congressmen. Two inspectors at one of our large boxes were appointed, and at the close of the election, when a box had been prepared with which to change the result of the election, the two negro inspectors positively refused to leave the room even for supper. Under this stress, one of the white managers, who was a doctor, told them this was one time when the colored and white folks would eat together; and he went out and returned presently with a number of boxes of sardines and crackers. He had, with a hypodermic needdle, injected croton oil, or some other violent drug, into the two boxes handed the Negroes. In a very few minutes the Negroes were sick and had to leave hurriedly, and the box showed at the count a big majority for the Democrats.

At the box at Bolivar where I lived at the time, there were five hundred negro voters and only about twenty-five white voters. One can imagine the difficulty of making that box show a Democratic majority. One favorite scheme was to mix bills of lading at the river and ship by mistake a ballot box to St. Louis while a coil of rope or bale of cotton was sent to the county site to be counted; or the ballot box might, accidentally, be dropped out of the window of a train; in fact, any trick might be employed that seemed to promise a chance of success.

The present generation can hardly realize that even up to 1895 there were numerous negro officers in Bolivar County. We used what was known as the fusion system, and that was to agree for the Negroes to have some of the offices, and the whites, of course, the best ones. While Bolivar County had two negro sheriffs, B. K. Bruce and J. E. Ousley, we never had any but white men for chancery clerk. At one time all the officers were black except the chancery clerk. The writer has appeared in court as a lawyer with all the court officials, the twelve men on the jury, and the lawyers on the other side, as well as all witnesses, being black. In fact this condition existed in the county until the constitutional convention of 1890 disfranchised the Negroes by legal means.

Almost every justice of the peace of the county was a Negro, many of them very illiterate and lacking in sufficient intelligence for their position. Let it be said to their credit, however, that they never, at any time, showed any prejudice against white men in their administration of justice; and, so far as the writer can remember, they administered justice as justly and fairly as their limited ability permitted.

As a fair indication of conditions of the time, I recall that a newly elected negro justice came to a lawyer near him, stated that he wanted the lawyer to help him with his docket and judgments, and told the lawyer that he expected always to decide the lawyer's cases in his favor, but he wanted the lawyer "always to read the claw in the law upon which it is to base my decision." Sufficient to say the lawyer always cited the "claw" and marked it, and the justice faithfully carried out the agreement during his terms of office.

In those days our districts were divided by lines running east and west. The river was known as the "front," and it was the custom of all justices to hold their courts at the levee, usually in the back of a saloon or on a porch; or, if the weather was warm, in the shade of a tree. It was the custom of the jury after hearing the evidence and arguments to proceed over the levee to consider their verdict. This recalls an amusing case, in which the writer was one of the lawyers, involving a Texas pony. One of the litigants was a big black preacher and the other a "likely looking" yellow girl, all bedecked with red ribbons and rather striking clothing. After hearing the argument, the jury retired over the levee as usual and quickly returned a verdict in the following words: "We, the jury, finds that Annie must have the horse with all our hearts."

In 1886, Dr. H. L. Sutherland, a real gentleman of the old school, was the mayor of the town of Bolivar, where I then resided. He was trying a case about a pair of smoothing irons used by washerwomen. A negro lawyer by the name of Rufe Richardson from Rosedale was opposing counsel to me, and during the argument, Richardson, addressing himself to the court, exclaimed, "Have I come down here all the way from Rosedale to cast my pearls before swine!" Immediately the hand of the court began moving towards one of the irons lying on the table, and the lawyer saw the movement just in time to get out the door as the smoothing iron hurled by the court hit the door casing.

In the eighties it was the custom of the circuit judge to hold his courts first at old Austin on the river, the county site of Tunica County, then at Friars Point, then Rosedale, then Greenville, and on down to Mayersville. A number of lawyers went from court to court; and, during court, accommodations for visitors were limited, many of the negro ligitants and witnesses sleeping in the courtroom, with several poker games in continuous session in the saloons adjacent. As facilities were limited, it was the custom to have a poker game in the grand jury room where there were a table and chairs; and I remember well hearing the negro deputy sheriff going to a poker game one morning and announcing, "Gents, the court am in session upstairs." This meant for the game to suspend and the grand jury to resume its sessions. Of the negro lawyers then in practice in the courts I can remember the names of but three, Rufus Richardson at Rosedale, one named Harris at Greenville, and A. B. Grimes at Mound Landing; the latter, I believe, is still living in the lower end of the county.

It was during one of these court poker games about 1883 that occurred an incident that has come to be used nationally as a joke ofttimes told and even now is worth repeating. A game was going on over a saloon in Rosedale known as the "Sky Parlor," and the luck was all going to one man who had only one eye. After a heavy loss, one of the players who had stood the losses steadily finally drew a big pistol from his hip pocket, laid it on the table by him and announced, "This game may be straight, but I want to say that if the luck don't change soon, I am going to shoot somebody's other eye out." It changed!

In the eighties there were twenty-three lawyers in the county, all of course living at towns along the river. A majority of them lived in towns away from the county site, Rosedale.

The writer, a young lawyer during this period, resided at Bolivar and practiced law somewhat like a doctor practices medicine in that he rode horseback from court to court. He carried with him in a pair of saddle bags just a code of state laws and oftentimes a Bible from which he frequently quoted with good effect to the negro juries before whom he appeared in behalf of clients.

In those days we traveled either on horseback or by steamboat. My business frequently called me to Rosedale from Bolivar, my home twenty miles distant, and in the spring when the river was high, it was so difficult to make the trip on horseback that I frequently took a steamboat, and if it was night, got off the boat at Terrene, where there was a wharfboat with rooms for travelers, and walked four miles down to Rosedale the next morning.

However, those were happy days after all; our people were a hospitable lot of folks who shared each other's troubles and burdens: and it was quite the custom for a family to visit another family for even weeks at a time. When over-crowded, we thought nothing of sleeping on the floor or a store counter. We attended dances, arriving before dark and dancing until daylight so that we could see how to get home, as there were few roads, and they were almost impassable in the winter. Our people cared little for money or position or fine clothes (our girls made their own clothes) and all we wanted was a comfortable place to live without ostentation, and a good horse and buggy.

The people of whom I write and who were the controlling influence in the county have nearly all passed to their final sleep; the cane has given way to the tractor and automobile; "the finger has writ and having writ has passed on," and just a memory is now all the few of us have left of those dark days of Reconstruction, as well as the happy days that succeeded them.

Appendix B

A Brief History of the Town of Mound Bayou

This small all-black town was built by two African American men, Isaiah T. Montgomery and his first cousin Benjamin T. Green, who were born into slavery as property of Joseph Emory Davis, the brother of Jefferson Davis (President of the Confederacy). Montgomery's father, Benjamin Thornton Montgomery, had been purchased in the slave market at Natchez. He had the advantage of a liberal education received from a former master in Loudon County, Virginia. His education encouraged Joe Davis to inspire other slaves. Isaiah's mother, Mary Lewis Montgomery, was also a slave from Virginia before her parents moved to slavery on to Joe Davis's plantation, Hurricane.

Isaiah never attended school, although his father, Benjamin, taught him the elementary matters and hired both black and white tutors for his children. When Joe Davis discovered that his slaves were receiving a better education than some of his family, he arranged for them to attend school together. It is said that neighbors put pressure on Joe Davis to stop this practice of an integrated system.

At the age of about nine or ten, Isaiah Montgomery was called to work in the office of Joe Davis. He later assumed the entire charge of Davis's public and private offices and held this responsibility until the outbreak of the Civil War. His father, Benjamin Montgomery, operated a mercantile business on Davis Bend with a high rating from Dunn & Bradstreet. Isaiah kept the accounts for Joe Davis's family and managed their plantations during the Civil War, when the Davis family moved inland for safety. Shortly after the War, in 1867, the Montgomery family purchased the four thousand acres plantations from Joe Davis for $300,000 at 6 percent per annum, for

Joe Davis wanted his plantations to be managed by this family and to be a home for his former slaves. The Montgomery family managed the property for eighteen years and it ranked as the third largest cotton producer in the South, receiving several prizes in international competitions. There were disagreements with the heirs to Joe Davis and there were also the recurrent overflows of the river. The Montgomery family surrendered the plantations and moved to Vicksburg, where Isaiah (Benjamin and Mary's son) opened a store. Benjamin died at Brierfield (the Davis plantation home) in 1878, after his wife Mary Lewis died there in 1875. This story illustrates to me how close yet separate the White and African American families were.

Isaiah Montgomery and George McGinnis, land agent of the Louisville, New Orleans and Texas Railway, began corresponding and arranged a meeting with the black Secretary of State, James Hill, where they negotiated the proposition for an all-black colony. The plan was accepted by the railway. On 12th July, 1887, Isaiah selected the site in Bolivar County at the junction between two bayous and an Indian Mound, for which the town was named. This site was about half way between Vicksburg and Memphis.

It was not easy. After the first eighty or ninety acres were cleared, the area was destroyed by flood.Isaiah Montgomery was a man of forty by this time and he and his Cousin Benjamin T. Green and seven other men joined in this adventure. They arranged for men to sleep on the train, some were posted to watch for wild animals at night. Green rigged up a groundhog sawmill, lay timber for homes and erected the first cotton gin. Montgomery purchased 840 acres at $7- $9 dollars an acre.The first women and children arrived in about February, 1888.

The longest tenure of mayor was Benjamin A. Green, the first child to be born in Mound Bayou and the son of the town's co-founder, Benjamin T. Green. He came to be known as 'Judge Green' and was the man that I met in the 1940s, during the war. He had been educated in the Mound Bayou System and afterwards at Fisk and at Harvard. During his tenure of forty one years, until his death in 1961, he oversaw the following establishments: The Mound Bayou Oil Company, The Mound Bayou Baptist College, the Bethel A. M. E. Church, the Bolivar County Baptist Seminary, the St. Gabriel's Catholic Mission, the Mound Bayou Bottling works, and the Taborian Hospital. He endeavoured to teach unity and train the inhabitants in self respect, decency and honor. They developed a public school system, a thriving cotton gin, a dress making business and a first class post office.

As late as 1953 the city owned over 37,000 acres of the richest land in the Delta, and the Bolivar County Farm Bureau's Negro Division was formed. Today the town boasts an Olympic Swimming pool and a recreational center and a uniquely constructed Housing Project.

Appendix C

The Jim Crow Laws: Mississippi (from online publications)

The state of Mississippi enacted 22 Jim Crow statutes, and a law restricting voting rights between 1865 and 1956. Six miscegenation laws were enacted; four school and three railroad segregation acts were passed. Three segregation laws were passed after the 1954 Brown decision. T he sentence for violating the state's 1865 miscegenation law was life imprisonment. In later years, the miscegenation laws became more complex. In 1880, those persons with one quarter or more Negro blood were considered, "colored." By 1890 the law had become more stringent, marking those with one-eighth or more Negro blood as non-white. In 1906 the miscegenation law was amended to include not only blacks but Asians as well in the list of unacceptable mates for Caucasians. During the Reconstruction era, Mississippi passed five civil rights laws, permitting miscegenation, protecting voting rights and barring public carrier and school segregation.

1865: Miscegenation (Statute)

Declared a felony for any freedman, free Negro, or mulatto to intermarry with any white person. Penalty: Imprisonment in the state penitentiary for life.

1865: Railroad (Statute)

Declared a felony for any free, free Negro, or mulatto to ride in any first-class passenger cars used by white persons. Penalty: Misdemeanour punished by a fine between $50 to $500; and imprisonment in county jail until fine and costs of prosecution are paid. Half of the fines to be paid to the informer, the other half to the county treasury where offense was committed.

1867: Barred court testimony discrimination (Statute)

Negroes given the right to testify on the same terms as white persons.

1867: Jury selection (Statute)

Negroes declared incompetent to serve as jurors.

1868: Barred public carrier segregation (Constitution)

All citizens had the right to travel on all public transportation.

1868: Voting rights protected (Constitution)

Removed limitation of suffrage to white people only.

1871: Barred anti-miscegenation (State Code)

Omitted miscegenation or intermarriage statute.

1871: Barred school segregation (Constitution)

All children from five to twenty-one years of age shall have in all respects equal advantages in public schools.

1872: Barred prison segregation (Statute)

No distinction on account of race or color or previous condition in working convicts.

1873: Barred public accommodation segregation (Statute)

1878: Education (Statute)

Prohibited teaching white and black children in the same school.

1880: Miscegenation (State Code)

Revised state code to declare marriage between white persons and Negroes or mulattoes or persons of one-quarter or more Negro blood as "incestuous and void." Penalty: Fine up to $500, or imprisonment in the penitentiary up to ten years, or both.

1888: Railroad (Statute)

New depot buildings were to provide separate rooms for the sexes and the races if deemed proper by the board. Equal but separate accommodations to be provided for white and colored passengers. Penalty: Misdemeanour for railroad companies failing to comply, with a fine up to $500. Conductors who failed to enforce the law could be fined from $25 to $50 for each offense.

1890: Miscegenation (Constitution)

Prohibited marriage of a white person with a Negro or mulatto or person who has one-eighth or more of Negro blood.

1890: Education (Constitution)

Separate schools to be maintained for white and black children.

1896: Education (Statute)

Separate districts established for the schools of white and black children.

1904: Streetcars (Statute)

Streetcars were to provide equal but separate accommodations for white and colored passengers. Penalties: Passengers could be fined $25 or confined up to 30 days in county jail. Employees liable for a fine of $25 or confinement up to 30 days in Jail. A streetcar company could be charged with a misdemeanour for failing to carry out law and be fined $100 or face imprisonment between 60 days and six months.

1906: Railroads (Statute)

Railroad commission to provide separate waiting rooms for white and black passengers. Separate restrooms were to be provided also.

1906: Miscegenation (Statute)

Prohibited marriage between a white person with a Negro or mulatto or a person with one-eighth or more Negro blood, or with an Asian or person with one-eighth or more "Mongolian" blood.

1920: Miscegenation (Statute)

Persons or corporations who printed, published or circulated written material promoting the acceptance of intermarriage between whites and Negroes would be guilty of a misdemeanour. Penalty: Fine up to $500 or imprisonment up to s ix months, or both.

1930: Education (State Code)

Required schools to be racially segregated, and the creation of separate districts to provide school facilities for the greatest number of pupils of both districts. In addition, authorized separate schools for Native Americans. (This assured a different quality of school in white and colored districts —csc)

1930: Miscegenation (State Code)

Miscegenation declared a felony. Nullified interracial marriages if parties went to another jurisdiction where such marriages were legal. Also prohibited marriages between persons of the Caucasian race and those who had one eight or more Asian blood.

1942: Voting rights (Constitution)

Instituted poll tax requirement. (in the middle of the war, who were the legislators? csc)

1942: Miscegenation (State Code)

Marriage between white and Negro or Asian void. Penalty: $500 and/ or up to ten years imprisonment. Anyone advocating intermarriage subject to fine of $500 and/or six months (fear of war brides csc)

1942: Health Care (State Code)

Segregated facilities at state charity hospital and separate entrances at all state hospitals.

1956: Education (State Code & Constitution)

Separate schools to be maintained. All state executive officers required to prevent implementation of school segregation decision by "lawful means." Governor may close any school if he determines closure to be in best interest of majority of children.

1956: Public carriers (State code)

Public carriers to be segregated.

1956: Public accommodation (Statute)

Firms and corporations authorized to choose their clientele and the right to refuse service to any person.

1958: Recreation (Statute)

Authorized governor to close parks to prevent desegregation.

1967: The Supreme Courted ruled on the issue in Loving v. Virginia, concluding that Virginia's miscegenation laws were unconstitutional. (102 years in a country where 'all men were created equal' that to this day hales Democracy the world over. csc)

Acknowledgements

Virginia Bass, acknowledged in the dedication, and two others made this book possible: Walter Raleigh Coppedge, Professor Emeritus of Virginia Commonwealth University, who grew up in Rosedale and has Mississippi Delta roots even deeper than mine, edited an early version of this book, and Scott Coopwood, the owner of *Delta Magazine*, allowed me full run of the archives in his office.

The first person who took such an interest in what I really wanted to do and gave me the confidence that I could write a book when I retired from legal practice was the late Helen Lane, who under the name of Helen Hudson wrote twelve novels, including two published when she was past ninety. Also encouraging were Travis Coopwood's (a child) reactions while I read the typescript to her. Besides embellishing memories of our shared childhood, my cousin, Jan Poitevent Davis Clark, enhanced my knowledge of our Poitevent family. Becky Brettell Shelby Smith read an early draft of the book and made useful suggestions. Eleanor Humphrey Schnabel provided information on the Mounds People and assisted with my research on the early Native American civilization. Her sister, Suzy Biename, sent me a photograph of their mother, Emma Knowleton Lytle. Julia Hamilton, who has authored seven splendid novels, read the typescript and led me to many helpful changes. Margret Schuchard, Reader Emeritus of English Literature of the University of Heidelberg, visited the Delta with me and proposed useful changes to both the first and second drafts of *Street*. Peter and Lyndy Davey, Thor Thorsson, my neighbour Olive Cornell, Louis de la Vergne, and Mimi Murphree read the typescript and offered helpful ideas. Jenny, Allen, and Drew Long graciously allowed me to reproduce a copy of the picture that their mother/grandmother, Martha Long painted of the commissary.

This book would not have been possible without the gracious hospitality of so many of my friends and relations in the Delta, who made sure that I was not just an absentee landlord. Ann Morrison Coopwood Bode and her late husband, Dr. Gene Coopwood gave an open house. Lucy Lee Maynard Lanoux and the late Elsie Maynard Milligan submerged me in their Delta stories, and their parents, the late George and Lucie Lee Maynard, gave me unstinted hospitality as did the late Emma and Stuart Lytle. The late Isabel and Billy Barksdale of Rosebud Plantation near Jonestown, Gwin and Nan Shelby, the late Gertrude Conner, Annie Anderson, Mary Lee Hall, and Rives and Ginny Neblett were responsible for some of the events in the latter part of this book: Rives's memory for detail embellished several scenes.

I am also deeply indebted to family genealogists who patiently devoted numberless hours of their retirement contacting and visiting relatives, crafting a picture of our forebears; the late Cass Knight Shelby, visited and wrote a personal story of every branch of the Shelby family in America; Thomas Graham Sinclair, wrote a scholarly book about my grandmother's Texas family; Isabel Poitevent Barksdale Maynard, wrote the story of the Poitevent family who fled France in 1684, the year before the Edict of Nantes was revoked, and held fast to their Huguenot values for several hundred years; and the late Florence Warfield Sillers, who edited a history of Bolivar County derived from vivid stories of the early settlers which should never go out of print.

Finally, thanks is due to Kate Lechter, who copy-edited *Street* with meticulous professionalism; Herman Payton, who designed a cover which far exceeded my suggestions; Neil White, who has been a most accommodating and congenial publisher; and my inimitable husband, Shelby Tucker, who will not read this book until it is published to avoid suggesting changes, but recorded many of my mother's stories over forty years ago and has opened many windows for me that otherwise would have remained closed.

About the Author

The Author was born in the Delta and lived in Shelby until she went to Tulane University at age 18. She owns part of a plantation which her grandfather bought in the 1890s from one of the town's first five settlers, a lone widow who came to the area with her great great grandparents in 1852. Although she has lived in England for most of her life since 1969, this land and her black nurse Lizzie kept her roots in the Mississippi Delta, returning most years for a visit and to inspect the crops.

She majored in Modern European History with a minor in American History at Tulane and later studied law at the College of Legal Education in London, was admitted to the Bar in 1974, practiced as a Barrister for five years, became a member of the Louisiana Bar, and later changed sides of the legal profession to become a solicitor in England and worked in civil litigation for a further fifteen years.

Her home has been in the center of Oxford, England with her husband, the writer Shelby Tucker, and various Jack Russell terriers since 1974. During intervening periods she has travelled extensively to 57 countries, through much of Africa, the Middle East, Asia and South America, sometimes hitch-hiking. Hence this book has been written with a certain amount of perspective. She claims that had she sold her land in 1969 and bought more property in England, she would have been a very rich woman today. She kept the land and wrote a book.

17777496R00240

Made in the USA
San Bernardino, CA
17 December 2014